"Pat Brans' new book is an insightful, and essential, guidebook to the wireless transformation of the enterprise, a must-read for any busy IT manager struggling to make sense of the wireless revolution and proliferation of mobile devices, solutions, and networking standards."

Editorial Director and CEO
WirelessReport.net—voices of the wireless revolution

"This is an excellent read for senior business and technology executives covering all the essential ground in what is really one of the hottest topics in boardrooms today."

—Chris Pearson
Global Head of Mobile Business Solutions
PWC Consulting

"I would recommend this book to any general manager or sales executive interested in the way business will be conducted in the future. Time is the essence of business, and mobile technology is the best way to optimize one's use of time. This book helped me define the roadmap to get there."

—Andre Surchat
Vice President General Manager
Avery Dennison, Southern Region Europe

"This book is a must-read for business managers looking to leverage mobile technology to enhance their competitive position today. Brans provides excellent insight into the technical issues that underlie the development of mobile software and applications for the global enterprise, and how mobile and wireless applications deliver tangible benefits to your business' bottom line."

—Randy Brouckman
CEO
Telispark, Inc.

"This book covers virtually all the key technology and business challenges associated with extending today's critical corporate applications—and tomorrow's innovations—to mobile workers. Especially valuable are the discussions and references to the tangible business benefits of deploying wireless and mobile solutions to the global enterprise."

—Steve Simpson
President and CEO
Extended Systems

Mobilize Your Enterprise

Achieving Competitive Advantage Through Wireless Technology

ISBN 0-13-009116-2

90000

9 790130 091160

Hewlett-Packard® Professional Books

HP-UX

Fernandez	Configuring CDE: The Common Desktop Environment
Madell	Disk and File Management Tasks on HP-UX
Olker	Optimizing NFS Performance: Tuning and Troubleshooting NFS on HP-UX Systems
Poniatowski	HP-UX 11i Virtual Partitions
Poniatowski	HP-UX 11i System Administration Handbook and Toolkit
Poniatowski	The HP-UX 11.x System Administration Handbook and Toolkit
Poniatowski	HP-UX 11.x System Administration "How To" Book
Poniatowski	HP-UX 10.x System Administration "How To" Book
Poniatowski	HP-UX System Administration Handbook and Toolkit
Poniatowski	Learning the HP-UX Operating System
Rehman	HP Certified: HP-UX System Administration
Sauers/Weygant	HP-UX Tuning and Performance: Concepts, Tools, and Methods
Weygant	Clusters for High Availability: A Primer of HP-UX Solutions, Second Edition
Wong	HP-UX 11i Security

UNIX, LINUX, WINDOWS, AND MPE I/X

Diercks	MPE i/X System Administration Handbook
Mosberger	IA-64 Linux Kernel
Poniatowski	UNIX User's Handbook, Second Edition
Roberts	UNIX and Windows 2000 Interoperability Guide
Stone/Symons	UNIX Fault Management

COMPUTER ARCHITECTURE

Kane	PA-RISC 2.0 Architecture
Markstein	IA-64 and Elementary Functions

NETWORKING/COMMUNICATIONS

Blommers	Architecting Enterprise Solutions with UNIX Networking
Blommers	OpenView Network Node Manager
Blommers	Practical Planning for Network Growth
Brans	Mobilize Your Enterprise: Achieving Competitive Advantage Through Wireless Technology
Cook	Building Enterprise Information Architecture: Reengineering Information Systems
Lucke	Designing and Implementing Computer Workgroups
Lund	Integrating UNIX and PC Network Operating Systems

SECURITY

Bruce	Security in Distributed Computing: Did You Lock the Door?
Pearson et al.	Trusted Computing Platforms: TCPA Technology in Context
Pipkin	Halting the Hacker, Second Edition
Pipkin	Information Security

Mobilize Your Enterprise

Achieving Competitive Advantage
Through Wireless Technology

Patrick Brans

Hewlett-Packard Company

www.hp.com/hpbooks

Prentice Hall PTR
Upper Saddle River, New Jersey 07458
www.phptr.com

Library of Congress Cataloging-in-Publication Data

A CIP catalog record for this book can be obtained from the Library of Congress.

Editorial/production supervision: *MetroVoice Publishing Services*
Cover design director: *Jerry Votta*
Cover design: *Talar Boorujy*
Manufacturing buyer: *Maura Zaldivar*
Executive editor: *Jill Harry*
Editorial assistant: *Kate Wolf*
Marketing manager: *Dan DePasquale*
Full-service production manager: *Anne R. Garcia*
Publisher, Hewlett-Packard Books: *Patricia Pekary*

© 2003 by Hewlett-Packard Company

Published by Pearson Education
Publishing as Prentice Hall PTR
Upper Saddle River, New Jersey 07458

Prentice Hall books are widely used by corporations and government agencies for training, marketing, and resale. For information regarding corporate and government bulk discounts, please contact: Corporate and Government Sales (800) 382-3419 or corpsales@pearsontechgroup.com.

All product or company names mentioned herein are the trademarks or registered trademarks of their respective owners.

All rights reserved. No part of this book may be reproduced, in any form or by any means, without permission in writing from the publisher.

Printed in the United States of America

10 9 8 7 6 5 4 3 2 1

ISBN 0-13-009116-2

Pearson Education LTD.
Pearson Education Australia PTY, Limited
Pearson Education Singapore, Pte. Ltd.
Pearson Education North Asia Ltd.
Pearson Education Canada, Ltd.
Pearson Educación de Mexico, S.A. de C.V.
Pearson Education — Japan
Pearson Education Malaysia, Pte. Ltd.

To the warmest and funniest family in the whole wide world:

Sylvie, Louise, and Paul

You are always asking just what it is I do at work.
Well, it goes like this...

Contents

9 Mobile Enterprise Security   205

B **Recommended Reading   327**

Glossary   331

Index   375

Foreword

When we got our first bulky, crackling cell phones ("for emergencies only," remember?) nobody predicted the quality, convenience, and reach of today's mobile connections. But after a few short years, whole countries leap-frogged a century of wireline development and built first-rate national networks with not a telephone pole in sight. A few years more, and the wired phone could join the rotary dial and manual switchboard in technology's attic.

Like early cell phones, the wireless modems of just a few years ago offered little promise for the future of mobile computing. But as with cell phones, accelerating technology development and integration are pushing us into a world where wireless data is effortless, reflexive, and universal. Companies that anticipate and plan for this new wireless world will flourish in it; those that struggle to catch up will, well, struggle to catch up.

Managing the Enterprise Marketing and Solutions Group at the new HP has given me a front-seat perspective on the development of corporate wireless computing. Right now I see levels of innovation, integration, and momentum that recall the cell phone explosion of a decade ago.

After years of struggle to make them work and roll them out, mobile computing devices, networks, and applications today have reached levels of utility and power that invite widespread business use. Fully-featured mobile devices—from compact, voice-activated Web phones through ruggedized custom tablet computers—now suit most business needs. Networks and "invisible" computing technologies meet utility-grade standards for coverage and reliability. Most important, business applications that have already transformed the wired enterprise—managing company finances, and relationships with customers, partners and suppliers—are finally ready to cut the wires.

Close behind them, entirely new, "mobile from the ground up" business e-services will deliver media-rich information, up-to-the-minute data access, or secure financial transactions to whoever needs them, wherever they are.

But none of these parts—devices, networks or applications—works alone. And perhaps the greatest progress has been made integrating these components into practical solutions to real business problems. This is a bread-and-butter issue here at HP. We make the nonstop computing infrastructure that powers the world's mobile service providers, working closely with them, applications software companies, and systems integrators, to deliver and support new services. Most of all, we are an enthusiastic wireless customer—driving hard to put mobile solutions in place for our own sales and service teams around the world. Lately, we have seen all these jobs get *easier* as the infrastructure, applications, and services fit together better than ever, and solutions grow more powerful by the month.

Nowhere is the growing momentum of wireless more apparent than at HP's Mobile e-Services Bazaars. These regional solution centers (combination laboratories and business incubators) bring technologists, applications specialists, consultants and end-users together to design, build, and evaluate next-generation wireless solutions. E-Bazaars give HP a window on the breakneck world of wireless data, an environment to collaborate with partners, and a guide to our own deployment of mobile solutions. With more than 400 partners worldwide, and applications ranging from banking to forestry, the Bazaars have shown us fully-integrated solutions that are powerful, cost-effective, inevitable, and ready.

Pat Brans' book is an up-to-date map of this new wireless business landscape. It will help you deploy mobile technology for measurable, sustainable, business value. Pat has been involved in mobile e-services since their earliest days. As a leader in HP's worldwide mobile solutions team, veteran end-user of mobile technologies, regular contributor to international conferences and standards committees, he has accumulated a world of knowledge and insight into wireless technology.

But *Mobilize Your Enterprise* is emphatically *not* about technology alone. Of course, the technology is here—from wireless networks to the latest application gateway models. But this book is "all business," with realistic solutions to genuine business problems. Every business reader will find value in this book:

*   Sales and service professionals will learn how to use today's wireless technology to improve productivity and how tomorrow's will transform their work life.

- IT managers will learn common-sense methods to balance data security and accessibility, and how to reduce the time, money, and risk of any implementation with a toolkit of decision tools and vendor-selection criteria.
- Business managers and CEOs will find a vision of the "bridge" from today's business processes to tomorrow's always-and-everywhere mobile business—with a plan for moving their company across the gap.

And readers throughout the world will learn how to design and implement mobile *solutions*, not just how to buy technology. This book will help you evaluate technologies and standards according to their business impact, and select vendor/partners with the vision and capabilities to address your specific business goals.

Pat insists, and I agree, that vendors should talk business, not technology. If a vendor cannot sustain a discussion of your business issues, in your business language, it may not be a conversation worth having.

Mobilize Your Enterprise puts your business on the wireless map, and illuminates the road ahead. Use it to connect your front line to the home office, to keep everyone instantly up-to-date, and to deliver new capabilities to your newest customers. Use it in ways no one has thought of yet. Use it to build, compete, and win.

When was it that we knew that wireless telephony would be really, really big? Probably about the time coverage became reliable and universal, the phones fit at last in our pockets and purses and worked for days without recharging. In other words, when we could finally take the technology for granted, and focus on making the call.

Wireless computing stands at that threshold. Now is the time to get ready—and this book is the place to start.

—Janice Chaffin
Senior Vice President
Enterprise Marketing and Solutions Group
Hewlett-Packard Company

Preface

There are some common mistakes technology vendors tend to make in an early market. They get confused by all the hype. But in an early market it is usually the supply side—not the demand side—that makes all the noise. This is self-perpetuating—one vendor hears noise from other vendors, interprets it as a market, and then generates some more noise. In many cases, the hype gets out of hand and people get all the wrong expectations. Unfortunately, in the midst of all that, no real buyers can be identified.

For example, two years ago many people thought there would be a real interest in performing financial transactions on a cell phone. Some were thinking that the average person would want to trade stocks from these small devices. The problem was that typical consumers had no desire to do so.

The hype would not have been so bad if it had stayed among a closed group on the supply side. After all, the suppliers themselves are at fault for not having identified buyers with real problems that could be solved through the new technology. Unfortunately, this was not the case. The general public got wind of these big ideas about a big emerging market, and the confusion spread to the demand side.

Following the early hype is a lot of disappointment and frustration. Few people realize that there was never such a market—just a lot of companies going to the same trade shows and recycling ideas, mistaking those ideas for something coming from potential buyers. People who were in the middle of this look for various scapegoats for the market's not having taken off. They never realize that in fact the market they were targeting never really had a problem that could be solved by the technology in the state it was.

Once companies go belly-up through all this and die-hard techies move on to the next hype wave, we start to hear a whisper—one that in fact has been there long before the technology hype drowned it out. This whisper talks about an industry or industries who have had some burning problem for a long time. That is what is called a market—somebody has a problem (the demand side) and somebody else has a solution (the supply side). This is not rocket science; any kid selling lemonade on a hot summer's day understands this.

Mobile technology has matured in the last two years. There are several good wireless data services available—and there are several good PDAs, tablet computers, and notebook computers with wireless capabilities built in. The technology is now at a state where real business problems can be solved—and it turns out that there *are* real business problems crying out to be solved. These are the problems resulting from lack of critical information when and where workers need it. This problem is particularly acute among mobile workers—especially those who spend a lot of time in front of customers.

Mobilize Your Enterprise: Achieving Competitive Advantage Through Wireless Technology is both a business book and a technical book. It explains the business value of mobile technology to the enterprise—and it explains the enabling technology in terms of its business value. As such, *Mobilize Your Enterprise* aims to help the following types of readers:

- *Executives*, looking to understand what mobile technology can do for your company: this book will arm you with answers to your business questions and it will give you a working knowledge of the technology that makes business value possible.

- *Sales Managers, Service Managers, Line of Business Managers*, looking for ways of optimizing the business processes of mobile workers: you will learn where mobile technology has business value and where it does not. You will learn enough about the underlying technology to be able to make sense of what vendors are telling you.

- *IT Managers*, looking to understand the mobility paradigm: this book will show you the different technologies that go into a mobile solution. It will also help you develop ways of talking about the business rationale for mobile technology to economic buyers in your company. You will learn the structure of the market, and what kinds of vendors you should call on.

- *Technology Vendors*, looking to further your knowledge of this market: this book will help you understand how the buyer sees mobile solutions. It will complement your understanding of the technology, and it will give you new insight into the competitive landscape.

Mobilize Your Enterprise: Achieving Competitive Advantage Through Wireless Technology) is a book to help you make decisions. I hope—and fully expect—that you will find the mobility paradigm a compelling way for your company gain an advantage. But if this book helps you decide that mobility does not make sense for your company, I will still consider that I have done my job.

Acknowledgments

Writing a book is fun! Most of the fun comes from kicking ideas around with people—and being exposed to so many different viewpoints. I have a lot of people to thank for helping me with this book.

First I would like to thank Bruno Castejon, a great boss and coach, for his encouraging words and useful ideas. I would also like to give special thanks to Joe Bono, Geoff Hogg, and Amjid Murtza for a thorough review of every one of the chapters. Thanks guys for ripping it to shreds—and especially for giving me feedback in ways that did not bruise my ego too badly.

I would also like to thank the following people for sharing their insight in this business, for cheering me on, and for their time spent reviewing different parts of the book: Erik Andersen, Ed Anderson, Gary Avery, Celia Bohle, Tommy Brans, Christian Brunet, Jon Coate, Bernard Desarnauts, Stephen Doddridge, Denny Georg, Joe Gerardi, Roke Ghodsi, Bill Grist, Simon Hartley, Caren Hochheimer, Cedric Jarkovsky, Dave Levine, Shelle Meacham, Jeff Medaugh, Pat Mulvanny, Claus Pedersen, Michel-Nicolas Poncet, Ian Rhodes, John Rhoton, Marc Rolfe, Louisa Saunier, Christian Sindel, Remi Vezat, and Lyonel Vincent.

And finally, I thank you, the reader, for your interest in mobile technology—one of the passions in my life.

Making the Case

The Future is Wireless

Well known science fiction writer Arthur C. Clarke once said, "any sufficiently advanced technology is indistinguishable from magic." This sounds about right. New technology is usually awkward and hard to use—and we are very aware of its presence. But as it advances, technology blends right into the background, fitting into our natural way of doing things. It becomes, well, magic.

How many of us think about the massive force of electricity coming into our homes? We do not need to be electricians to turn on a light, use the refrigerator, or turn on the TV.

However, we almost have to be computer scientists to boot up a computer and use the Internet. The difference is that we have been using electricity for over a century now, whereas computers and the Internet are still quite new.

Human nature does not change to conform to technology. It is the technology that changes to fit in with our natural way of doing things. Successful scientists and engineers invent things that people have wanted all along.

Granted, in some cases people do not know what they want. They are just not able to imagine things that are too far out. For example, 200 years ago, I doubt many people imagined sharing gazillions of bits of information instantaneously with others around the world.

No, not many people thought about these kinds of things. But still there were a few who did. These were the people who believed in magic.

TECHNOLOGY VERSUS MAGIC

A corollary to the proposition "any sufficiently advanced technology is indistinguishable from magic" might be the following:

If you want to know where technology is going, just think about what people would do if they could work magic. Over time, technology will approach that.

That sounds a little strange at first. Let's examine this idea a little closer. One hundred fifty years ago my ancestors would have loved to be able to go back to Europe from time to time to visit the families they left behind. And they would have given anything to be able to have a conversation with those same people a few times a week. Back then if you even moved a few hundred miles away, you pretty much broke ties with everyone you left behind.

Few people ever dreamed that technology would one day make travel and communication so easy. But with mind-boggling advances in transportation and communications technologies, we now have air travel, which allows us to move from one continent to another and still come home to visit regularly. We also have extensive telephone networks, which allow us to hold a conversation between virtually any two points on the globe.

We can also take the more recent examples of the Internet and email—technologies that have made it possible for us to get back in touch with long-lost friends. This was the stuff of magic only a few years ago.

Human nature is constant. We want to go out and explore new things, but at the same time be able to keep in touch with the home base. It is the clever engineers who reconfigure things around us to make this possible.

The Magic of Companies

What about groups of people, for example, companies? Can we also say that the things they wish for determine the direction of technology?

I think so. Companies are big buyers of many different kinds of technology—at least they are when they see a business value. For example, advances in transportation and communications technologies have brought great value to businesses. They have brought on the magic of global teams, thereby extending the reach of companies, and bringing them into markets they could only dream of penetrating previously.

Telecommuting allows companies to tap into a workforce that may have otherwise been out of reach. This, of course, is also beneficial to employees, because it allows them to live where they want.

Consider J. Paul Getty. He may have been the first transcontinental tele-commuter when he ran his California oil empire from Europe in the 1930s. Why did he do this? Because he liked living in Europe, and using the telephone allowed him to conduct business from wherever he chose.

Now consider another famous industrial pioneer: Henry Ford. He wanted to make cars available to the masses and the magic that allowed him to do this was electricity. Before we developed the technology to harness electricity, water was a principal source of power. This meant that manufacturing had to occur near the water mill. Electricity changed that by making it possible to line workers up on an assembly line and bring power to the various pieces of equipment. Needless to say, the impact was astounding!

Again the most recent example of magic is the Internet. The Internet has made it possible for large companies to disseminate large quantities of information to employees. Thanks to the simple ideas behind HTTP and HTML, the sharing of documents is now easy and intuitive.

It appears that with companies the same rule holds true. Clever engineers eventually figure out ways of providing what the companies want. In other words, the direction of the engineer's efforts is toward the wishes of people or companies.

This means that to understand the direction of technology as a whole, we can just think about what people and companies want. One way of doing this is to imagine that we are not constrained by the laws of physics—or let's say we will imagine we can work magic.

Friction-Free Sales and Service

Let's try the following exercise and see where it takes us. For the sake of this book, we are interested in companies as a whole, because we want to know how they can be made more competitive.

What would companies do if they could work magic? An obvious response is that they would magically generate revenue without incurring cost. Maybe one day this will be possible, but for our purposes, that is looking a little *too* far into the future.

Reeling in our imagination a little bit, let's try this one: Companies would really like for all of their employees to have telepathic powers that allow them to access any information available to the company, at any time, and from any place. Likewise, if companies had their way, any new information attained by an employee would instantly be made available to the rest of the company.

Think of how powerful this notion is. The lack of information would no longer constrain the business processes of mobile employees. Any traveling professional would be connected to what is happening at the home base.

Perhaps the kind of worker who would gain the most from this magic would be customer-facing employees, because the result would be a sort of *friction-free* sales and service, with the benefits listed in Box 1–1.

All employees who interface with customers would have perfect knowledge—or at least as perfect as the information that comes into the company. They could answer questions immediately and accurately, they could quote prices instantaneously, and they could even enter orders on the spot.

This would mean that prices could be changed on a daily basis to reflect instantaneous market conditions. Nobody would have to worry about propagating the updates.

Because orders would be taken on the spot, it would be easier to sell goods and services at a higher price—as a rule of thumb, the quicker the order can be taken, the higher the price. Furthermore, in taking the order, the salesperson would be able to reserve the inventory and promise a delivery date.

Field engineers would be dispatched more efficiently, based on skill set, proximity, and availability. When they reached the problem spot, they would have perfect knowledge of technical specifications and problem history reports.

After rendering services, a bill could be generated immediately. The bill could then be sent in the mail, or it could be magically output on a nearby printer. Either way, the company cash flow would be improved because the turnaround on being paid for services would be greatly reduced.

Traveling professionals would no longer experience dead time. They could communicate with colleagues, schedule meetings, and be alerted to problems that need their attention. Or they could participate in some sort of interactive training.

Last but not least in my mind, employees' lifestyles would be improved. People would not have to make special trips to the office to fill out annoying reports or to fetch documentation. They would no longer be so closely tethered to the office.

Box 1-1   The Value of Friction-Free Sales and Service

Through friction-free sales and service:
- All employees have perfect knowledge.
- Orders are taken on the spot.
- Engineers are dispatched automatically based on skill, proximity, and availability.
- Engineers have immediate access to problem history and all technical documents.
- Bills are generated immediately.
- Trips to the office to fill out reports are no longer necessary.
- Employees can work while traveling.

This all sounds pretty good, but it is probably a good idea to take a reality check here. Just how close can we expect technology to approach this magic?

TECHNOLOGY THAT WORKS MAGIC

It turns out that technology *can* approach that magic—starting now. Employees could be equipped with small wirelessly enabled devices, allowing them to communicate with their enterprise applications to retrieve and update information in real time.

Maybe the first time we saw this kind of setup was in the old *Star Trek* episodes with the communicators that linked Captain Kirk with *his* enterprise, the *Starship Enterprise*, and allowed him to interact with the ship's computer via a user-friendly voice interface. He did all this without a network to route calls!

But what I am talking about really is not *that* far-fetched. What I am talking about is made possible by the convergence of technologies that have developed along the five lines shown in Figure 1–1: *wireless networks, battery, CPU/memory, user interface,* and *enterprise applications.*

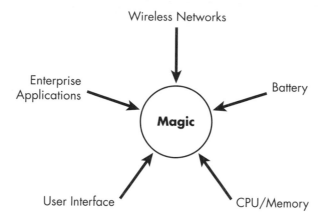

FIGURE 1–1   The 5 axes of enabling technology.

To get an idea of where things are going, we should first review how far we have already come in these areas.

How Far We Have Come

You may already have a good feel for how far we have come along these lines over the last few decades just by thinking about your own experiences. I, for one, have a few vivid memories of early mobile phone technologies.

Wireless Networks

The very first time I saw a wireless phone was about 25 years ago when a kid in my neighborhood showed me what looked like an oversized walkie-talkie. He had to dial several series of numbers to get connected, and only a handful of people could use their phones simultaneously in a given area of coverage.

The mobile phone system was called mobile telephone service (MTS). The reason several numbers had to be dialed was that two different logical connections had to be established: one from the phone to the mobile network, and one from the mobile network to the fixed-line recipient. There was absolutely no privacy—it was easy for somebody else to listen in on the call. Nobody really cared anyway, because most users were hobbyists.

What we know as cellular networks today did not come into commercial use until the early 1980s. The cellular model is based on a confederation of contiguous cells (radio coverage areas) linked to a network that routes calls, handles billing, and provides various other services. In the 1980s, this new arrangement, along with new signaling techniques, made it possible to support many more users. But the coverage was still patchy, and it was still pretty expensive to use. Consequently, people generally only used their cell phones for emergency situations, both business and personal.

From the 1980s to the 1990s digital transmission techniques made it possible to jump an order of magnitude in the number of users that could be supported per cell. These techniques also reduced the amount of interference, thus making calls clearer.

Just stand around the downtown area of any city in the industrialized world and you are likely to see several people engaged in a phone conversation as they are walking along. That is progress!

Batteries

Similar things can be said about battery technology, which has helped to make portable computing devices possible. Just a little over 10 years ago, only important executives who needed to be reachable at all times had "mobile" phones.

In fact, the mobile part was questionable, because the battery was about the size of a car battery. Furthermore, it had to be recharged frequently. Aside from access limitations resulting from spotty network coverage, the lifetime and recharging characteristics of the battery meant that the phone was frequently turned off.

Designs based on nickel cadmium (NiCad), followed by those based on nickel metal hydride (NiMH), offered increasingly attractive storage densities. Then lithium-ion designs improved on that, bringing on a new generation of batteries that were smaller, longer lasting, and couldn't be overcharged. Now we carry mobile phones around in our pockets that are so small we forget they are there.

Finally, the latest, greatest battery designs are based on lithium polymer. These batteries, which we are starting to see in commercial products, are not only lightweight, they can also be bent into shapes that allow them to fit into the nooks and crannies of small computing devices.

CPU/Memory

When discussing developments in the area of CPU, we need only evoke Moore's law, a term coined by the press in reference to an article published in *Electronics* in 1965. In "Cramming More Components into Integrated Circuits," Gordon E. Moore predicted that roughly every year we would see a doubling in the number of transistors that could be squeezed onto a single chip. His prediction was that this would hold true up until 1975.

This prediction did not hold true to the letter—it turns out to be more like every 18 months that technology and the economics of production allow a doubling in transistor density in commercial microprocessors. But the underlying point was right on. We have indeed enjoyed an exponential increase in the power of integrated circuits—and it has lasted a lot longer than 1975.

In fact, cramming more transistors into a given amount of space actually has two nice consequences. The first is that more logic can be carried out per unit of space. The second is that, because the transistors are closer, the chip can operate at a higher speed.

As for memory, I remind you what Bill Gates said a little over a decade ago when challenged on the memory limitations imposed by the DOS operating system. He is quoted as saying that "640K of memory ought to be enough for anybody." The public easily digested this comment at the time. We accepted this software-imposed limitation, because it was not too far off the hardware limitations.

But since then we have all been amazed at the rate of increase we have enjoyed in the amount of random access memory (RAM) and the amount of disk space (secondary memory) that comes with a standard PC. In fact, thanks to compact flash (CF) memory, we can now store over 100 megabytes of data in a personal digital assistant (PDA). CF "remembers" without drawing power. The result is you don't need a hard disk on your PDA. You can store all that data in compact flash.

Today's PDAs have a CPU that is more powerful than a PC of a few years ago, and they take over 100 megabytes of memory. That is real progress!

User Interface

With the increased processing power, and with clever new algorithms, a tremendous amount of progress has also been made in the area of user interfaces. We have gone from text-based to graphics-based interfaces. And now, handwriting recognition is not only possible, it is widely used on PDAs.

Primitive voice interfaces are now possible. But there is still a trade-off between recognition of a variety of voices and accents versus recognition of a large number of words. It is hard to have both, since each requires a lot of computation.

Maybe the best way to understand the importance of a good user interface is to consider the surge in popularity of the Internet in the mid-1990s. This was brought on by the introduction of the browser interface, which significantly enhanced usability, and therefore, brought us much closer to magic.

In fact, the browser has been so successful that most major software applications have been modified to accommodate the browser as a primary user interface. This is certainly true for the large enterprise applications—those applications, such as customer relationship management (CRM), that make some sense of all the data we can now amass on powerful storage systems.

Enterprise Applications

Enterprise applications are the fifth axis of interest to us. We have also seen a great deal of progress in this area.

In the past, all data was stored on a large mainframe—and it was a cumbersome task to do anything meaningful with that data. However, large enterprise applications have really grown up in the last decade with enterprise resource planning (ERP), supply chain management (SCM), customer relationship management (CRM) systems, and various human resources applications that allow meaningful organization of critical company information.

Using these applications, companies operate much more efficiently, tracking sales funnels and optimizing the supply chain. Any salesperson in the company can get a view of the history of interactions with a customer. Products can be built to order, which allows more flexibility in configurations that can be offered to the customer, and, at the same time, it minimizes the need to stock up beforehand.

And let's not forget another important enterprise application—the ubiquitous corporate-wide email system. Only computer geeks used email 10 years ago. Now almost every large company is absolutely dependant on a corporate-wide email system for both internal and external communication.

Near-Term Expectations

Now that we have reviewed how far things have come along the five axes during the recent past, let's take a survey of what we can expect from these technologies in the near future. This will give us an idea of how close we will come to friction-free sales and services in the next few years.

Wireless Networks

We can soon expect fast data services from our cellular networks. We can also expect improvements in the coverage area. Most mobile telephone operators in the world have plans to migrate to third-generation (3G) mobile telephony. The carriers in the United States are no exception.

Third-generation mobile networks will provide high-speed data services—around 2 megabits per second. This means the bandwidth you will get on a mobile link will compete with that which you get on current digital subscriber line (DSL) links at home!

The peculiarity of the U.S. market is that the carriers are using different technology now, which means that the migration path to 3G may be different from one network to another. For example, Sprint PCS is rolling out a data service known as radio transmission technology (1xRTT), whereas AT&T Wireless is rolling out general packet radio services (GPRS). These two fast data services, which I cover more extensively in Chapter 6, take their respective networks down the path toward 3G.

You may have heard about some of the disappointments in the actual bandwidth achieved with GPRS networks. One of the limiting factors has lied in the early generation of GPRS handsets. The problem is that the handset has a lot more processing to do. All that extra work generates a lot of extra heat and drains the battery too fast.

This is not the first time a state-of-the-art handset component has lagged behind the network standards. For example, when work started on the GSM standards, no existing CPU could handle the amount of processing necessary to support the protocols. But the designers of GSM took Moore's law into account, and correctly assumed that microprocessor technology would quickly catch up.

Batteries

Indeed these handset issues are resolved through improvements in battery and microprocessor technologies. We are now just about in the middle of a transition from the use of lithium-ion batteries to lithium polymer. What will this mean?

It is thanks to lithium-ion designs that we have the current generation of lightweight batteries that in turn have made the current generation of mobile devices possible. Lithium polymer designs result in even lighter batteries that can take on odd shapes that fit into the nooks and crannies of small equipment.

This malleability is a very useful property, and will help deliver even more magic by allowing devices to get even smaller. However, lithium polymer represents only an incremental improvement over lithium-ion in terms of *storage density*, which is the amount of energy that can be stored in a given size or weight of battery.

In fact, the next order of magnitude improvement we'll see in storage capacity will likely come in the form of fuel cells, which aren't actually batteries in the strictest sense. These cells are recharged with some kind of fuel—the current thinking is that diluted liquid methanol works best.

Fuel cells should be more powerful than lithium-ion by an order of magnitude. It is likely that we'll start seeing commercial use of this new portable power source within two or three years.

CPU/Memory

Even as portable power sources are improving, we continue to see astounding progress in microprocessors. The main factor bringing about these improvements is the increase in the number of transistors that can be placed in a given unit of space (*transistor density*). At higher transistor densities, chips require less power to perform a given set of tasks.

In 1965 Moore did not expect the exponential increase in processing power to last as long as it has. He was only thinking of the next 10 years—up to 1975. But Moore has recently stated that he now expects this kind of progress for the next 20 years!

In addition to the tremendous advances in transistor density, we are likely to continue to see advances in techniques to optimize how processors work and how memory is accessed. By making assumptions about the way most programs work, chip designers can have a processor perform tasks ahead of time. If the assumptions are correct, the predictions about the tasks that will need to be performed are usually right.

These kinds of optimization are commonly used in memory fetching. For example, it is usually assumed that bytes stored in consecutive memory locations will be needed by a given program at around the same time. Working on this assumption, several bytes are read at a time. It turns out that, on the average, this is optimal.

User Interface

Improvements in processing power have helped bring about great improvements in user interfaces. Voice recognition systems either learn the speech patterns of a small number of users and recognize a large vocabulary, or they are able to make out the words of a large speaker base, but use only a limited vocabulary. Right now it is hard to get both, but if Moore's predictions hold true, this issue should be resolved by the progress in microprocessor technology.

Still, the real hope lies in natural language processing (NLP). Remember that human nature remains constant, and technology eventually catches up, fitting right in with our way of doing things. When user interfaces make people speak or write in unnatural ways, we are all too aware of the presence of technology. One day, through NLP, we will achieve the state of advancement

Captain Kirk enjoyed when he spoke to his ship's computer as if he were speaking to a human being.

Enterprise Applications

The areas in which we can expect to see improvements in enterprise applications are in the integration of applications from different vendors, in the pre-packaging of functionality, and in the way these applications provide functionality specifically needed by the mobile worker.

A lot of work is being done to standardize the way applications from different vendors exchange information. Most importantly, efforts are being made to get different applications to work together in a coordinated fashion to improve business processes.

In the early days a lot of customization was required to get large enterprise applications to do something useful for a company. This was due in part to the variety of software and databases that were already installed and running within a given company. It was also due to the lack of maturity of the enterprise applications themselves. In the future these applications will be more shrink-wrapped, and will require less customization.

This is all good to hear, but the improvements that are probably the most important to the mobile enterprise are those around tailoring applications' functionality to the needs of the mobile worker. Software vendors are assuming that an increasingly large part of their user base will be using small, wirelessly enabled devices, and these users will be highly mobile.

Indeed all of the major developers of enterprise applications are working mobility into their software. One thing we will be sure to see will be software that makes use of information about the location of the user. This software would behave differently, and it would provide different data, depending on where the user is at the time.

Long-Term Outlook

Given the magic companies would like to work, and the direction of the supporting technology, I can say with confidence that within five years most companies will equip a large part of their workforce with small, wirelessly enabled devices with some clever user interfaces that will allow those employees to access enterprise information anytime and anywhere. Furthermore, it will all seem very routine to us.

This is probably not an earth-shattering prediction to you. There is a lot of talk in the press about what will be possible with wireless in the near future. But how far is your company along the path toward being a mobile enterprise?

I hope you have started to prepare for the future. Those companies whose work force is not equipped with such devices will be at a competitive disadvantage in many ways, including those shown in Box 1–2.

Box 1–2   Consequences of Not Mobilizing

Those companies who do not master mobile technology will be at a disadvantage in the following ways:

- They will have longer sales cycles.
- It will take longer for them to perform repairs.
- Their dispatch costs will be higher.
- They will miss opportunities to close sales.
- They will fumble around and look clumsy in front of customers.
- It will take them longer to generate bills for their services.
- They will waste time during travel.

It is just a matter of time before mobile technology becomes a fundamental business tool. Sooner or later, each and every successful company will have to learn to use it.

THE IMPACT ON IT PLANNING

If we believe that the mastery of mobile technology will make such a big difference, we have to start developing an idea of when exactly we should take on this new paradigm. At a minimum, most companies should be assigning a team of people in the IT department to start developing expertise in mobility.

Planning for Security

This team should understand the security implications of mobility, especially since the mobile solutions with any significant impact will have to access data *inside* the firewall. The goal of the mobile enterprise is to have employees carrying small devices. Almost by definition, these devices tend to get lost or stolen pretty easily. The mobility team must ensure that there are adequate authentication mechanisms in place in the geographies where it will make sense to equip the workforce with mobile solutions. It is also important to protect data that resides on the device itself to prevent malicious individuals from stealing company information from a portable computer left lying around.

Planning to Deploying New Applications

Another key job of the mobility team should be to examine any new purchases of large applications with an eye to determining if mobility can be fit in at a later date. One of the things to be concerned with is the flexibility of the application output to be adjusted to a variety of devices, most of which have smaller screens than those on a desktop PC. Likewise, the content from the same set of smaller devices has to serve as input to the application. This could be built directly into the application, or it could be done by a front-end "transcoder," which may be developed either by the same vendor or by a separate one. In the latter case, it is highly desirable that the application interface be in the form of HTML, or better yet, extensible markup language (XML). This makes it much easier for the transcoder to do its job.

New Business Processes

Another thing to look into is how the application developer plans to modify the application behavior to more naturally fit the new ways it would be used. For example, it should take advantage of the fact that the user is likely to be standing in front of a customer while using the application. Response time is therefore critical, and different kinds of information will be useful in this situation. For example, the customer-facing employee has to have quick access to the status of previously placed orders, or problem history.

Location-Based Features

The developer might also be planning to develop something specific to mobility into the application, such as location-based features. There are two aspects to location-based features. One is actually determining the coordinates. The other is doing something sensible with that information.

Coordinates can be obtained either by using a global positioning system (GPS) or through queries to the network. In the case where GPS is used, the position can be determined more accurately. However, it only works when the user is outside. This also assumes that an extra GPS module is carried by the employee, either as part of the data device or as a separate piece of equipment. This module then has to communicate the coordinates back to the application.

Wireless network operators can also determine a user's position, but the resolution is not very good. There are several ways of doing this, and they will be described in greater detail in Chapter 6. Regardless of how the network determines a user's coordinates, the application has to get that information from the network. This will require special logic from the application.

Once the position is determined, something useful has to be done with it. The obvious application of this information is to dispatch engineers based on where they are now. To do this right, geographic barriers, such as rivers, have to be taken into consideration. For example, an engineer can be 100 yards from the site in question, but if there is a river between the two, it may take him or her several hours to get there.

Some other uses of position information are to do things like find office buildings, restaurants, or hotels. For this to work right, the application needs access to a substantial database of these kinds of places. That could come with the application, or the application could make use of a database from another vendor. Either way, special logic is needed.

We cover location-based services in more detail later. The point to take away from this discussion is that now is the time to start asking your software suppliers what their plans are in this direction. This is part of the job of the mobility team in the IT department.

Addressing the Paradigm Shift

I would compare the impending paradigm shift to that brought on by the Internet and the Web. At the point where we knew that Web interfaces would dominate, the forward-looking IT departments started asking their large application vendors what their plans were to allow for a browser interface to their applications.

It became imperative that applications requiring two or more computers to communicate do so over TCP/IP. It was clear then that those applications that didn't fit the Internet/Web paradigm boxed their users into a dead end.

The same will be true as we shift to the mobile enterprise. Those applications that continue to assume users have a large screen and a fixed-line connection will take users down a dead-end path.

Immediate Actions

To prepare your company for the new paradigm, the mobility team has some immediate actions to take. Box 1–3 lists the most important ones.

Box 1–3   Immediate Tasks for the Mobility Team

The mobility team should start on the following:

- They should develop expertise in mobility.
- They should plan a security infrastructure for mobility.
- They should start evaluating new applications in terms of how they will evolve toward wireless.

How much further should companies go at this point? In the next chapter we explore this question further—and I provide guidelines you can use to determine how far your company should move now.

SUMMARY

If companies could work magic, they would make it such that all of their employees have telepathic powers that allow them to access any information available to the company, at any time, and from any place. Likewise, any new information attained by an employee would instantly be made available to the rest of the company. This would be of enormous benefit, resulting in *friction-free sales and service*.

The solutions that will approach this magic are made possible by developments in technology along five axes: wireless networks, battery, CPU/memory, user interface, and enterprise applications. These technologies have made huge advances over the last few years; and it is already clear that, in the near term, we will see more big advances.

Because there is a strong need to mobilize an enterprise, and because this is now possible, we can be sure that within five years most companies will equip a large part of their workforce with small, wirelessly enabled devices that will allow employees to read and update critical enterprise data.

Since this will certainly happen, IT departments have to start preparing now. At a minimum they should assign a team of mobility experts to rethink the security infrastructure and to view any new purchases in terms of an evolution toward the mobile enterprise.

The remaining question is, in addition to developing mobility expertise and making sure new applications have a path toward mobility, what other steps should be taken at this point? The next chapter sheds some light on that question.

Today's Possibilities

Now is the time to start thinking about how your enterprise will take on wireless technologies. What timeline makes sense to you? Should you plan a massive rollout today? This all depends on the state of the technology, the state of the industry, and the attitude of your company.

It seems pretty obvious that the state of the technology is of utmost importance. We have already touched on how far the relevant technologies have come—and how far we think they will go in the near future. Now we will look at the state of the technology today.

We must also consider how well developed the industry is. For even if the technology is in the right state, it is not until the industry matures that the products and standards are developed to allow the technology to be easily purchased and used. Without mature products and standards, mobilizing the enterprise can be a difficult undertaking indeed.

Finally, the attitude of your company is to be considered, because we need to think about how well your company generally takes on new technology. Are you generally early adopters of productivity-enhancing tools?

THE CURRENT STATE OF TECHNOLOGY

Let's examine the current state of the technologies along the five axes that we are counting on to bring us friction-free sales and service. This will help us make a decision as to whether or not the mobile enterprise makes good business sense today.

Networks

In this book we are mostly concerned with wireless networks that offer public access over a wide area, that is, distances of kilometers or miles. These networks use frequencies that are licensed by a government body (such as the Federal Communications Commission in the United States) and they are built around code division multiple access (CDMA) or global system for mobile communications (GSM), for example.

This is different from those networks using unlicensed frequencies, and for which the radio signaling only covers small areas, that is, distances of 10s or 100s of meters or yards. These networks are wireless local area networks (WLAN) and they are based on 802.11b, HiperLAN2, or HomeRF.

This is also different from personal area network (PAN) technology, like Bluetooth. We touch on WLAN and PAN technologies in Chapter 6; but they are on the periphery of our principal area of interest, which is the business of providing workers out in the field with wide area network services.

Public Wireless Networks in the United States

The development of wide area wireless networks in the United States has taken a different course than it has in most other industrial nations. The difference lies in the role the government has played. In the United States, the government has licensed spectrum to network operators without mandating networking standards. In many other parts of the world, governments have mandated the use of GSM.

The issue here lies in the compatibility between handsets and networks. It is very difficult to develop a handset that will conform to all the different frequencies and signaling standards. The result is that a given handset will be compatible with one or a small number of wireless network standards.

In those countries where the government has exercised tighter control over the standards used, a cell phone works with all of the networks in that country, as well as with networks in many other countries. In the United States this is not the case—and that is a far cry from magic!

However, there is at least one advantage to having a more loosely controlled competitive environment. In such an environment, companies get more innovative. Qualcomm, for example, has developed some really good technology for fast data services on CDMA networks.

We might compare the industry structure in the United States to what we would experience if the different television networks were to use different transmission techniques. Some would offer higher resolution and better quality viewing than others. But a given TV set would not work with all channels. As it is today in the television industry, because the different networks operate using the same standards, and because an industry has grown up around that, we are stuck with low-resolution television.

It turns out that the wireless data industry in the United States is even more complicated than that. There are different kinds of wireless networks that have sprung up for various reasons in the past to provide various services that were in vogue at the time. Several of these networks can now offer some kind of wireless data service. For our purposes, we can classify them into three different groups. These are paging networks, dedicated data networks, and cellular networks. Let's see what each offers us today.

Paging Networks

In the late 1980s an industry grew up around paging. This was originally based on a one-way protocol, that is, the person being paged received data, but he or she could not send anything back.

However, thanks to the clever innovators at Motorola, two-way paging is now possible. This technology, called ReFLEX, offers *downstream* (from the network to the handset) data rates that are higher than the *upstream* (from the handset to the network) data rates. It is a common—and usually valid—assumption that users receive more data than they send. For this reason, the downstream data rate is often greater than the upstream data rate. Table 2–1 shows the bandwidths offered through different versions of ReFLEX.

TABLE 2–1 Versions of ReFLEX Available Today

Version	Downstream Data Rate	Upstream Data Rate
ReFLEX 25	9.6 kbps	up to 6.4 kbps
ReFLEX 50	25.6 kbps	up to 9.6 kbps

Networks based on ReFLEX include Arch Wireless, Metrocall, SkyTel Communications, and WebLink Wireless. Services offered include email and limited Internet access.

Since paging services can also be offered through dedicated data networks, and soon most cellular networks as well, it appears that networks based on two-way paging are at a competitive disadvantage. Customers will want richer features that can be more easily offered through the other networks.

Dedicated Data Networks

Networks designed specifically for data services are well established in the United States. Table 2–2 summarizes these networks and the data rates offered.

TABLE 2–2   Dedicated Data Networks in the United States

Specification	Leading Provider	Data Rate
Mobitex	Cingular Interactive	8 kbps to 19.2 kbps
ARDIS	Motient	4.8 kbps to 19.2 kbps

Mobitex is a standard that was developed by Ericsson and Swedish Telecom Radio in the early 1980s, and was subsequently opened up to other manufacturers in the mid-1990s. This protocol operates on cellular frequencies and offers data rates of 8 kbps. With a newer generation of base stations, data rates of 19.2 kbps can be achieved. The largest Mobitex operator in the United States is Cingular Interactive.

Advanced Radio Data Information Service (ARDIS) was developed by Motorola and IBM to support their field organizations. From the beginning, a key feature of ARDIS has been to provide reliable in-building communications. It does this at data rates of either 4.8 kbps or 19.2 kbps.

ARDIS has since been bought by Motient, who has combined this with its satellite services to provide coverage in both metropolitan and rural areas.

Cellular Networks

Most cellular network operators offer some kind of data service in addition to their bread-and-butter voice services. Today, U.S. cellular operators are serving up the following alphabet soup for data users: CSD, CDPD, SMS, GPRS, and cdma2000 1x (aka 1xRTT).

For this discussion we need to distinguish between first-generation (1G), second-generation (2G), and two-and-a-half generation (2.5G) networks. First-generation networks use analog signaling, whereas 2G and 2.5G networks use digital signaling. Two-and-a-half generation networks is a convenient term used to refer to 2G networks that have taken an evolutionary step toward 3G by providing fast data services.

Table 2–3 is a bit of a simplification, because, for example, GPRS and cdma2000 1x are mutually exclusive. That is, whether a network takes on GPRS or cdma2001 depends on whether the network is currently based on GSM or CDMA. No one network will offer both.

We cannot really speak of data rates for SMS, which is a messaging protocol. What we can say is that it is slow; and it can only reasonably be used as originally intended, that is, for sending and receiving short messages.

TABLE 2–3   Data Services Available through Cellular Networks Today

Protocol	Generation	Average Data Rate
CSD	1G, 2G, 2.5G	9.6 to 14.4 kbps
CDPD	1G	9 kbps
SMS	2G, 2.5G	NA (Messaging only)
GPRS	2.5G	28 to 40 kbps
Cdma2000 1x	2.5G	28 to 80 kbps

The following is a further explanation of the data services offered by cellular operators today:

- *Circuit Switched Data (CSD)* is the easiest data service for operators to provide. It works much like a modem works on a fixed-line voice network, that is, a voice channel is used to transmit bits and bytes. Because this only works once a connection is established, it does not have the same *always-on* properties of the packet-switched services.

  To use CSD, a modem is required. This can be an integral part of your phone or PDA, or it can be on a PDA card or sled. If you need voice communications anyway, the best way to go is to have the modem on the phone, and connect your notebook computer or PDA to the phone via a serial cable or via one of the short-range wireless options, such as infrared (IR) or Bluetooth.

  Using CSD, the maximum data rate you get will range from 9.6 to 14.4 kbps. The advantage to CSD is that it does not require any additional network infrastructure, so you get data service anywhere voice service is available.

  A step up from CSD is high-speed circuit-switched data (HSCSD). This protocol combines two or more circuits to provide a higher data rate, but because it ties up more than one voice circuit, it cuts down on the amount of voice traffic that can be supported. For this reason, HSCSD has not been widely deployed in the United States.

- *Cellular digital packet data (CDPD)* provides an always-on service over existing voice channels. Like CSD, it transmits data using a wireless modem. However, unlike CSD, with CDPD a dedicated voice circuit is never established. Instead, data is transmitted during idle time on several voice circuits.

  To perform the fancy technique of finding idle voice circuits, and quickly stuffing data onto them, special equipment is required at each cell site. In addition, other special network equipment is required to route the CDPD traffic within the network and between the network and the Internet. The CDPD equipment within the network also provides encryption and user authentication services.

So far CDPD operates only on 1G networks. While theoretical data rates are up to 19.2 kbps, the average data rate is around 9 kbps.

- *Short Messaging Service (SMS)* started out on 2G networks. This protocol borrows the signaling channels that are normally used for coordination between the various network components to perform things like call setup, call accounting, and prepaid account debit.

  As the name indicates, SMS allows only the sending and receiving of short messages of up to 160 characters in length, or a little more with some variations on the standards. This is not enough to allow true Internet services. However, it has become a popular way for teenagers in Europe and Asia to communicate, and abbreviated vocabularies have been developed to overcome the limited service.

  Business users may also use SMS for limited communication, such as sending messages or alerts. The usefulness of SMS to the business user ends there.

- *General packet data service (GPRS)* is the evolutionary path for GSM networks on their way to 3G. That is, GPRS is the 2.5G for these GSM.

  We are now seeing a rollout of GPRS in the United States, and although the theoritical data rate of this protocol reaches up to 144 kbps, there are some issues that result in the real data rates being much lower. As mentioned previously, one issue is the amount of extra processing a handset has to do to "speak" the protocol. Another issue is the contention by other users for the same transmission slots. And finally, there are some latency issues—delays in the time it takes to send data, because some negotiation has to take place between the sending side and the network before data can actually be sent.

- *cdma2000 1X* is an evolution from cdmaOne networks on the path to 3G. CDMA stands for Code Division Multiple Access. The 1X is an abbreviation for 1xRTT, which in turn is an abbreviation for Radio Transmission Technology.

  cdma2000 1X is being rolled out now and it will offer increased voice capacity in addition to fast and efficient data service. It does not suffer the same issues as GPRS around processing power, bandwidth contention, and latency. While it is a superior protocol, its use is restricted to cdmaOne networks. Theoretically, 1xRTT can acheive data rates of 144 kbps, but real data rates are lower.

Analysis of Wireless Data Today

I warned you things were complicated in the United States! And I am sure you had already figured that out before you picked up this book. But let's take a look at what this means to the mobile enterprise right now.

Today it makes a lot of sense to get wireless data services from the paging or dedicated data networks. This is their business, and they are pretty well established. In the short term, it is well worth your while to consider making use of the services offered by these networks.

However, it is most likely that over the long term, the wireless data magic we need will be delivered as an overlay to existing wireless voice networks. The expected data services will be at a good bandwidth. Furthermore, since our need to talk is not going to go away, the network that provides both voice and data services will be more attractive in the long run than those that provide only one and not the other.

Two-and-a-half generation data services are being rolled out aggressively. Even as we wait for complete coverage, there are already enough good data services to start mobilizing parts of your enterprise now. But for the time being, we will have to proceed with caution, because not all of the data services work together, and the coverage is still spotty.

If you want to start mobilizing your enterprise using the network services that are likely to be successful in the long run, that is, the *always-on* data services offered through cellular voice networks, a key criterion for exactly which parts of your enterprise should be mobilized now is the geographic area where such services are needed. You will want to focus on areas where *always-on* data services already exist.

Another thing to take into serious consideration is the use of CSD, which would mean that although you do not get the *always-on* features you would get from a packet-switched service, it is simple, and you get coverage anywhere you get voice coverage.

Still another creative way of doing things today is to use a voice interface on a cell phone. If the set of functions your mobile workers need are relatively simple, voice menus and voice interaction may work just fine. The advantages are that it is an easy interface to use (all you have to do is talk and listen), and you get coverage anywhere you get voice coverage.

One other alternative that should be considered today is desktop synchronization. This is a good compromise to a full-blown wireless solution. And in fact, even when you get perfect coverage, it will probably still make sense to have some sort of regular desktop synchronization to pass large amounts of data between the handheld device and enterprise applications.

Battery Technology

As mentioned in Chapter 1, we are now in the midst of a transition from the dominance of lithium-ion battery designs to the dominance of lithium polymer battery designs. Since lithium polymer cells are lighter and more malleable, we can expect to see a new generation of smaller devices.

However, we will not see a tremendous improvement in how long we can go without recharging. In fact, what works against us here is that, in our greed, we ask for more and more power from batteries. Transmission requires extra processing, which draws more power. Fancy computing and graphics also draw more power.

Engineers of small computing devices have already had to develop some pretty clever techniques to make the best use of available power. This has made a significant difference between the various brands of mobile phones and computers.

With the exception of the laptop, the battery life of these devices looks pretty good for the mobile enterprise. Laptops can only be used for a few hours before the battery is drained. Fortunately though, when you are not using your laptop, you can put it in hibernation mode, in which there is very little drain on the battery.

When we start adding PDA functions to a phone, or when we start building transmission capabilities into the PDA, subnotebook, and notebook computer, batteries drain much faster. A device that acts both as a computer and a transmitter has a much higher energy requirement.

Furthermore, all other things being equal, the faster the data networks get, the faster the device consumes the available power. In fact, one of the reasons the first generation of GPRS phones are not hitting full GPRS speeds is because of power consumption and issues around heat dissipation. Before we achieve the ultimate magic, we need some major improvements in the battery technology itself, and probably also in the techniques used to manage power consumption.

However, what we have today will already allow us to make some big improvements in our business processes. Therefore, battery technology is not a roadblock for the time being.

CPU/Memory

There are a plethora of handheld devices commercially available today. We cover the most popular ones in Chapter 5, but for right now we are interested in the kind of processing power and amount of memory generally available in these devices. This will help us determine whether or not now is the right time to start mobilizing the enterprise.

Three chip manufacturers currently dominate the handheld industry: ARM, Intel, and Motorola.

The ARM processors are made by the company ARM Ltd., which was originally known as Advanced RISC Machines. This company was a spin-off of a collaborative effort between Apple computer and a company called Acorn.

ARM now specializes in developing processors for small devices, including cell phones and PDAs. They have 32-bit processors and some proprietary techniques for reducing the amount of memory needed to store programs targeted for 32-bit processors. ARM has patents on this technique, and they license the use of these design features to other companies, including Intel and Motorola.

Using its license on ARM technology, Intel sells the StrongARM processor. Intel, of course, also continues to manufacture the chips for which it is famous. In fact, while not designed for small devices, some of the old Intel chips are used in handheld devices today.

For example, one interesting approach is that of the company Research In Motion (RIM), who produces the popular BlackBerry pager. These pagers, beautiful for their simplicity, use the rather old Intel386 as a central processing unit. BlackBerry pagers do not do a whole lot, so this processor is a very appropriate choice.

Motorola manufactures the DragonBall processor, which is used by PALM and Handspring devices. Motorola now also licenses ARM technology to produce its own ARM-based chip, the MX1. These processors may also be used by PALM and Handspring in the future.

The amount of RAM you get with a PDA today ranges from under 1 Mbyte to more than 64 Mbytes—and most PDAs allow you to add even more memory. Today you get more memory on the PDA than the 640 Kbytes you were allotted on a DOS machine in the mid- to late-1980s. And we used to use those things as business tools back then!

As demonstrated by the success of the BlackBerry pager, you do not need a lot of processing power to perform some of the basic business tasks, such as sending email, using calendaring, and retrieving a little text output from enterprise applications. Most of the current generation of PDAs are a lot more powerful than that, making better user interfaces possible, and running more substantial business applications.

It seems that as far as CPU and memory goes, today we have the magic we need to mobilize the enterprise.

User Interface

Nowadays we can get computing devices that are so small they cannot be used in traditional ways. The screen is too small, and there is not much room for a usable keyboard. The race is on for the ideal user interface.

If we go back to the theory that the direction of technology can be determined by simply imagining what people would do if they could work magic, we might say that user interface technology will evolve in such a way as to approach a direct transfer of ideas from a person's head to the device.

And by the way, if we consider the basis for most Western alphabets, that is, phonetics, we might conclude that these alphabets are no longer adequate. With all the information thrown at us these days, having to read words and sound them out in your head is a very slow process. The oriental characters are better in this regard because you can pick up an idea at a glance.

Many people think that voice interaction technology is the way to go. After all, this is the most natural form of communication for us. Furthermore, we have already gotten used to seeing people walk around public areas talking into small microphones. The first few times you saw this, you may have thought the people were talking to themselves, but now it is a pretty routine sight in most metropolitan areas.

For applications requiring only a limited vocabulary, you can get a pretty good voice recognition system that can be used by multiple users in your company. Employees can communicate with this system through a cell phone.

For more sophisticated applications, a PDA is needed. Most PDAs now come with handwriting recognition technology. Those devices based on the Palm OS require the user to learn the graffiti alphabet, but this can usually be mastered in 10 or 20 minutes. PDAs based on PocketPC, on the other hand, learn the user's natural handwriting.

PDAs also offer onscreen and fold-out keyboards can be bought as attachments. For larger devices, like the notebook computers, keyboards work just fine.

For most business functions, the state of user interface technology is sufficient. Some brief training may be required to get people comfortable using the handwriting interfaces and onscreen keyboards of a PDA.

Enterprise Applications

A question we cannot overlook is whether or not the information the mobile worker needs is organized in a meaningful way. What data and applications will actually improve the business processes of the mobile worker? What is state of the art of these applications and how can they be made available on small devices?

The enterprise applications that are most important to the mobile worker are email, customer relationship management (CRM), enterprise resource planning (ERP), and supply chain management (SCM). Email would not normally fall into the same category as CRM, ERP, and SCM, but I have lumped them all together in this discussion because they all process important company information that the mobile worker needs.

Email systems, of course, allow the exchange of electronic mail across the company. They may also provide other functionalities, such as contact, calendar, and shared repositories of subject-specific information to allow employees to share insights and best practices.

Box 2–1 summarizes the email functions that are of interest to the mobile enterprise and that are available today.

Box 2–1   Email Functions for Today's Mobile Enterprise

Mobile Enterprise Functions from an Email System

- **Messaging:** sending and receiving email
- **Personal Information Management (PIM):** name and address information for contacts and calendar functions
- **Shared databases:** news groups or other subject-specific databases allowing employees to share knowledge on an area of interest

CRM is designed to allow companies to get to know their customers better by tracking customer interaction at the different points at which a customer comes into contact with the company. Such points of contact include casual inquiries, sales calls, product ordering, service calls, Web site visits, and phone support. At each point something can be learned about the customer. This information can be tied together so that the customer gets consistent service, and the company gets a better understanding of buying patterns, preferences, and so on.

CRM can be a great help to sales and service people, providing information about the customers they serve. It is also a useful marketing and planning tool, since so much can be learned about buying behavior. However, it only works as long as it is kept up to date.

Box 2–2 summarizes the CRM functions that are of interest to the mobile enterprise and that are available today.

Box 2–2 CRM Functions for Today's Mobile Enterprise

CRM Functions for the Mobile Enterprise

- **Opportunities:** Tracks sales opportunities along with an estimated probability of closing the deal, the potential amount of the deal, next steps that must be taken, and the date at which closure is expected.
- **Contacts:** Tracks the people in a client company, including information about their importance with respect to various sales opportunities.
- **Forecasts:** Computes how much revenue a given sales person is expected to generate over some period of time.
- **Leads:** Tracks customer leads.
- **Dispatch:** Sends an engineer to a site needing support.
- **Service ticketing:** Allows an onsite engineer to generate a service ticket so that a given problem can be tracked globally.
- **Product catalog:** Contains information on all the products for sale. Ideally there are cross-references, which allow up-selling and cross-selling.
- **Time and expense:** Assists service engineers and consultants, since time and expense information can be entered for an invoice to be generated immediately.

ERP provides functions to support a broad set of internally focused activities, including manufacturing, materials management, finance, and human resources. The idea is to allow the different departments in a company to work off the same databases, so that data is not duplicated. When data is duplicated, it becomes very difficult to prevent the different copies of the data from diverging over time.

This covers an awful lot of ground—and as you probably already know, ERP systems are very complicated, requiring a great deal of integration and customization. For our purposes, we are interested in the fact that part of what ERP covers involves the generation of invoices and ordering of parts and materials. These are functions required by customer-facing employees.

Box 2–3 summarizes the ERP functions that are of interest to the mobile enterprise and that are available today.

Box 2–3   ERP Functions for Today's Mobile Enterprise

ERP Functions for the Mobile Enterprise

- **Parts ordering:** Allows an onsite engineer to order parts needed to repair equipment.
- **Order status:** Enables a salesperson or engineer to check the status of an order in real time.
- **Invoice generation:** Ensures that an onsite engineer or consultant can cause an invoice to be generated for services rendered.

Supply chain management (SCM) is designed to make the supply chain more efficient. Part of this is the whole business of just-in-time inventory, or allowing salespeople to sell products that are not in inventory, but for which you can count on the supplier to deliver just in time to fulfill the order. That is, you do not buy the components, configure the product, stock it, and then sell it. Instead you wait until you get an order before buying the components. Then you configure it and ship it.

There are all sorts of advantages to doing this. First of all, you do not have to tie up money in inventory. Second, in cases where your selling prices fluctuate frequently, and especially when they tend to move in a downward direction, you minimize the risk of being stuck with inventory that costs you more than what you can sell it for. One other advantage is that you have a higher potential to offer more flexible configurations, since you have not taken a guess at the configuration the customer will want.

Box 2–4 summarizes the SCM functions of interest to the mobile enterprise that are available today.

Box 2–4   SCM Functions for Today's Mobile Enterprise

SCM Functions for the Mobile Enterprise

- **Available-to-Promise (ATP):** Allows a salesperson to quote and promise delivery to customers in real time by reserving capacity and materials as far down the supply chain as necessary.
- **Monitor and Control Orders:** Enables a salesperson to detect in real time any exceptions in order fulfillment that may be occurring somewhere in the supply chain.

It is important to note that the definitions of the various classes of enterprise applications vary from vendor to vendor—and some of the functionality shown above in one category may actually be offered through a different software suite in some cases. For example, order status might be checked through

ERP or through SCM, depending on the software vendor, and depending on how your company is set up.

Since different vendors sell CRM, ERP, and SCM software suites, and since those that are best in class at one category are not so in another, it makes sense for a company to buy different application suites from different vendors. In addition, it usually turns out that these applications are bought over a long period of time, during which relationships change, different vendors dominate, and so forth. In either case, the result is most companies have enterprise applications from different vendors, and these applications are generally not designed to work with one another.

The applications we are most interested in for mobilizing a workforce can be seen in Table 2–4 along with the leading vendors of each category of application.

TABLE 2–4   Enterprise Applications Important to the Mobile Enterprise

Application	Leading Vendors
Email	Microsoft, IBM
CRM	Siebel, SAP, Oracle, PeopleSoft, E.piphany
ERP	SAP, J.D. Edwards, PeopleSoft
SCM	i2 Technologies, SAP, Manugistics

In many organizations, information needs to be exchanged between the different software suites. For example, ERP and CRM may need to share price lists. For this sharing to occur, unless the ERP software and the CRM software are provided by the same vendor, some integration work will have to be performed. There are a variety of ways of interfacing the different applications—and there are a variety of levels at which such an interface makes sense, such as at a business process level, at an event level, at a messaging level, or at a database level. Today, the most popular way of getting some of the big enterprise applications to work together is through a class of middleware products called *enterprise application integration* (EAI), which are a prepackaged set of connectors (sometimes called adaptors) that know how to talk to various applications and translate the output from one form to another.

Broadly speaking, there are two ways of extending these applications so that they are accessible from mobile devices. The first is for the application vendor to modify the application so that it produces output specific to a class of devices, and likewise accepts input from the same class of devices. The application vendor may also include options for synchronization and caching for cases where network coverage is minimal.

The second—and preferable—way of extending these applications to mobile devices is to use a wireless application gateway (WAG), which translates output between one or more applications to the format expected by one or more classes of mobile devices. Some advantages to this approach are shown in Box 2–5.

Box 2–5 The Advantages of Using a Wireless Application Gateway

Advantages to the Wireless Application Gateway

- It is easier to support several classes of devices, and to extend the device catalog to new devices, because the WAG specializes in this. The alternative—having each enterprise application understand a multitude of devices—is frightening.
- One WAG can mobilize all your enterprise applications. It can also combine the features of the different applications in ways that specifically accommodate the mobile worker.

As we have just seen in the above discussion, there already exists a rich set of applications that can really help our mobile workforce. We also have ways of integrating them. In the future we can look toward improvements in how they are integrated at a business process level, and we can also expect these applications to start offering functionality that assumes real-time use by a mobile worker. That is, as enterprises mobilize, the vendors of enterprise software will start designing functionality to fit the new usage patterns.

In conclusion, while we can look forward to a certain number of improvements, enterprise applications are not a roadblock to mobilizing the enterprise today.

Analysis of Today's Technology

From the above discussion, we conclude that the biggest inhibitor to mobilizing your enterprise today is network technology. Data coverage is still spotty and there are too many different transmission techniques and protocols, offering too wide an array of latency and bandwidth. The effect is a lot of confusion among buyers.

That said, with the current state of network technology, we can already put together solutions that allow employees to access critical enterprise data from handheld devices. As shown in Box 2–6, three things that should be considered now are the use of CSD, the use of a voice interface, and the use of synchronization and caching techniques.

In the meantime, the network issues will be resolved. We *do* know how to build faster, more capable networks today and they *are* being rolled out. It is just a matter of time before the transmission inhibitor is lifted, opening up the floodgates. I for one do not want to be standing in the way when this happens.

Box 2–6   Approaches to Consider Today

Ways to Extend Your Reach Now

- **Use circuit-switched data (CSD) for data transmission.** This is just like placing a phone call and using a modem. Anywhere you have cell phone access, you can use CSD to establish a data connection.
- **Use a voice interface.** If the functionality you need only requires a simple interface, it could probably be done through voice menus. As is the case when using CSD, when using a voice interface, the coverage area you get is that of the cell phone.
- **Use synchronization and caching.** This stores information in the hand-held device for places where there are holes in network coverage. Given the current generation of enterprise applications, many of the functions the mobile worker needs do not require real-time access anyway.

To show what we can put to use today, let's map the functions we can get out of our enterprise applications to our options for extended reachability. This is shown in Table 2–5.

At each of the intersections we will apply a rating based on the old Clint Eastwood movie, *The Good, the Bad, and the Ugly.* For this exercise, *good* means it works fine. *Bad* means that we can get it to work, but it might be a little awkward and inefficient. And *ugly* means you should run for the hills if anybody suggests it. Do not even attempt to use it.

TABLE 2–5   Enterprise Applications and Options for Extended Reachability

	CSD	Voice Interface	Synchronization
Send/receive messages	Good	Bad	Good
Contacts	Good	Good	Good
Calendar	Good	Bad	Good
Shared DB	Bad	Ugly	Good
Opportunities	Good	Good	Good
Customer contacts	Good	Good	Good
Forecast	Good	Good	Good
Leads	Good	Good	Good

TABLE 2–5   Enterprise Applications and Options for Extended Reachability

	CSD	Voice Interface	Synchronization
Dispatch	Bad	Good	Ugly
Service ticketing	Good	Good	Ugly
Product catalog	Good	Bad	Good
Time/expense	Good	Good	Good
Parts ordering	Good	Good	Ugly
Order status	Good	Good	Ugly
Generate invoices	Good	Bad	Good
Available-to-promise	Good	Good	Ugly
Monitor/control orders	Good	Good	Ugly

It appears that with our three options for extended reachability, we can put together some real solutions today. Later in this chapter, and throughout Chapter 3, we explore which set of functions can improve business processes for various job categories.

THE CURRENT STATE OF THE INDUSTRY

Let's now turn our attention to the new industry forming around the mobile enterprise. We will do this by taking a look at the demand side (the buyers) and the supply side (the sellers).

The Demand Side

To understand the state of the industry, we first look at the demand side. More than anything else, this will drive the maturity of the industry. As the demand grows, companies will fall all over themselves to fill the different niches in the new ecosystem of players.

For this analysis, it is important to note that mobilizing an enterprise represents a discontinuous change to the enterprise. This is as opposed to a change that is continuous, or not requiring new behavior on the part of the user. The mobile enterprise is a discontinuous change, because it brings about a transformation in the way a company operates. New infrastructure is required, new skills are needed to operate the new infrastructure, and new vendor relationships have to be established. Furthermore, employees using such tools have to learn the new technology and modify their way of working.

The uptake of discontinuous changes by a population is best modeled by the Technology Adoption Life Cycle, which was most recently popularized by Geoffrey Moore in his series of books on high-tech marketing, starting with the hugely successful book, *Crossing the Chasm*.

This model is very useful in understanding the dynamics of a high-tech market. But it actually predates high-tech as we know it today. It comes out of a study dating from the middle of the 20th century on how American farmers took on new strains of seed potatoes. The study found that there were a few farmers who took on change early, but most of them waited to see how their peers fared with the new seeds. That is, most of them needed references before taking on the new way of doing things. Then there were those who resisted change and took to using the new strains only when they felt they had to. Only a small set of farmers fit into this latter group.

It appears that this model actually tells us something more fundamental than just how high-tech markets behave. It tells us some things about human behavior, and how much we act like herd animals.

When change is upon us, a few individuals will make a decision to move on their own. In the high-tech model, these are the *technology enthusiasts* and *visionaries*. However, most people will wait to see others around them act; they are the *pragmatists* and *conservatives*. Finally, there are the *skeptics*, who resist change as long as possible.

In the animal kingdom, those individuals in the herd who sense danger early—and act quickly—survive longest. At the other extreme are those who ignore the danger until the last minute. These individuals are a favorite of the predators, because they are good for dinner. Wow, this actually sounds a lot like modern industry!

The Technology Adoption Life Cycle model can help us in evaluating when and how we should make our way toward the inevitable mobile enterprise, by helping us understand the demand side of the equation. This is key, since it is the demand side that will drive the industry. As Figure 2–1 shows, visionaries are currently taking up our new paradigm.

While most companies would like to work the magic of allowing all employees to have telepathic access to company information no matter where the employees are, there just are not a lot of companies who have jumped on the bandwagon yet. Most are waiting for the stampede to begin. A small set will even wait until after the stampede, only to find themselves overtaken by predators.

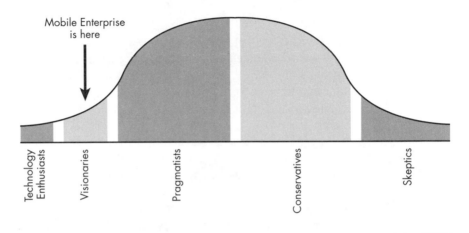

FIGURE 2–1 Mobile enterprise in the technology adoption life cycle.

The Supply Side

Now let's see what is happening on the supply side of the equation. Because the large majority of the population has not started taking on this new way of operating, the industry is not yet in a state of maturity. It is currently a fragmented industry. That is, a large number of companies have devised an even larger number of ways of accomplishing the same thing. De facto standards have not yet been established. As the industry matures, consolidation will occur. And you can be sure that many of the companies now trying to establish themselves as vendors for the mobile enterprise will not survive in the long run.

In Chapter 11, where we start shopping around for solutions, we go into detail on the different companies offering products for the mobile enterprise. But for now, to get an understanding of the overall shape of the market, let's take a brief look at the kinds of companies that sell products for the mobile enterprise:

- *Enterprise application vendors* have an interest in making their software accessible from small, wirelessly enabled devices. Over time, they will make some fundamental changes to the functions provided by their software to accommodate the new usage patterns, taking advantage of the fact that frequently the user is at a client site—and, in fact, he or she may be standing right in front of a customer while using the application. But for now, in this early market, most of the enterprise application vendors are only modifying their applications so that the output fits the smaller screens of the handheld devices. They may also be doing fancy things with caching and synchronization to help out in spots where network coverage is not available or where the bandwidth is relatively low.

- *Device vendors*, that is, companies producing cell phones, PDAs, tablet computers, and notebook computers, are also interested in selling in a big way into this market. Most of the vendors of computing devices (PDAs, tablets, and notebook computers) have already made the necessary changes to their products to allow them to communicate over public wireless networks. One of their biggest headaches is the same headache cell phone manufacturers have been suffering a long time now. That is, there are just too many wireless data protocols out there right now—and no device can do them all, so a choice has to be made. You as the buyer should be careful to understand what this means to your company in terms of areas of coverage and bandwidth that are possible with a given device. You should also take a look at what kinds of network subscription and airtime charges you are locking yourself into.

- *Systems integrators* have developed expertise in wireless data networks and they are interested in going to market with this expertise, along with their expertise in EAI. They also see a good market for a consultative sale, whereby they come in and advise companies on how their business processes can be improved through the use of mobile solutions. Until the day mobilizing your enterprise can be accomplished with a shrink-wrapped solution, and until the accompanying business process changes are well understood, systems integrators will have a big role to play in this market.

- *Wireless application gateway (WAG) vendors* are those companies selling wireless protocol gateways (e.g., WAP gateways), and those selling transcoding engines. There are other terms for this class of products, such as *multiaccess portals*, *multichannel portals*, and *multidevice portals*. The idea is pretty much the same: something has to stand in between the enterprise applications and the handheld device to translate the output from one into the format expected by the other. Ideally, the WAG will be able to render content on a multitude of devices, and it will have connectors or adaptors enabling it to interface with a multitude of enterprise applications. Any significantly mobilized enterprise will depend on a WAG for the time being.

- *Wireless network operators* see big business in this market for selling network subscriptions and airtime. And they are also seeking new revenue opportunities by *hosting* a WAG or even some of the enterprise applications. The benefit to the mobile enterprise is that they could probably pay for the services on a subscription basis and would not have to run a lot of extra infrastructure in their own IT department. The downside is that they become much more dependent on one network operator.

- *Platform vendors* see an opportunity to sell more hardware and specialized middleware to ensure things like load balancing, high availability, additional security, and network management. Frequently, the enterprise application vendor or the WAG vendor will make the choice of infrastructure platforms. It is up to the buyer to make sure the right choice was made, and to insist on a change if necessary. This is especially true when your IT department will be tasked with operating the new equipment.

We have just gone over the state of the industry that is growing up around the discontinuous change brought on by wireless data technology applied to the enterprise. It is now time to take a close look at how you and your company might fit into the Technology Adoption Life Cycle.

VISIONARIES VERSUS PRAGMATISTS

Since only visionaries are now mobilizing their enterprise, the question is whether you are a visionary or a pragmatist. (I am assuming that you would not fall into the conservative or skeptic group, because if you did, you probably would not be interested in a book like this.) To help answer this question, we will reference how Geoffrey Moore describes these personality types in *Crossing the Chasm:*

- *Visionaries* do not look around for well-established references to make a decision. Instead, they rely on their own intuition and vision. They are not in love with technology as an end in itself, but they see it as a way of jumping ahead and gaining significant business advantage. Visionaries understand that there will probably be hurdles to overcome in being early adopters of a new category of products and solutions, but they are ready to move ahead anyway in order to leap ahead of the competition.

- *Pragmatists*, on the other hand, wait to see how others have fared before they take on a discontinous change. They are risk averse. They want complete products and solutions, and they want to buy them from well-known companies. Pragmatists are looking for incremental improvements, rather than major leaps ahead. They generally do not attract a lot of attention to themselves.

It is instructive to review past discontinuous changes to see where vision-aries achieved long-term competitive advantage through their foresight, and through courageous decisions to act early. Here are just a few:

- Henry Ford was an early adopter of electrical power. He quickly realized that this new source of power allowed him to line up machines in what became the assembly line. This is something that could not be done pre-viously when machines had to sit next to a water mill to derive power. The result was mass production, and Henry Ford really won big on that!

- Microsoft was an early adopter of corporate email. From the early 1980s they used it for internal communications. This was a productivity-enhancing tool at all stages of the company's growth and today more than ever, they continue to use email. In addition to that, they understand it so well that they can now sell corporate email systems to their custom-ers. And they are tremendously successful at doing so!

- Hewlett-Packard was an early adopter of telecommuting technology in the early 1990s. The result was that the company could tap into a larger pool of skilled workers. It also increased workforce loyalty.

- Dell Computer was an early adopter of using the Internet to sell products and optimize the supply chain. The result has been that Dell has a lower cost structure than its competitors.

Perhaps early adopters of mobile technology will also leap ahead. Only the future will tell. In any case, it is something with which every enterprise will have to come to terms sooner or later. For this reason, it is important to at least start understanding what it is all about.

THE CAUTIOUS VISIONARY

We went over several examples of where visionaries won big in the past. And it usually is the case that first movers gain a competitive advantage over those who wait. Another way of saying this is "the early bird gets the worm."

This is not to suggest that it would be a good idea to run out and mobilize your entire enterprise right now. A better approach would be that of the *cau-tious visionary*. Move forward, but limit your risks. And there are indeed a number of risks you need to be aware of. These are summarized in Box 2–7.

Box 2–7   The Cautious Approach

Risks the Cautious Visionary Will Mitigate

- **Cost overruns:** Because the industry is immature, and there are still various holes in the ecosystem of products offered, a good deal of integration has to be performed. This can be a recipe for runaway costs.
- **Network coverage:** You have to make sure you have the network services in the places where they are needed. Mountains and other barriers may interfere with good coverage.
- **Security infrastructure:** It will usually be the case that your mobile employees need to access data inside the firewall from small, wirelessly enabled handheld devices. Before we can deploy mobile applications, infrastructure has to be in place to allow proper authentication of the users of these devices. This typically includes software and/or hardware on the device itself, and an accompanying software component as part of the IT infrastructure.
- **Uninterested users:** Your users may not really want to be hassled with a new way of doing things. You have to be prepared to give them proper training up front, and you should have a way of unintrusively monitoring usage to see what works and what does not work.
- **Poor user interface:** In fact, if the new tools are not a delight to use, you are likely to have even more uninterested users. You should make sure the tools have an intuitive interface and are enjoyable to use. It needs to be as easy as magic!
- **Lost or stolen devices:** This presents two distinct risks. The first is the risk of having a malicious individual read the data sitting on the device that has been lost or stolen. The second risk lies in the speed of replacement. An identically configured device is needed to get the employee back up and running.

The cautious visionary will have a plan to mitigate the risks that apply to his or her particular situation. He or she will start out by equipping only those employees with a real need for mobile solutions, and for which there can be a quick return on investment (ROI).

JOB FUNCTIONS WITH IMMEDIATE ROI

The kinds of people we want to equip first with mobile solutions for the enterprise are those that have job functions for which such solutions really make a difference. These are the job functions where we can get a quick return on investment from the use of mobile technology. A likely class of jobs would be those where information is needed in real time, and where having that information makes a big difference.

Another criterion for selection would be that we want our early users to be good and eager users of the new technology. If they are not generally good users of technology, and if they have little interest anyway, they are not likely to get your company off to a good start on the path to mobilization.

It is also good to choose users who have a relatively high profile. You want to show off the fact that your company is trying new things. You probably want the world to know that your company is forward thinking. Of course, this approach backfires if your initial mobile project is a flop. But with a little careful planning, including a good understanding of the potential pitfalls and how they can be overcome, there is no reason your project should fail.

Given the three criteria—quick ROI, good early users, and high-profile users—perhaps the first set of users should come from the following four types of job functions:

- *Sales*: salespeople have a high need for accurate information in real time. The quicker and more accurately they can answer the customer's questions, the faster they move toward closing a sale. With information at their fingertips, they are much more capable of up-selling and cross-selling. They can retrieve instantaneous prices on various configurations, and they can see quickly how much of a margin they can make on a given sale. After a customer visits, a salesperson should be able to update opportunity information. For example, he or she should be able to provide a new estimate on the probability of closing, the potential size of the deal, and anything new about customer contacts.

- *Services*: field service engineers, utility meter readers, insurance claims adjusters, and generally any job function that requires several trips per week to a customer site to perform some service could use a good dose of mobile technology. Employees working these jobs need to be dispatched to each location—and once at the location, they need to have technical information on the fly. Frequently they need to communicate information back to the office, including pictures. (For example, the insurance claims adjuster needs to bring pictures back to the office.) They may have to order parts or check on the status of parts previously ordered. They may also have to generate trouble tickets so others in the company can track a given problem. Finally, once services are rendered, the field worker has to be able to enter information so that an invoice can be generated. The faster the invoice is generated, the quicker you get paid.

- *Consultants*: need to be able to fill out travel expenses, and enter time and materials, so that invoices can be generated. These employees have a high profile, because they are usually in front of customers. Their jobs are to be experts in some area, and this expertise is greatly enhanced when the consultant has a huge source of information at his or her fingertips.

- *Traveling professionals*: a sort of catch-all category of any employee who frequently travels (which includes all those job functions listed above), and needs a way of overcoming the overhead of wasted time brought on by such travel. They need to be connected to their work, sending and receiving email at all times from any location. They need to be able to receive alerts when something critical requires their attention. They need to be able to schedule meetings and have access to the calendars of their colleagues to know who is available and when. These people may also need to submit travel expenses, or enter some other kind of report. An additional feature that would be nice to put in the hands of the traveling professional would be the ability to perform some sort of online training while sitting around waiting for airplanes.

FUNCTIONALITY REQUIRED

Table 2–6 maps the different functions we would like to get from our enterprise applications to each of the job categories we would like to equip with mobile solutions today. We can cut out all the fat, providing each kind of employee with only those functions for which real-time access would be a critical element in enhancing job performance. Note that the functions, *forecasts* and *leads,* are not listed as critical functions for any job category. This is because nobody absolutely *needs* this information right away.

This exercise is somewhat subjective, as each company will have a different definition of the job categories described above. For this reason, I invite you to try this exercise on your own, using real job categories from your own company.

TABLE 2–6   Application Needs by Job Category

	Sales	*Service*	*Consultant*	*Traveling Professional*
Send/receive messages			Critical	Critical
Contacts			Critical	Critical
Calendar	Critical	Critical	Critical	Critical
Shared DB		Critical	Critical	
Opportunities	Critical			
Customer contacts	Critical			
Forecast				

TABLE 2–6   Application Needs by Job Category (Continued)

	Sales	Service	Consultant	Traveling Professional
Leads				
Dispatch		Critical		
Service ticketing		Critical		
Product catalog	Critical	Critical		
Time/expense		Critical	Critical	
Parts ordering		Critical		
Order status	Critical	Critical		
Generate invoices		Critical	Critical	
Available-to-promise	Critical			
Monitor/control orders	Critical			

Given this analysis, and revisiting Table 2–5, we get a feel for how much of the critical functionality can be provided to each of the job functions using the options for extended reachability: CSD, voice interface, and synchronization.

SUMMARY

Although the technological underpinnings of the magic companies would like to work are not at the ideal state of advancement, today we have what it takes to provide real business value.

The industry is still immature, meaning it has not settled on standards. Not all niches have been filled, so a good deal of custom integration may be required. The immature nature of the industry also means that many of the vendors providing products in this space will not be around in a few years.

Those companies that move forward and start to look at how to mobilize are likely to have the most effective workforces of the future. However, at this point companies should move forward with caution, choosing a set of job functions where wireless technology provides a quick payback. They should pilot mobile solutions on those job functions and in specific geographies with adequate network services.

Today's Business Value

In the previous chapter we looked at some of the functions that can be made available to the mobile employee. These functions come from enterprise applications already installed and running within many companies. They have been paid for, and are just waiting to be put to good use by the mobile employee.

We have identified four job categories where mobile solutions make sense now: *sales*, *service*, *consulting*, and *traveling professional*. These are jobs where it is critical to have quick access to information and for which it is important to communicate updates back to the rest of the company. The best way to start mobilizing your enterprise is to apply mobile solutions to these job functions and carefully study the return on your investment. Prove that it makes sense here before moving on.

We now take a closer look at some of the problems faced by employees performing these jobs. We will see how by applying mobile technology, we can expect to improve their business processes.

SALES

The nature of the sales profession varies from industry to industry—and it varies greatly according to whether the products being sold are high volume and low value or low volume and high value.

Selling high volume/low value products usually involves visiting several customers per week—and the visits are usually relatively short in duration. In such a situation, the salesperson equipped with a mobile solution is better prepared to answer questions on the fly, quote prices in an instant, and bring business to a close by entering an order.

Mobile solutions may also help in situations involving low volume/high value products, but the emphasis is less on providing immediate answers to customer questions, and more on allowing access to CRM functions, such as opportunity management and contact history.

In general, a salesperson's time can be broken up into five broad activities:

- Preparation
- Travel
- Customer time
- Follow-up activities
- Administrative tasks

Mobile technology can help reduce preparation time, make the customer time more productive, and accelerate follow-up activities. In those cases where the salesperson is traveling by means other than driving, a mobile solution can provide a means for doing something productive, such as administrative tasks, email, or online training.

Information at Your Fingertips—Literally

Mobile solutions put information at the salesperson's fingertips. This is convenience at its best, since during a sales call a customer may ask the salesperson a variety of questions, including questions about:

- The status of a previously placed order
- The price and availability of a product
- Whether some unusual configuration is possible

It is usually impossible for the salesperson to anticipate all of these questions, especially since many of them come up spontaneously during the course of discussion. So there is frequently no way to prepare the answers ahead of time. When such questions come up, the salesperson has to either call somebody back at the office, or jot down the questions and call the customer back later. There is usually nobody back at the office standing by to answer such questions and if there were, you can imagine the overhead. The upshot is that the customer's questions usually cannot be answered during the visit, thus requiring more of the salesperson's time to follow up and thus interrupting the momentum of the interaction, which may have otherwise moved toward a close.

By equipping the salesperson with a mobile solution, most of these questions can be answered during the customer visit. This results in a better interaction. The customer feels that he or she can bounce around ideas about different configurations and different combinations of products. Because the questions can be answered through mobile technology, the conversation moves on to more important issues, and the sale moves more quickly to a close.

Price Quotes and Product Availability

When the conversation moves on and the customer is ready to discuss pricing, the wise salesperson has done enough preparation to have this information available—at least for the standard product set. But prices tend to change in response to market conditions, or as part of a promotional campaign. So the salesperson has to have prepared the right version of the price list ahead of time.

Or perhaps the salesperson may not be prepared to quote prices of unusual configurations or of unusual combinations of products. And if he or she attempts to go down that path, there is no easy way of knowing how much profit can be made on a given configuration or combination of products.

Again a mobile solution can help out by allowing the salesperson real-time access to an instantaneous price list. This means that prices can be changed on an hourly basis if necessary, with no worries about propagating the updates to all salespeople. In this case, the mobile solution also cuts down on the amount of preparation work the salesperson has to do in anticipation of questions concerning price.

Unusual configurations can be considered, and prices quoted. The same goes for different combinations of products. The salesperson has the flexibility to brainstorm different possibilities, quoting prices on each one, and privately viewing the margin his or her company would make in each case.

The salesperson can also check and promise availability of products and configurations. This takes him or her one step closer to taking an order. A good CRM system can also help in assessing whether a customer should be offered more discounts or other incentives.

Orders and Delivery

Once the customer's questions have been answered, and different possibilities explored, the customer is now ready to place an order. Without mobile solutions, this whole process may have required several visits, spanning several days. With mobile solutions, this can all be done during one visit. And as it is today, to take an order, the salesperson probably has to do some paperwork and make a trip back to the office to enter the order. With a mobile solution, we can cut down on a lot of this tedium, no longer requiring the trip to the office for order entry, or order reentry.

Furthermore, the salesperson can promise delivery of the product or configuration as the order is taken. Again, all of this is addressed in the same visit—and the chances of errors in the order are greatly reduced, since paperwork and extra travel can be eliminated.

Up-Sell and Cross-Sell

Today, most salespeople do not have an easy way of knowing which alternative products can be offered—there are just too many possibilities. So when a customer requests one product, the salesperson may be lucky enough to be able to recommend a better alternative, or to recommend purchase of a related product that is usually of interest in combination with the one requested. However, more often than not, the salesperson is not prepared. It is just too complicated for mere mortals.

The convenience of a mobile solution eliminates this problem. The salesperson selects the requested product, and a back-end application suggests an up-sell or a cross-sell as appropriate. Sufficient information could also be stored on the handheld computer so that the wireless connection to the back-end application is not necessary. Thus a synchronized, or offline, solution would also work here.

The advantage of using a mobile solution is that more sales can be made, and higher-value products can be sold.

Forecasts

Between customer visits, a salesperson may want to check up on how he or she is doing with respect to quota for the quarter or for the year. Using a mobile solution, the sales rep can view sales forecasts as they change, and have a better understanding on how well he or she is doing with respect to quota. Having this information makes it possible to react early to a bad situation, thereby increasing the likelihood of recovering gracefully.

Opportunities/Customer Contacts

In cases where more than one salesperson is dealing with the same customer, it can be difficult for each one to follow the progress of the others. It simply requires too much overhead, and is fraught with errors brought about by mis-communication. Once again, the mobile solution can help us out.

If each salesperson is equipped with a handheld device that allows access to opportunities—that is, for each customer or potential customer, the kinds of deals that are currently on the table, the probability of closing the deal, the deal potential, and the expected date of closure—a much more concerted approach can be taken, thus making the whole process more efficient, and increasing the chances of winning the deal. Since the mobile devices make it easy for a salesperson to update the opportunity information—on the way back to the car, for example—your company can track progress.

Tracking customer contacts is another benefit of mobile solutions, since information can be easily shared. In a flash a salesperson can learn who in the company has the authority to make which decisions. In certain scenarios this kind of immediate access can make or break a deal! Retrieving information, providing answers in an instant, is key in today's ultra-competitive market.

Benefits

The power of mobile technology translates to real benefits to the salesperson. These benefits are summarized in Box 3–1.

Box 3-1 Principal Benefits to Salespeople

Mobile solutions can help salespeople:
- Shorten sales cycles
- Make fewer trips to the office to do research or to enter orders
- Require less preparation time
- Close higher-value sales through up-selling and cross-selling
- Complete administrative tasks during travel time
- Coordinate sales efforts between colleagues

It is worth noting that many of these benefits can be derived from a solution based on a mixture of online and offline access. Where the salesperson is accessing information that does not change throughout the day, the information can be preloaded onto the salesperson's portable computing device.

In cases where the information changes frequently, a wireless connection is required. However, this does not necessarily require fast data service from a network operator. As we shall see in Chapter 6, circuit switch data (CSD) is sufficient in many cases.

SERVICE EMPLOYEES

We noted that the sales profession varies from industry to industry. For our purposes, service is an even broader job category. As far as we are concerned, it includes any worker who regularly goes to customer sites to perform tasks or collect information. This would include field support engineers, utility meter readers, insurance claims adjusters, and workers performing site surveys.

In many cases, service workers need to be dispatched, and they have to know how to get from one customer site to another. Once at the customer site, they usually need access to technical documents. They may also have to order parts. Often, they will be performing work for which the client is billed. In these cases, they have to fill out reports on the service rendered so an invoice can be generated and sent out as soon as possible. In some cases, service employees have to take pictures of something they are working on and bring those pictures back to the office for examination by other experts.

Let's explore how mobile solutions can change the nature of these responsibilities.

Dispatch

Frequently, dispatching a field engineer requires a well-staffed dispatch center. When a problem is recognized, somebody has to call in to the center to get an engineer to the trouble spot. The person answering the call will then consult the schedules of the engineers with the appropriate skill set. It is never easy to keep these schedules up to date, so a call has to be made to the selected engineer to see if he or she *really* is available. This process may include paging the engineer.

In any case, there is a lot of overhead here. First of all, the dispatch center is needed. Second, it is hard to be sure of the validity of a schedule. Third, the dispatcher has to wait for a call back from the engineer to confirm availability. And last, but not least, it is frequently difficult to know which engineer is closest to the trouble spot at the time of the call. After all, the closest engineer is the one who is most likely to get there the quickest.

All of these problems can be minimized or even eliminated when mobile technology is used for dispatching. The dispatch request can even come from another employee—for example, a salesperson—who is also equipped with a mobile solution.

Once a request has been made, a call management system, which may be part of the CRM suite, looks up engineers by skill, proximity, and availability. Schedules are kept up to date, because as the engineer moves about, he or she easily updates their location through the mobile device. A higher-end solution would involve the use of a global positioning system (GPS) to automatically track the location of the engineers. In any case, schedule and current location is made available to the call management system, which uses this information to make dispatch decisions.

An alert is sent to the selected engineer who then accepts or rejects through the click of a button. It is even possible to send the engineers directions to the trouble spot.

Parts Replacement

When an engineer looks over the product in question, it may turn out to be necessary to order replacement parts. Currently, this requires some paperwork, and it may be difficult or even impossible to know when those parts can be delivered.

This is not so with a mobile solution. The engineer can order parts through a mobile interface, and a back-end system can return an acknowledgment along with a delivery date. The engineer then informs the customer, schedules a return trip, and moves on to something else. Since the engineer does not have to go back to the office to enter the order, it is possible to service a greater number of customers on any given day.

Trouble Ticketing

In many cases, when a critical problem occurs, the customer wants to be assured that the problem is being tracked. The customer wants to be able to call any support center and get definitive answers without having to explain the problem repeatedly to each new representative.

One way of doing this is through "trouble ticketing." That is, a unique reference number is assigned to the problem, and all status updates are logged against this number. When a customer calls a support center, he or she provides the ticket number and the support person at the other end of the line can immediately see the history and current status of the problem.

The service worker equipped with a mobile solution can easily generate a trouble ticket from the customer site, and can check on status against an existing ticket. The engineer can also enter new status against a ticket.

Problem History/Technical Documents

When a field engineer is dispatched to fix a problem, it is sometimes necessary to get a report on the history of other problems that may have occurred in the past with the same piece of equipment. It is also useful to get information on known errors, or service notes, with the model in question. Getting this information may require a special trip to the office or the engineer may lump several such work items together and go back to the office to get the problem history and service notes on all of them in one trip. In both cases, the result is a lot of extra delay in getting to a trouble spot.

It may also be necessary for the engineer to go back to the office to retrieve the latest technical documentation on the equipment in question. This contributes to the delay.

Mobile solutions applied to these situations allow the engineer to view the problem history and technical documentation on a portable computing device at the customer site.

Billing

Once a service has been rendered, a bill has to be sent out. Otherwise, you are not likely to get paid. Today, the most common way of generating a bill is by filling out paperwork and then making a trip back to the office to enter the information into a computer system. Of course, this may also be done from the engineer's home if the engineer is set up to do so. But in either case, entering the information requires extra work and possibly extra travel. It also means the bill cannot be sent out immediately.

Filling out these reports can be so annoying that the service worker may choose not to do so for small services that may have been requested "spontaneously" during a visit. For example, during a visit the customer may say something like, "By the way, while you are here, can you have a look at this other problem?"

Everything takes the path of least resistance, and field engineers are certainly no exception. In most cases, they just go ahead and fix the problem, and do not bother to do the paperwork necessary to bill for the extra services.

With mobile technology a report can be made on a handheld device immediately after services are rendered. Then all relevant information can be transmitted back to the office so that an invoice is generated and sent out.

Since this process is so much more convenient, it is more likely to get done. This means more services are billed. The whole business of processing of invoices is sped up, thereby decreasing accounts receivable. Because a bill is sent out sooner, on the average, payment will be made sooner.

Benefits

Mobile technology provides a powerful, new set of tools to the service worker. Box 3–2 summarizes how these tools improve business processes.

Box 3–2 **Principle Benefits to Service Workers**

Mobile solutions can help service workers:
- Shorten service cycles
- Reduce dispatch costs
- Order parts more quickly
- Coordinate support
- Access problem history and technical documents instantaneously
- Get paid more quickly for services rendered
- Bill for absolutely all services
- Make fewer trips to the office

As is the case for the salesperson, much of this power can be delivered with a solution that is based on a mixture of online and offline access. Where a large volume of information is required, data can be preloaded onto the portable computing device of the service worker.

Throughout the day, the service worker may make updates to the data stored on the device. Where wireless connection is available, he or she can upload the changes to the enterprise applications.

CONSULTANTS

Consultants spend a lot of time with customers. They generally do not bill for each small task they perform. Rather, they tend to offer expertise the customer might not otherwise have. Their value usually lies in their knowledge of some subject matter. This value is naturally increased when the proper material is at their fingertips.

Information Access

Information can be provided through access to shared databases, for example, those offered through an email system. Or it might be provided in a knowledge management (KM) system at the enterprise. And perhaps the simplest way of providing the consultant with access to a great deal of information is to give him or her a mobile device with a browser and Internet access.

For the consultant, a wirelessly enabled notebook computer might be the most appropriate device. Consultants generally have time to wait for a full boot-up, and they tend to spend enough time with the client so that he or she is actually expected to come equipped with a notebook computer.

Email Access

The consultant also needs access to email to exchange ideas and ask questions of colleagues. He or she has to have a way of bouncing ideas off other people back in other company locations. This improves the quality of the service that can be provided, and it means service can be rendered more quickly.

It is not always possible to send and receive email when you are at a customer site or moving about between customer locations. Therefore, a small device with a wireless connection will really help the consultant connect to the rest of his or her company to exchange information as needed.

Staying Up to Date

The more a consultant appears to be up on things, the more credible he or she is with the customer. The consultant needs to appear technically savvy. It is actually even more important to *really* be technically savvy. Mobile solutions can help do both.

Since what we are talking about is cutting-edge business technology, there is no better way of showing that your company is forward looking—and that your consultants are really up on the latest technology—than to equip consultants with mobile solutions. Let them use it in front of everybody. This could give your company a boost in credibility.

If your consultants are talking to customers about improving business processes, then you absolutely have to show up with tools that improve your *own* business processes. Let your consultants understand firsthand what it is to improve their own business processes. Practice what you preach.

Benefits

Box 3–3 summarizes how mobile technology can improve the business processes of consultants.

Box 3–3   Principal Benefits to Consultants

Mobile solutions can help consultants:
- Provide quicker answers to questions
- Stay in touch with other experts
- Increase credibility with customers

Notebook computers and PDAs are the devices of choice for consultants. As is the case with service workers, consultants usually need large quantities of data that can be preloaded onto the portable computing device. Additionally, there may be information exchanges that require wireless access. For example, a consultant may need to browse the company intranet.

THE TRAVELING PROFESSIONAL

All of the jobs discussed so far require a good deal of travel, and are therefore included in the overall traveling professional category. But this category also includes managers who travel a lot, and just anybody who, for whatever reason, spends a lot of time in airports and hotels.

To paraphrase a famous quote, "Business travel is hours of boredom punctuated by a few cell phone calls." Not only is it boring, but travel comes with a lot of overhead to the company—not just in terms of the cost of getting from one place to another. Perhaps even more expensive is the wasted time and the problems resulting from being out of reach.

Performing Administrative Tasks

While sitting around in an airport, sitting in an airplane, or just plain old sitting around waiting for something to occur, the traveling professional can use a mobile solution to do expense reports, perform online training, read up on news headlines, and perform a variety of other tasks that might have otherwise required a trip in to the office or a dialing in from home. Much of this can be done through offline access, and does not require constant wireless coverage.

Alerts

The traveling professional can be alerted electronically when certain events occur. For example, if the professional is an IT manager, he or she can be alerted when systems management software detects a critical condition, such as downtime. Alerts can be sent out for a number of events, including a stock price crossing some threshold, a new order being taken, or a personal emergency. For alerts to work, wireless coverage absolutely has to be there.

Mobile technology can also enable a traveling professional to send alerts to other employees.

Email

Connected to a corporate email system, the mobile solution can allow an otherwise bored and idle traveling professional to connect to the rest of the company and do useful things. This means that he or she does not have a big backlog of email upon returning to the home office. It also means he or she can be just as responsive while traveling as while at the office.

Meetings

Mobile solutions can allow the traveling professional to schedule meetings and to be included in meeting scheduling while he or she is out on the road. You no longer have to make several phone calls to see who is available for a meeting you want to schedule. Instead, you can just use the same calendaring system you use when you are back at the office.

Other employees can more efficiently schedule meetings to include employees who are not around when the scheduling occurs. Currently, this process may take a day or so. The result is that meetings have to be scheduled far in advance, and your company's ability to react immediately is greatly impaired.

Benefits

Box 3–4 summarizes how mobile technology can improve the business processes of the traveling professional.

Box 3–4   Principal Benefits to Traveling Professionals

Mobile solutions help traveling professionals:

- Waste less time
- Be automatically alerted to situations needing attention
- Stay connected through email
- Schedule a meeting or be informed that others have done so

As is the case for the other job categories, a mixture of offline and online access is appropriate for the traveling professional.

THE REST OF THE COMPANY

We have gone over the benefits we can expect to get out of mobile solutions when applied to the four job categories of our immediate concern: *sales, services, consultants,* and *traveling professionals.* By equipping these employees with mobile technology, the rest of the company also benefits.

For example, CRM is kept up to date. If you make it easy for your customer-facing employees to enter updates on the way out of the customer office and into their car, you are more likely to have a CRM system that is of real use to your company. This is great for performing marketing campaigns and for coordinating funnel activities.

Furthermore, if you can track what is happening in your sales funnels, you can predict downturns and upswings earlier. A great example of this is that Siebel Systems was able to predict the recent economic downturn early by using its own CRM system to detect a decrease in early customer visits. Since early customer visits lead to orders, which then lead to sales, a decrease in the number of early customer visits probably means a decrease in revenues several months later.

Acting on this information, Siebel was able to respond to the downturn before it happened. That is what I call practicing what you preach!

Box 3–5 lists some of the benefits the rest of the company derives from being able to reach the traveling professional.

Box 3–5   Benefits to the Rest of the Company

Mobile solutions help the rest of the company:

- Create better marketing campaigns
- Track funnels better
- Stay in touch with traveling employees
- Satisfy employees

In a few years, once we have reached a state of real magic, it may be very hard to tell who is traveling and who is in the office without actually going over to their desk to have a look.

SUMMARY

Even today with network technology not yet where we want it to be, mobile solutions can bring us some real business value. Since it is inevitable that most companies will mobilize, and since those who lag behind risk being at a competitive disadvantage, it is well worth your while to get a good start by applying this technology to those job functions where business value can be demonstrated early on. Prove it works on these employees and then plan a bigger rollout.

A key to gaining wide acceptance within your company is to be meticulous about measuring the benefits. In Chapter 12 when we start to plan a pilot, we will discuss ways in which the benefits brought out above might be measured in an objective way.

Closing the Gap

The Anatomy of a Mobile Enterprise

In the first part of this book, I made the prediction that within five years from now most companies will equip a large part of their workforce with wirelessly enabled portable devices. This will allow mobile workers to access critical information in real time. Those companies that have a mobile workforce and fail to provide that workforce with these tools will be tomorrow's losers.

In the first part of this book we also looked at the current state of technology. We saw that while technology is not yet at an ideal state of advancement, it is already good enough for us to start mobilizing the enterprise right now. It may or may not make sense for *your* particular company to start now, but in any case, you should understand this imminent paradigm shift and make a conscious decision as to when and how your company will take it on. Finally, at the end of Part I, we discussed the business value that can be derived from mobile solutions today.

In short, Part I addresses the *why*. In Part II we will address the *how*. How can you put together a mobile solution with today's technology? How can you ensure that such a solution will scale upward and take you into the certain future of wireless? We try to answer those questions in the next six chapters.

THE GAP BETWEEN WORKERS AND INFORMATION

The problem we set out to solve is that there is a large gap between the mobile worker and critical information—the critical information that lives behind the company firewall.

Recently your company has probably made much of that data available to remote workers over fixed-line Internet connections. However, access is only available where there is a computer and a fixed-line connection.

Your company has probably set up a virtual private network (VPN) so that the remote worker can access data as if he or she were sitting in the office. This VPN is made possible through authentication techniques that provide some proof the user is who he or she claims to be—and through cryptographic techniques that prevent eavesdropping.

To many of us it is already routine to work remotely in a secure fashion. While this concept is relatively recent, we almost take it for granted. We can be sure that one day in the near future we will be working from wireless terminals just as routinely.

Today is not that day. Today many of our business processes are suffering from a bottleneck that occurs when we do not have the right information where we need it and when we need it. In other words, as shown in Figure 4–1, there is a gap between the mobile professional and the enterprise applications that manage the information he or she needs. As long as this gap exists, your mobile workers will be out of step with the rest of the company. Their productivity will not be as high as it could be and they will miss opportunities.

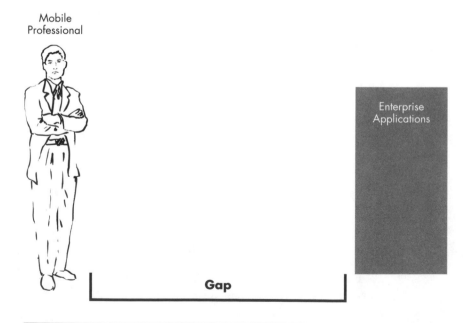

FIGURE 4–1 The gap.

The mobile professional is not the only one affected by this problem—the rest of the company also suffers as a result of this gap. Mobile professionals have difficulty in feeding information back to the company. In the best case, they can call colleagues and talk about things they have learned or they can connect to the company intranet from a hotel room. Neither way is adequate.

When you share information with a colleague through a phone conversation, the sharing stops there. You have only passed the information to one other person, and nothing is recorded.

By the time you connect to the company intranet from a hotel room, you may have forgotten a number of things. Fatigue may have set in, thus causing a precipitous drop in your motivation to share information. In some cases, new information needs to be shared much sooner. By the time you get to your hotel room, it is too late.

BUILDING BLOCKS TO BRIDGE THE GAP

Let's now look at how we can solve this problem. The functional components needed to bridge the gap between the mobile professional and critical information are in bold italics in Figure 4–2.

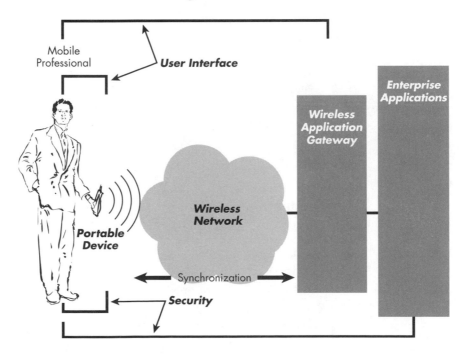

FIGURE 4–2   Building blocks.

Let's now take a brief look at each of the building blocks. In subsequent chapters we will discuss them at length. Here we go into just enough detail to get an understanding of how these components work together and how they might be configured to provide a solution to your compelling business problems.

Portable Computing Devices

The mobile professional will need a computing device that can be carried around. There are a variety of devices to choose from: data-enabled cell phones, personal digital assistants (PDAs), Smart Phones (hybrid phone/ PDA), tablet computers, or notebook computers. Your selection will likely depend on a variety of factors, including cost, boot-up time, the size of the keyboard and screen, and how much your mobile workers are willing to carry around with them.

Some of the other considerations will be whether or not the device needs to be ruggedized and what kinds of add-ons are important. If your field engineers are working in a rough area, ruggedized devices might be necessary. If your field workers need to take pictures, you might consider a camera add-on.

You will need to understand the different kinds of portable computing devices available today, and how they are likely to evolve. Combinations of devices are also worth considering.

You may decide to select different devices for different job functions. Managing these devices will become an important function of your IT department. There will need to be ways of replacing lost or stolen devices, performing backup and restore, and upgrading software with little or no user intervention.

Portable computing devices are discussed in detail in Chapter 5.

User Interface

You will need to think through an appropriate interface to ensure acceptance of this new paradigm. After all, you cannot expect your sales and service force to spend a lot of time figuring out how to use the new tools. These tools should be intuitive, and even fun, to use. If your mobile solutions are not a delight to use, they probably will not be used.

The user interface will depend on the device chosen. You cannot fit an entire Web page on a cell phone or a PDA and you cannot expect users to enter large quantities of data on a cell phone. On the other hand, it is probably not a good idea to have users work through a voice menu from a notebook computer.

Most companies will select more than one kind of device, since different job functions have different requirements. If this is the case with your company, you will want to avoid buying and operating a new version of each of your enterprise applications for each device. For this reason, you will want to use a wireless application gateway, which you or a systems integrator can configure to reformat application output according to the device from which the application is being accessed.

User interfaces will be discussed throughout Chapters 5–9.

Wireless Networks

Needless to say, wireless networks are fundamental to the mobile enterprise. You should understand how these networks work, and perhaps more importantly, you should understand their limitations. There are several networking standards and several network operators. This makes it very confusing to the consumer.

As discussed in the first part of this book there are networks that are designed specifically to provide data services. These networks have a head start on cellular networks, which are now beginning to provide useful data services. You should consider both options, and make an informed decision on which one best fits your needs.

Forced by regulation to offer the capability of determining the position of a subscriber, cellular network operators will soon be able to offer location-based services—services that provide local information to the user, help the company track workers, or help workers make their way to a destination.

You as a buyer will have to get comfortable with wireless network technology. For this reason, we discuss this subject in detail in Chapter 6.

Wireless Application Gateways

The job of the wireless application gateway is to take care of the characteristics of small devices and wireless networks on the one side and interface with enterprise applications on the other.

There are special constraints of mobile networks, such as low bandwidth, unstable connections, and high latency (the time it takes a bit to get from one end to the other). The wireless application gateway works within these constraints, so your enterprise applications do not have to be modified to be accessible to mobile professionals.

Different workers may be using different kinds of portable computing devices. The wireless application gateway interfaces with enterprise applications and reformats the data from those applications so that it fits on the small screens of mobile devices. It can present application output differently depending on the device being used.

Data exchanges between mobile workers and the enterprise applications may occur in different ways: data may be prefetched and aggregated on the wireless application gateway, it may be fetched from enterprise applications on demand, it may be *pushed* to the mobile worker without a request, or it may occur in the form of synchronization. A good wireless application gateway will be able to operate in all of these modes.

We explore wireless application gateways in detail in Chapter 7.

Enterprise Applications

The critical information your mobile workers need belongs to enterprise applications you may already be using. You will need to understand which information can be obtained from which applications, and how it can all be integrated to provide a *meta-application* tailored for the mobile workforce.

There are several classes of application-managing information you need to make available to your mobile workers. These include enterprise resource planning (ERP), supply chain management (SCM), customer relationship management (CRM), knowledge management (KM), and email. You will have to know which applications hold the information needed by your mobile workers.

Enterprise application integration (EAI) also plays a role in how you mobilize your enterprise. You may already be integrating several of your applications using EAI middleware. In this case, you might use this same middleware to extract the data needed by mobile workers.

We go into detail on enterprise applications in Chapter 9.

Synchronization

In many cases, the information your users need can be preloaded on to the portable computing device. This is true for information that does not change throughout the day—or for cases where it does not matter if the user gets a version of the information that is slightly out of date.

Users may also perform updates throughout the day and then synchronize with enterprise applications later. This works well when it is important to capture the information immediately, but no urgency to share it with the rest of the company.

In these cases, synchronization is important. Synchronization can occur over a fixed line connection, for example, over the Internet or on the company LAN. It can also occur over a wireless connection when the quantity of data to exchange is relatively small. For example, if a mobile professional is working in an area where there is little or no network coverage, he or she can capture data on the device and then synchronize from a place where there is adequate network coverage.

I discuss synchronization throughout Chapters 5–9.

Security

The mobile enterprise comes with a new set of vulnerabilities. Portable computing devices get lost and stolen more easily than desktop computers. Any sensitive data on those devices has to be encrypted. Some mechanism should be in place to allow only authorized users to access the device.

You cannot control all use of portable computing devices—and there are already a number of computer viruses that target these kinds of small computers. For these reasons, virus protection software should be used.

Some of the other vulnerabilities are similar to those you encounter when setting up a way for employees to work from home. That is, you have to be concerned with eavesdropping and unauthorized access to applications behind the company firewall.

You will need to think through security from the beginning. You will have to take a new look at your company's security policy and update it for this effort. You should think through the vulnerabilities, think about the value of what you are protecting, and the motivation of potential intruders. Apply the appropriate set of countermeasures to protect your company's intellectual capital.

Security is discussed in detail in Chapter 9.

DIFFERENT SOLUTION CONFIGURATIONS

The different components of the mobile enterprise can be arranged in different ways, depending on what you are trying to accomplish.

Access to One Application

If you only want to make one enterprise application available to your mobile workers, you can have the wireless application gateway functionality built

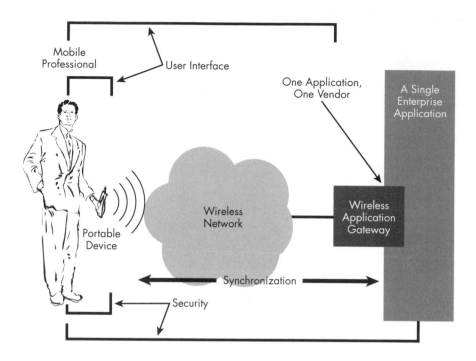

FIGURE 4–3   Mobilizing a single enterprise application.

into that one enterprise application. Most large vendors of enterprise applications have already developed this capability, shown in Figure 4–3.

An advantage to this approach is that since the company providing the wireless application gateway is also providing the enterprise application, they are intimately familiar with the application being presented to the mobile worker. The result is a look and feel that is similar to what you get when you use the same application on a desktop computer. Application upgrades may also be smoother—you can rest assured that when you get an application upgrade, the mobile interface is upgraded in lock step.

A disadvantage to this approach is that only one enterprise application is made available to your mobile workers. If you also want them to be able to access a different application, they have to sign out of the first one and then sign into the second one. Each application may take up a lot of memory on your portable computing device, so it may not even be possible to run more than one on the same device.

Access to Several Applications

If you want to make several enterprise applications available to your mobile workers you will need to use a wireless application gateway that is separate from any one application. This configuration is shown in Figure 4–4.

In this case, the wireless application gateway is provided by a company that has nothing to do with any particular enterprise application. An advantage to this approach is that you can create a separate application for your mobile workers. As we shall see in Chapter 8, this is quite appropriate, since your mobile workers have different needs than those sitting in front of a desktop computer.

This separate application can extract data from several enterprise applications and present the data in a way that makes sense to the mobile worker. In other words, the mobile application fits nicely into the business processes of the mobile worker.

A disadvantage to this approach is that you have to develop a relationship with a separate vendor. Upgrades to your enterprise applications may be complicated, since you have to make sure the wireless application gateway is compatible with the newer versions of the enterprise applications.

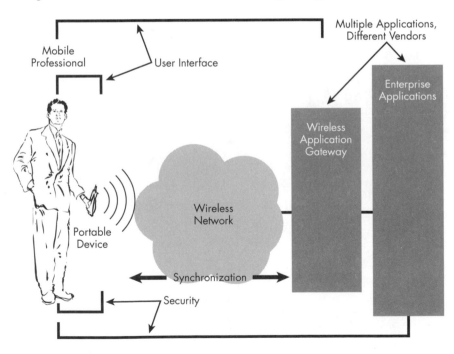

FIGURE 4–4 Mobilizing multiple enterprise applications.

A Subscription Service

Some wireless network operators are offering hosted solutions. That is, as shown in Figure 4–5, they run the infrastructure needed to mobilize one or more applications. The most popular case of this is wireless access to email.

An advantage to the subscription service is that you pay less money up front. You also benefit from not having to operate the wireless application gateway. The network operator does this for you.

There are a few problems associated with a subscription service. The first concern is security. If the data you want to send to mobile workers is not something you want to share, you have to make sure the data remains encrypted between your company intranet and the portable computing device.

Another big concern is that by using such a subscription service you may become too dependent on one network operator. You want to retain the ability to switch operators easily. It is important to be able to switch based on services offered and based on prices. If you are locked in to one operator, you weaken your position to negotiate.

Finally, you cannot synchronize your portable computing devices with the enterprise applications through the wireless application gateway. This means

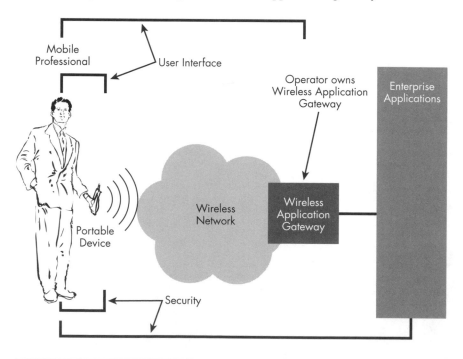

FIGURE 4–5   Hosted wireless application gateway.

that the wireless access to these applications takes a separate path than the synchronization process. The logic may not be the same, resulting in the need for extra work to make the wireless access and synchronization compatible.

CHOOSING THE RIGHT KIND OF SOLUTION FOR YOU

Having seen the different ways of mobilizing your enterprise, you will need to think through which one is right for you. Each configuration has a different pricing model and requires a different amount of work from your IT department to deploy and manage the solution.

Mobilizing a single application may seem easy at first glance. However, it may not be the least expensive. Furthermore, it ties you into using just that application. The mobile version of the application may not be sufficiently tailored to the needs of mobile workers, which are not the same as the worker sitting in the office in front of a desktop computer.

The subscription service is appealing in that it is easy to get started and the upfront costs are relatively small. However, you lock yourself in to using one network operator. There are also security issues—you do not want your sensitive enterprise data to pass unencrypted through another company's network. One other problem is that synchronization through a fixed-line connection can be quite complicated, since the synchronization process does not involve the same platform that provides the wireless access.

The solution configuration that offers the most flexibility is the one where multiple enterprise applications are mobilized, that is, the wireless application gateway is provided by an independent vendor. Even if your short-term intention is to just access one application, by having a separate wireless application gateway you keep open the possibilities for extension. This configuration also offers the best possibilities of presenting enterprise data in a way that better fits the business processes of a mobile worker.

You will need to talk to different kinds of vendors depending on which kind of solution fits your needs. If you want to mobilize just one enterprise application, you should talk to the vendor of that application. If you want to mobilize more than one application, you should talk to either a systems integrator or a wireless application gateway vendor. If you want a subscription service, you should talk to a wireless network operator.

You might also talk to device vendors and systems integrators for all of these cases. They may offer additional insight and they may have partners with whom they work to provide different kinds of solutions.

In Chapter 11 I talk more about the structure of the industry and the different classes of companies selling products and solutions to mobilize your enterprise.

SUMMARY

The problem we are trying to solve is rather obvious. We are trying to close the gap between the mobile worker and critical information. In doing so, we will create a new paradigm that will revolutionize the way we work.

The building blocks of the mobile enterprise can be arranged in different ways depending on your needs. You can mobilize a single application or you can mobilize multiple applications. You can also subscribe to a service that provides wireless access to one or more of your enterprise applications.

The most flexible configuration is one where the wireless application gateway is independent of any enterprise application. This kind of solution allows you to provide mobile workers with access to multiple back-end systems and it allows you to develop a new application, which extracts data from the various back-end applications and puts it together in a way that fits the needs of the mobile worker.

It is important to become familiar with the technology behind a mobile solution. This will help you make choices and select vendors. For this reason, we go into detail on the building blocks of the mobile enterprise in Chapters 5–9.

Portable Computing Devices

The most prominent feature of the mobile enterprise is the small computer each employee carries with him or her to access critical information. These are the tools mobile professionals use every day. Either they like their portable computers or they do not. In selecting which device they use, pay careful attention to their needs and prejudices.

You should also think about the impression such devices leave with your clients. After all, your mobile professionals are your company's ambassadors. In large measure, the outside world will form its opinion of your company as a result of contact with these representatives. If your mobile professionals operate in a smooth manner, the world is likely to have a good impression of your company. If, on the other hand, your company's representatives are clumsy and they carry around a lot of stuff they do not know how to use, they are likely to leave a bad impression. To this end, you should choose your portable computing devices carefully. Features, usability, and even fashion should play a role in your selection.

In this chapter I talk about the different kinds of portable devices that are available for use by your workforce. I specifically call out the cases where one is more appropriate than another, and I discuss different combinations you should consider.

ENTERPRISE REQUIREMENTS OF PORTABLE DEVICES

One indicator of the state of the industry around portable devices is the number and variety of products and accessories on the market. As in any early market there is a good deal of fragmentation. A lot of different players are vying for market share. They are approaching this business in different ways, using different standards, and emphasizing different features. Eventually many of these companies will get nudged out and a few winners will emerge. Once this happens the industry will settle on de-facto standards.

However, this is unlikely to happen anytime soon. The underlying technology is changing too quickly—forever making new things possible and allowing new entrants into the market. For you, the buyer, the result is a lot of confusion. You are now confronted with new possibilities that may be applied to your competitive advantage, but you cannot do so without first cutting through all the noise and understanding what is real and what is just a bunch of fluff. Those who fail to make the difference between hype and reality run the risk of jumping in front of a parade that is heading down the path of industrial disaster.

Of course, the danger of standing still as the parade marches by is that your competitors may jump out in front and lead the way in your industry. How many times have we seen this in the past? A paradigm shift of the magnitude we are now witnessing will eventually change just about everybody's business. Those who pick it up early and forge a clear path ahead will be able to leap frog over the competition.

It all comes down to understanding this new technology and determining how, if at all, it applies to your business. The good news is that for our purposes we *can* make some sense of the fragmentation around portable computing devices. Let's start out by thinking through what it is a mobile enterprise might require of portable devices. We can do this by looking at two sets of parameters:

- *Functional requirements*: What are the features you require of portable devices? Table 5–1 can be used as a guideline for thinking through the kinds of questions to ask when selecting what is most appropriate for the job functions you have in mind.

- *Economic and practical considerations*: What does owning such a device entail? Table 5–2 lists the economic and practical considerations that should be taken into account when you choose portable computing devices for your workforce.

Maybe you have a few parameters to add to the lists in Tables 5–1 and 5–2. Only *you* know the full set of requirements for your specific case. What is important is that you start out with a list or lists similar to what is shown in these two tables. This will facilitate an objective evaluation of the portable devices.

TABLE 5–1   Feature Requirements of Portable Devices

Factor	Questions and Concerns
Wireless access	• Do you need the device to have direct access to a public wireless network? Which networks do you want access to?
Synchronization	• Which applications and data do you need to synchronize and what kinds of synchronization procedures are acceptable?
Indoor/outdoor use	• Do you need to use the device inside? If so, you will have to consider in-building network coverage, and you will have to consider how good the display is indoors.
	• Do you need to use the device outdoors? If so, you will have to make sure the display is readable under sunlight.
Size	• Do you need the device to be small enough to put in a pocket?
	• Does the screen have to be small enough not to interfere with face-to-face conversation?
Weight	• Does the device have to be especially light?
Multimedia	• Do you need to be able to view videos or listen to audio recordings?
	• Do you need to be able to record video or audio?
Add-ons	• Do you need to add a bar code reader, a camera, global positioning system (GPS), or something else?
Ruggedization	• Are you going to operate the portable device in a dusty environment, in hazardous weather, or in a place where it will have to withstand shock?
Battery life	• How long do you need to operate without being plugged into the wall?
	• How much time can you tolerate for recharging the battery?
Boot-up time	• How long can you wait for the portable device to boot up?
User interface	• Do you need color display?
	• How would you like to enter data?
	• How much screen space do you need?
	• Do you require the ability to make phone calls?

TABLE 5–2   Economic and Practical Considerations

Factor	Questions and Concerns
Cost	• How much does it cost to buy and maintain?
Popularity among thieves	• Do people like to steal this kind of device?
Ease of replacement	• How easy is it to acquire a replacement? Do you have to stock up or can you just go to the store and buy a new one?
	• How easy is it to acquire parts and add-ons?
Compatibility	• Does the portable device use standards that are going to prevail?
	• Is the device compatible with other hardware and software to which it must interface now and in the future?
Aesthetics	• Is the device going to show a good image of your company?
	• Will your mobile professionals be proud to carry it around?

Remember also that part of what you will have to do is match the tool to the job function. For each job function there may be a different set of needs; and as such, you might choose a different portable computer for each professional role.

THE RANGE OF DEVICES AVAILABLE

For the most part, we can place portable computing devices into the five categories shown in Box 5–1. The devices you will be considering will probably fall into one of these classes.

Box 5–1   Categories of Portable Computing Devices

The following are devices that the mobile professional can use today:

- **Cell phones:** most cell phones on the market today offer some kind of data service. Most offer a short messaging service (SMS) and many also offer wireless access protocol (WAP) services that allow a minimal form of Web access.
- **Personal digital assistants (PDAs):** we are now seeing a tremendous amount of advancement and market uptake in PDAs. Due to the small size and relatively high computing power of these devices, they are fast becoming a favorite among mobile professionals.
- **Smart Phones:** we are just now starting to see viable products that offer both the capabilities of cell phones and PDAs. This is a powerful combination whose proponents view it as the device to end all devices.
- **Tablet computers:** these are computers with a large screen and no built-in keyboard. Input is through a stylus. The idea is that using these computers is like using a tablet of paper.
- **Notebook computers:** so far these have been the portable computing device of choice. Many people have gotten rid of their desktop computer and now just use a notebook, which they can carry around outside of the office. At the same time, many notebooks are powerful enough to use in the office just like a desktop computer.

These devices differ in terms of features and computing power. They also differ in terms of cost, size, weight, battery life, and boot-up time. To get an idea of how these devices compare, it is useful to plot a rough graph positioning them by functionality versus inconvenience, as is shown in Figure 5–1.

Keep in mind that what someone calls a useful feature is highly subjective. Likewise, what is considered an inconvenience will differ from company to company and from person to person. How you rate features and inconveniences will depend on the job function where the device is to be applied, as

Trade-Offs in Choosing Portable Devices

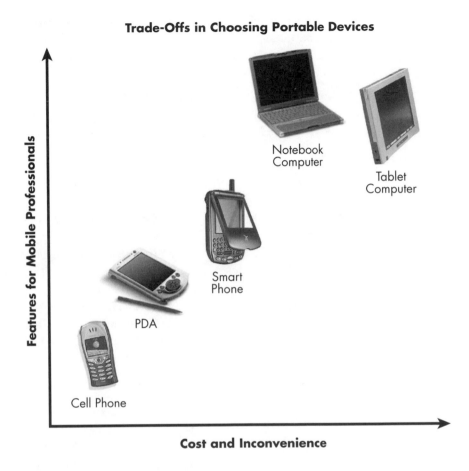

FIGURE 5–1   Rough positioning of portable devices.

well as on personal preferences. For these reasons, Figure 5–1 should only be taken as a very rough plot of features versus cost and inconvenience.

As you see, tablet computers are graphed as having fewer features and more inconveniences as compared to notebooks. Why then would anybody want a tablet instead of a notebook? Those people who prefer tablets have very specific needs. For example, many people want a computer they do not have to open to view the screen. They want to be able to view data on a large screen using a device they can hold in one hand. Tablets are also generally more resistant to abuse. They can take a coffee spill—notebooks cannot.

You may also be wondering why two-way pagers are not included on the list of portable computing devices. The reason I have left these devices out is that pagers by themselves are of limited usefulness to the mobile professional. Those that will enjoy long-term success in the marketplace are the ones that are either part of a cell phone or that offer PDA functionality as well. The Motorola V.200 is an example of the former and the RIM Black-Berry is an example of the latter. These devices are included in the discussions on cell phones and PDAs, respectively.

CELL PHONES

Mobile professionals are already using a cell phone—so much so that in many cases, it is taken for granted. Nowadays, carrying a cell phone is like carrying around a wallet and keys.

But do not forget how powerful a tool the cell phone is. After all, this is how mobile professionals make calls and this is how other people can reach them virtually anywhere. There is no doubt that the cell phone has already greatly enhanced the efficiency of workers on the move. But what can the cell phone do to help you access enterprise applications?

In cases where exchanges are relatively small, the cell phone might be the portable computing device of choice. For example, you can send a dispatch order including the address of the next trouble site to a technician's cell phone. The engineer can accept or reject this request and even get a little more information on the problem by clicking on a universal resource locator (URL).

Another case where the cell phone is a sufficient tool for accessing enterprise applications is where you are using an application that offers a voice menu with voice recognition. Your mobile professional can navigate the menus and enter data by speaking. As long as the list of things that need to be said remains small, this could work quite well. However, be careful when there is a high degree of variation in what needs to be done from individual to individual or from session to session. Voice recognition technology is still quite primitive. You can get hung up having to repeat yourself several times before becoming so frustrated that you just give up on using a voice application altogether.

In these two examples, there is no need to get a sophisticated portable device. If your problem is simple, do yourself the favor of keeping the solution simple. Stick with using cell phones.

Choosing a Cell Phone

Your choice of cell phone will go hand in hand with your choice of wireless network provider. The service provider will support only a certain set of phones. Often, they will provide the phone and the subscription as a package.

Which phones are supported by the operator will depend on which wireless network technology is being used—and in many cases, on which partnerships the operator has with handset manufacturers.

Cell Phone Features

The basic functions offered by the current generation of cell phones are voice calls, caller ID, voice mail, short messaging service (SMS), and address lists. There are several additional features that are of interest to the mobile professional. Box 5–2 lists some of the important ones.

Box 5–2   Additional Cell Phone Features for Mobile Professionals

Some additional cell phone features that are important to the mobile professional are:

- **Wireless application protocol (WAP)**: to allow a limited form of Internet browsing.
- **Messaging**: allowing users to send mail messages via a paging service.
- **Voice activation**: to allow you to initiate phone calls or other simple commands by speaking to your phone.
- **Infrared**: to allow you to *beam* information to another cell phone that is only a foot or so away and pointed at your phone. Infrared is also a useful way to connect a computer to the phone to allow the computer to use the data services of the phone.
- **Bluetooth**: to exchange information with other devices within 10 meters without having to point the devices at one another. Bluetooth is also an excellent way of providing data services to a computer. The computer can control the phone via the Bluetooth connection. You can do all this without removing your phone from your pocket.
- **Predictive text entry (T9™ or iTAP™)**: to ease data entry by reducing the number of keystrokes needed to enter a word.
- **Speakerphone**: for hands-free communication.
- **Synchronization**: to synchronize contacts and calendar with your desktop or notebook computer.

A WAP browser, messaging, and special data entry features all serve to make your cell phone a little more like a data device. In fact, a cell phone with these features might be the right tool for many mobile professionals.

WAP Browser

Many phones come with a WAP browser. WAP, which is the acronym for *Wireless Application Protocol*, allows limited Web browsing from a mobile phone. It does this through protocols that are adapted to the peculiarities of wireless networks. WAP includes a markup language, called wireless markup language (WML), which takes into consideration the limited screen and data-entry capabilities of a mobile phone.

You cannot directly access the same Web pages you would through the Web browser on your desktop PC. Either the Web site you access is written for WML or a portal has to be used to pick out fields from a Web page and package them for WML. Typically, network operators have a portal, which allows access to a limited number of sites.

Most of the cell phones on the market today offer a WAP browser that conforms to the 1.1 version of WAP, even though the WAP Forum has already released both WAP 1.2 and WAP 2.0 specifications. The biggest change from WAP 1.1 to WAP 1.2 is the *push* feature. This allows a message to be sent to the phone without the user first having to make a request. WAP 2.0 is a major revision aligning WAP more closely with standard Internet protocols.

Messaging

Some phones provide an *always-on* messaging service. A good example of this kind of phone is the Motorola V-200, shown in Figure 5–2.

This mix of telephone and messaging is best offered on networks with a two-way paging service. The messages can be *pushed* to the phone much like a paging message, that is, the user does not have to ask if he or she has mail.

FIGURE 5–2   Motorola V-200 phone-pager. Courtesy Motorola, Inc.

The network just sends it to the device as it arrives. The user checks mail when convenient and can usually be sure that the device has received the latest messages automatically.

Data Entry

One of the major limitations of the cell phone as a data device is the size of the keyboard. Most phones are limited to 12 keys—the 10 keys used to dial numbers and two special keys: "*" and "#". These same keys are used to enter letters of the alphabet and punctuation. Depending on the menu context, the phone will interpret keystrokes as either a number or a letter. When the keys are interpreted as letters it may take three or more strokes to get the right letter. For example, you have to hit the "2" key three times to select the letter "c."

T9 Text Input

An improvement on this is the system devised by the company Tegic Communications, which was acquired by America Online in 1999. This data entry system, called T9 Text Input, was originally developed to assist people with severe disabilities. Using special glasses that detect eye movement, a person can make a selection. Since it is impossible to focus on enough different places to make up a full keyboard, each selection maps to more than one letter. To resolve the ambiguity, the T9 system uses a database of commonly used words to propose an ordered list of possibilities to the user based on his or her selections.

The same principal was applied to handheld devices with limited keypads. For example, on an Ericsson T39 cell phone, if you type the sequence 5-6-8-3, the T9 software allows you to select one of the two words "love" or "loud," or the segment "jove."

Most of the phones on the market today use T9 for data entry.

iTAP™

Motorola developed its own algorithm for predictive text entry. This system, called iTAP™, is similar to T9. As the user types, the system narrows down a list of possible word segments based on a dictionary of 35,000 preconfigured words and any words the user has added. The order of words in the list is based on the commonality of the word and on the user's past selections.

Whether you use T9 or iTAP will depend on which software the phone manufacturer has licensed. Either system is sufficient for light data entry and short messaging. For more intense data entry, you will need a keyboard.

FIGURE 5–3 Ericsson Chatboard®. Courtesy Sony Ericsson Mobile Communications.

Keyboards

Some cell phones offer a small keyboard as an accessory. An example of this is the Ericsson Chatboard®, shown in Figure 5–3.

The chatboard is attached at the bottom of the phone and allows key selection with your thumbs. The usability is similar to that of email pagers, that is, you are not likely to win a contest in typing speed. However, for messaging it does the job quite well.

PERSONAL DIGITAL ASSISTANTS (PDAS)

Apple Computer coined the term *personal digital assistant* (PDA) in reference to its Newton MessagePad device, which was first released in 1993. This first PDA did not become very popular due in large part to the difficulties with its handwriting recognition. It was just too hard to enter data accurately.

Three years later in 1996, Palm Computing released the Palm Pilot. This was the first successful PDA. The thinking behind this creation of Jeff Hawkins, a founder of Palm Computing, was that a handheld device should not be a PC crammed into a smaller form factor. Instead, it should provide a small set of simple functions tailored to the needs of people on the go. At the same time there had to be a way for the device to synchronize with a desktop computer. In this way, the user could keep only one version of his or her schedule and contact list. The Palm Pilot used a simple letter recognition scheme that worked very well. This scheme, called *Graffiti*, allowed users to easily enter simple text using a pen-like instrument (a *stylus*).

The Palm Pilot device was so well received by consumers that it kicked off a new industry. Within a few years, several other companies jumped on to ride this new wave with their own handheld products. Today there are at least two dozen different brands of PDAs on the market. All offer the six basic functions shown in Box 5–3.

Box 5–3   Basic functions of a PDA

The basic functions of a PDA are:
- **Calendar**: to set appointments
- **Directory**: to store phone numbers and address information
- **Notes**: to take notes
- **Calculator**: to perform arithmetic
- **Alarm**: to wake you up or remind you of an event
- **Task List**: to track a set of things you intend to do

Many PDAs also offer word processing, spreadsheet, and time and expense applications. In addition, there are a variety of third-party applications developed for these small computers. The built-in software features, and the third-party applications available for a PDA, are determined by the operating system it runs.

Indeed, the OS is the biggest factor that sets one PDA apart from another. While there are several different operating systems powering PDAs today, three dominate:

- Palm OS
- Pocket PC
- EPOC

These operating systems have gained popularity among independent software developers who have collectively produced a rich set of applications from which you can choose. Fortunately for us, many of the software developers have created applications specifically targeting the mobile professional.

Palm OS-Powered PDAs

Companies that make Palm OS-powered PDAs include Palm, Inc. and Handspring. PDAs from these two companies are shown in Figure 5–4.

FIGURE 5–4 PDAs running Palm OS. Left image courtesy Palm, Inc. Right image courtesy Handspring, Inc.

To synchronize with the desktop, a system called HotSync is used. This requires a program to be installed on the desktop to interface with the PDA. In order to initiate synchronization, the user places the Palm device in its cradle and presses the HotSync button. Users may synchronize with both Mac and Windows desktop computers.

For data input, the user has a choice between an onscreen keyboard or the Graffiti system for letter recognition. The onscreen keyboard can be accessed when the cursor is in a text field. The layout is like that of a QWERTY keyboard.

Most users prefer Graffiti. Under this scheme, the user draws letters on the screen with a stylus. The letters have to be written in a special way. The Graffiti system recognizes letters by the shape of the stroke of the stylus, and by the origin and direction of the stroke. With the exception of the letter "X," every character can be written with only one stroke of the stylus. It takes most people less than 20 minutes to learn Graffiti.

Pocket PC-Powered Devices

Windows CE is an embedded version of the Windows family of operating systems. This embedded operating system is modular, allowing different frameworks or packages to fit to different classes of devices. The package used for PDAs is called Pocket PC; and the PDAs it runs on are called the same thing—Pocket PCs. Companies that make such PDAs include HP and Casio. Pocket PCs from these two companies are shown in Figure 5–5.

FIGURE 5–5   Pocket PC devices. Left image courtesy Hewlett-Packard
Company. Right image courtesy Casio, Inc.

To synchronize with a desktop computer, the user places the PDA in its
cradle and synchronization commences automatically, that is, in contrast to
Palm PDAs, users of Pocket PCs do not have to press a button to start synchronizing. On the Pocket PC, synchronization is through a system called
ActiveSync, which, like HotSync, requires a program on the desktop and one
on the PDA. ActiveSync supports synchronization with Windows desktops,
but not with Mac desktops.

Data entry can be accomplished through an onscreen keyboard, much like
that of the Palm devices. The user may also work with a letter-recognition
scheme or a full-blown handwriting recognition scheme called the *Transcriber*.

The Pocket PC letter recognition scheme is called *Character Recognizer*.
Like its Palm OS counterpart, Graffiti, Character Recognizer identifies letters by
the shape of the stroke, as well as by the point of origin and the direction of the
stroke. It is even easier to learn to write for Character Recognizer than it is for
Graffiti, since with the former the letters look more like the way you really write.
This being said, in either case you can master the system in a matter of minutes.

If your handwriting is really good, and if you are really patient, you
might try the Transcriber. Using this system for data entry you write whole
words at a time using printing style, cursive style, or a combination of the
two. The system interprets your handwriting and shows you the result. You
can then correct any of the Transcriber's mistakes.

Unfortunately, unless your handwriting is really good, you will spend a
lot of time correcting the Transcriber's interpretation of what you have written. This method of data entry is not yet magic enough to be useful.

EPOC-Powered Devices

A British company called Psion developed the EPOC operating system to run its line of organizers. This particular operating system attracted several phone manufacturers, who, under pressure to develop more sophisticated phones, were looking to standardize an operating system for cell phones. In 1998, Psion, Motorola, Panasonic, Ericsson, and Nokia formed a joint venture, called Symbian, to take ownership of EPOC as standard operating systems for cell phones. EPOC is now sometimes called Symbian OS. To minimize confusion I will continue to refer to it as EPOC.

Because EPOC is designed specifically for cell phones, the resulting devices are actually Smart Phones, that is, they are PDA/Phone hybrids. We will revisit this concept in the next section.

Two companies with EPOC-powered devices on the market today are Ericsson and Nokia. Examples of devices from these companies are shown in Figure 5–6. EPOC is so flexible that two EPOC devices from different vendors may look very different and offer different user interfaces.

The devices running EPOC generally have a keyboard for data entry. These keyboards are too small for heavy-duty touch-typing, but they are much easier to use than a stylus and onscreen keyboard.

A system called EPOC Connect provides a number of services including data synchronization, file management, backup and restore, email, contact, and calendar synchronization. Connect uses an open architecture that allows device manufacturers and other software vendors to add different interfaces

FIGURE 5–6 PDA/phone hybrids powered by EPOC. Left image courtesy Sony Ericsson Mobile Communications. Right image courtesy Nokia.

and extensions. For this reason, Connect may look different on different devices. The device manufacturer may even brand its version of connect differently; for example, Psion brands its version "PsiWin."

RIM

We now talk about a device that does not quite fit in one of the five categories I laid out in the beginning of this chapter. There is a maverick in every herd. I am referring to the series of devices called BlackBerry™ developed by the company Research In Motion (RIM). These devices run a proprietary operating system and they use data-only networks. They have become very popular because they do one thing very well: wireless email.

BlackBerry uses the DataTac and Mobitex wireless data protocols, which are offered by the network operators Motient and Cingular Interactive, respectively. These networks have extensive coverage and in-building communications are very good. I cover DataTac and Mobitex in Chapter 7.

BlackBerry devices are frequently classified as two-way pagers or email messengers. However, I am classifying them as PDAs, because, as you can see in Figure 5–7, these devices have many of the features typically found in a PDA.

With BlackBerry handhelds, synchronization occurs wirelessly. As email arrives, and as calendar and contact information is changed, updates are *pushed* to the device. In the reverse direction, as users make updates on the device, the change is propagated to the enterprise wirelessly. Since Black-Berry handhelds make use of networks with extensive coverage—networks

FIGURE 5–7   RIM BlackBerry™ devices. Courtesy Research In Motion Limited.

that work well both inside and outside—the devices can be kept up to date pretty easily.

Data entry is through the built-in keyboard. The keys are small, making it impossible to touch type. But as long as there is not too much data to enter, these small keyboards work just fine.

RIM has also released a Smart Phone, which is shown in the section following this one on Smart Phones.

Accessories

In looking for PDAs for your mobile professionals you should consider the kinds of add-ons that will be needed, and whether they are available on the devices you like. Some of the more popular add-ons are shown in Box 5–4.

Box 5–4   PDA accessories for mobile professionals

Some important PDA accessories for the mobile professional are:

- **Keyboards**: The more data entry you have to do, the bigger the keyboard you need. Letter recognition and onscreen keyboards just will not cut it for heavy data entry. There are several full-sized external keyboards that can be used with PDAs. These keyboards can be folded up to about the size of a PDA when they are not being used.

- **Communications cards**: You may want a Bluetooth card to have the PDA control your cell phone and use its data communications services. You might also want to have a card that allows you to access the data services of your wireless operator.

- **Phones**: There are accessories that add telephone functionality to PDAs. This turns the PDA into a Smart Phone (see the next section for more on Smart Phones).

- **Barcode readers**: Many mobile workers need to scan bar codes. These workers can use barcode readers that plug into their PDAs.

- **Cameras**: Some job functions can benefit from the ability to take pictures and send them immediately back to the office.

- **Global positioning system (GPS)**: In industries such as transportation, or in cases where dispatch and routing are important, a GPS receiver could come in handy. GPS receivers can plug into your PDA.

Be careful to match the accessory to the make and model of PDA you are using. Aside from differences in the operating systems running on various PDAs, there are also differences in the type and number of add-on slots. The result is that the buyer has to be a little more careful in choosing accessories.

SMART PHONES

Smart Phones are devices that perform the functions of both phones and PDAs. This idea has been around for a few years now. Some of the early instances of Smart Phones met with limited success, representing the worst of both worlds. They were both bad phones and bad PDAs.

However, in the last year we have seen a turnaround with several companies producing good Smart Phones. Not surprisingly, there are two kinds of companies that are well positioned to develop these *hybrid* devices: phone manufactures and PDA manufacturers.

Telephone Manufacturers that Make Smart Phones

The telephone manufacturers that have successfully developed Smart Phones include Motorola and Nokia. Figure 5–8 shows the Smart Phones from these two companies. The Motorola Accompli 009 runs a proprietary operating system called *Wisdom OS*; the Nokia 9290 runs the EPOC operating system.

FIGURE 5–8   Smart Phones from phone manufacturers. Left image courtesy Motorola, Inc. Right image courtesy Nokia.

Cell phone manufacturers have the advantage of being prepared to produce and sell millions of devices per month. They have the production capacity, the channel agreements, and the support structure. A strike against the cell phone manufacturers is that they have less of an understanding of computers, operating systems, and software development.

PDA Manufacturers that Make Smart Phones

The PDA manufacturers that have successfully developed Smart Phones include Handspring and RIM. Figure 5–9 shows Smart Phones from these two companies. The Handspring Treo runs Palm OS; the BlackBerry 6710 uses Sun Microsystems' Java 2 Micro Edition as its core OS.

PDA manufacturers have a better understanding of computing devices. However, they do not have as good a relationship with telephone operators, which are an important sales channel for voice-communication devices. We will certainly see a lot of other Smart Phones coming from PDA manufacturers in the next year.

FIGURE 5–9 Smart Phones from PDA manufacturers. Left image courtesy Handspring, Inc. Right image courtesy Research In Motion Limited.

The Downside of Smart Phones

While proponents of Smart Phones claim that these will be the devices to end all devices, a lot of other people are hesitant. The biggest problems with Smart Phones have to do with how they can be used. Many are too big or awkward to hold to your ear. Some offer microphones and earplugs to eliminate this problem. However, if you are using a microphone or an earplug, then you have to be prepared to set them up quickly when you get a phone call. Either that or you have to walk around with your microphone and earplug on at all times.

Another problem is that with many of the Smart Phones there is no real keyboard, rather, there is an onscreen keyboard and a stylus. This means that you can't feel the keys and dial without looking. It makes working with a menu more difficult because you have to constantly move the device from your ear back down to where you can see the onscreen keyboard to type a selection.

As we shall see later in this chapter, instead of using a Smart Phone, it might be better to have a Bluetooth-enabled cell phone and a PDA that uses the cell phone for communications services.

TABLET COMPUTERS

Tablet computers are devices that can be used sort of like a heavy tablet of paper. You enter data with a pen and the screen is always exposed.

There are several kinds of tablet computers. The biggest distinction for our purposes is between those that can do very little without a network connection and those that have a hard disk and operate well in standalone mode. The former group is sometimes called a Webpad. This kind of tablet is not so interesting for the mobile professional. After all, it would not be wise to depend on an ever-present wireless network connection—not yet, at least. For this reason, we will eliminate Webpads from our discussion. All of the tablet computers I mention here have a built-in hard drive.

Tablets are a lot like notebooks. The big differences are:

- Tablets generally have less RAM and hard disk space.
- Tablets run at a lower clock rate.
- Tablets do not have an integrated keyboard.
- Tablet screens are permanently exposed.
- Tablets can generally withstand more abuse.

Fujitsu makes tablet computers. An example of a tablet from Fujitsu is shown in Figure 5–10.

FIGURE 5–10   Tablet computers. Copyright Fujitsu PC Corporation.

There is a lot of variation in the size of tablet computers. This, of course, makes a difference in how easily the screen can be read. It also makes a difference in how easy it is to carry around.

If you need to enter a lot of data, you might consider buying an external keyboard that can connect to the tablet—either through a cable or wirelessly. You can imagine the situation where the tablet is carried around by a field technician throughout the day. As the technician goes from site to site, he or she can view large amounts of data and make a few updates using the pen. At the end of the day, the technician sits down and enters larger amounts of data using a keyboard.

Notebooks

The notebook computer has become the portable computing device of choice. The thinnest and lightest ones are so easy to carry around, you forget you are carrying a real computer. However, do not be fooled by size and weight—these little things pack a powerful punch.

At the other extreme are the more powerful—and therefore, larger—notebooks that can be used as a replacement of the desktop computer. These notebooks can do so much that it is hard to justify having both a notebook and a desktop computer.

The kinds of notebooks at the two extremes—ultra-thin and desktop replacement—may be used by different kinds of mobile professionals. You might also consider the variety of notebooks that lie between these two extremes.

Ultra-Thin Notebooks

Today, there are several notebook computers on the market that are 1-inch thick or less and weigh less than 4 pounds. These ultra-thin notebooks run at

FIGURE 5–11   Ultra-thin notebooks. Left image courtesy Casio, Inc. Center image courtesy Hewlett-Packard Company. Right image courtesy Dell Computer Corp.

clock speeds of at least 600 MHz, have at least 20 gigabytes of hard-disk space, and come with at least 128 megabytes of RAM.

Manufacturers producing these portable computers include Casio, HP, and Dell. Example products from these companies are shown in Figure 5–11.

Two of the biggest reasons notebooks have gotten so small and light are:

- *The choice of material*: these marvels of engineering are encased in lightweight metal such as titanium, magnesium, and aluminum.
- *Smaller chips*: the current generation of chips are much smaller, weigh less, generate less heat, and consume less power.

Ultra-thin notebooks are wonderful tools for the traveling professional who needs a powerful computing device, but cannot afford to carry around more luggage.

Desktop Replacement

There are many notebooks on the market today that can replace the desktop computer. There is no longer a good reason to have both. So many mobile professionals are opting for the notebook they can carry around while traveling, and then bring into the office, where they perform the intensive tasks that used to require a desktop computer.

Companies making high-end notebooks include HP and Dell. Notebooks from these vendors are shown in Figure 5–12.

FIGURE 5–12 Desktop replacement notebooks. Left image courtesy Hewlett-Packard Company. Right image courtesy Dell Computer Corp.

The high-end notebooks run at a clock speed of at least 1.7 GHz, they come with at least 256 megabytes of system memory, they have a high-resolution screen, and they offer at least 20 gigabytes of hard drive space. As is the case with the ultra-thin notebooks, these computers benefit from the current generation of smaller, more powerful processors.

Features for the Mobile Professional

Notebook computers come with a variety of built-in and optional features that are useful for the mobile professional. Some of these are shown in Box 5–5.

Box 5–5 Notebook Features

Notebook features for the mobile professional:

- **Wi-Fi (802.11b)**: wireless LAN comes built in to many of the notebook computers on the market today. Workers on the go no longer have to rely on a cable to gain access to the corporate LAN. Thanks to wireless LAN, they can move about the office and still stay connected. Wireless LAN also allows them to access the Internet at so-called *hotspots*, such as coffee shops, hotels, and airports.

- **Bluetooth**: Bluetooth cards can be used to have your notebook control a cell phone and make use of its data communication services.

- **Network cards**: for public network access using data services such as CDPD or 1xRTT (see Chapter 6 for more on these technologies). Using these cards, the notebook can gain direct access to the data services of your wireless network operator, such as AT&T Wireless or Sprint PCS.

- **Fingerprint authentication**: a fingerprint authentication system is built in to some notebooks, or one may be added on. This provides useful security.

Another thing to consider is how tough the notebook is. How much of a beating do you need it to take? As we shall see in the next section, many companies make ruggedized notebooks.

RUGGEDIZED DEVICES

In many cases your mobile professionals are working in a rough environment where a portable computing device is likely to be dropped, exposed to harsh weather conditions, and so on. In these kinds of situations you should consider investing in ruggedized portable computers. Several companies make these industrial devices. But exactly what does it mean for a device to be ruggedized?

Rugged Defined

Most ruggedized devices use the same internal components as any other portable computer of their class. The difference is that they are cased in material resistant to harsh conditions. In addition, a ruggedized device will usually have a display that can be easily read outdoors. Frequently, the shape of the device is adapted to the conditions under which the device is to be used.

The industry has not yet settled on an overarching definition of rugged. However, there are several aspects of rugged—*sealing*, *shock resistance*, and *operating temperature range*—that are measured in standard ways. The trouble is, there are different standards for measuring them. The other problem is that even within a given standard, there are different ways in which manufacturers interpret the standard. Make sure you ask a lot of questions and compare products from different companies if you need rugged devices.

If you are shopping around for ruggedized devices you may see references to some of the military standards, for example, MIL-STD 810. These standards indicate a set of criteria against which equipment should be tested. These criteria are meant to address the effects of things such as low pressure, extreme temperature, temperature shock, rain, humidity, sand, dust, shock, explosion, and other hazardous conditions.

Manufacturers may reference military standards to indicate how their equipment was tested. Once again, though, the standards may be interpreted differently from one manufacturer to another. Ask a lot of questions when shopping around.

Sealing

In the United States, the National Electrical Manufacturers Association (NEMA) defines standard ways of rating sealed enclosures. On a worldwide basis there is a different standard that meets the same need. The International Electrotechnical Commission (IEC) defines this standard, called the Ingress Protection (IP) standard. In looking for ruggedized devices you may see references to either of these two standards where manufacturers wish to express the degree to which their device is sealed.

Table 5–3 shows the NEMA ratings that are relevant to our discussion.

TABLE 5–3   NEMA Enclosure Ratings

Type	Protects Against
1	Dust (but the device is not completely dust tight), light, and indirect splashing
3	Dust, rain, and sleet
3R	Rain, sleet
4 and 4X	Windblown dust and rain, hose-directed water
5	All dust (the device is completely dust tight)
6	Temporary water immersion
7	Flammable gases in enough quantity to be explosive in an indoor area
8	Flammable gases in enough quantity to be explosive in indoor and outdoor areas
9	Combustible dust in indoor and outdoor areas
10	Mining conditions
11	Corrosive effects of liquids and gases.
12	Dust, falling dirt, dripping noncorrosive liquids
13	Dust, spraying water, oil, noncorrosive coolants

IP ratings are expressed as "IP" followed by two separate numbers. The first number is in the range 0 to 6. The second number falls within the range 0 to 8. Table 5–4 shows the meanings of the two numbers. No protection is indicated as IP00, and at the other extreme is maximum protection, which is represented as IP68.

TABLE 5–4   IEC Ingress Protection (IP) Ratings

IPxy, where x and y are different numbers

1st #	Protection Against	2nd #	Protection Against
0	Nothing	0	Nothing
1	Solid objects of 50 mm, for example, hands	1	Drops of water falling straight down
2	Solid objects greater than 12 mm, for example, fingers	2	Falling drops of water when device is tilted at 15 degrees from vertical
3	Solid objects greater than 2.5 mm, for example, tools and wires	3	Splashing water at an angle of up to 60 degrees
4	Solid objects greater than 1 mm, for example, small tools and wires	4	Splashing water from all directions
5	Dust	5	Water jets
6	All contact—completely dust tight	6	Powerful water jets
		7	Temporary immersion in water
		8	Continuous immersion in water

Some manufacturers will ignore the NEMA and IP ratings altogether and simply indicate the level of sealing. This might be expressed in terms of rainfall per hour, duration of water immersion, or the size of objects from which the device is protected.

Shock

Shock is usually expressed in terms of a drop onto cement from a specific height. There may also be an indication on how many drops the device can withstand.

Be careful when evaluating manufacturer claims on shock resistance. How well a device survives a shock may depend on what the disk drive does at the instance of impact. Some manufacturers make equipment with disk drives that continue operating during and after impact. Others take a looser interpretation of shock resistance.

Temperature

Manufacturers usually indicate the temperature range under which their device can operate. In some cases, there may also be a need for devices to withstand a sudden temperature change—temperature shock.

Maybe you need a device that can be placed on the hood of a car during a summer in Arizona. Maybe you need a device that can be left outside during a winter night in North Dakota. There are people who work in these extreme temperatures and they may need to be equipped with computers.

Resistance to temperature shock may be important in cases such as the one where a worker in Arizona is loading frozen food. He may step out of the summer heat into a walk-in freezer carrying a portable computer with him. The computer has to continue working under this sudden change in temperature.

Ruggedized PDAs

Rugged PDAs are housed in a protective substance like magnesium alloy, polyurethane, or carbon fiber. Companies that produce ruggedized PDAs include Symbol and Intermec. Examples of PDAs from these companies are shown in Figure 5–13.

Rugged PDAs can be dropped onto cement from a height of several feet and continue to operate. Some products can be dropped repeatedly; others can only withstand a limited number of drops.

FIGURE 5–13   Rugged PDAs from Symbol and Intermec. Left image courtesy Symbol Technologies. Right image courtesy Intermec Technologies Corp.

Ruggedized Tablets

Rugged tablets are housed in the same kinds of protective substances as rugged PDAs. Companies making these industrial tablets include Getac and Two Technologies. Tablets from these two companies are shown in Figure 5–14.

In most cases, a keyboard can be attached to these tablets. Alternatively, the keyboard might have a wireless connection to the tablet.

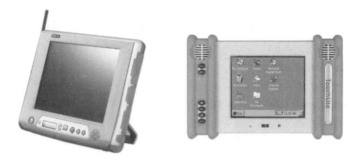

FIGURE 5–14   Ruggedized tablet computers. Left image courtesy Getac, Inc. Right image courtesy Two Technologies, Inc.

Ruggedized Notebooks

Rugged notebooks are housed in substances such as magnesium, polycarbonate, and aluminum. Many companies that make these tough devices started out by doing business with the military. Who operates in a rougher environment than the military? Who requires more reliability?

FIGURE 5–15   Rugged notebooks. Left image Dolch NotePAC
(www.dolch.com). Right image courtesy Getac, Inc.

Companies that make ruggedized notebooks include Dolch and Getac.
Notebooks from these companies are shown in Figure 5–15.

Special consideration is given to padding the rugged notebooks. Keyboards
have to be tightly sealed and they may also have glow-in-the-dark qualities for
night operations. Disk drives have to be protected against vibration and shock.

INTERESTING COMBINATIONS OF DEVICES

Many mobile professionals prefer a combination of two or more mobile
devices, rather than trying to find one device that performs all functions. By
doing this they keep some of the functions separate. One part of the whole system can be replaced without requiring a change to the other parts. Or maybe
they have different needs in different situations and carry one device or another
depending on the situation.

Notebook and PDA

Mobile professionals may be equipped with a notebook and a PDA. In this
case, the notebook should probably have the power of a desktop computer,
that is, it should be the main computer. If you continue to use a separate desktop, things get a little more confusing with three computers to synchronize.

The PDA and the notebook are synchronized so that the latest information is on both devices. In cases where there is enough time to boot up the
notebook, and where the larger device does not get in the way, the notebook
can be your device of choice. In cases where you need a small, light device
that switches on immediately, the PDA is the right choice.

Cell Phone and PDA

A cell phone with a PDA is another useful combination. The cell phone provides the data communications services. The PDA performs the computing and provides a more powerful user interface.

These two devices could be connected via an infrared link. In this case, the two devices have to be in close proximity and have to be pointed at one another—that is to say, the infrared ports of the two devices have to be lined up. This is awkward and can only be done when the worker is stationary.

Alternatively, the two devices could be connected with a serial cable. In this case, the worker has more liberty of movement. He or she can walk around while operating this way. However, it is still a bit cumbersome to have to carry around the extra cable and have the two devices wired together.

The third alternative, and my personal favorite, is to have the cell phone and the PDA connected with Bluetooth. As you will see in Chapter 6, Bluetooth can allow two devices to connect wirelessly without having to be aimed at one another. They just have to be within 10 meters of each another. In fact, you can leave the phone in your pocket and just use the PDA, which will connect to the cell phone and make use of its data services.

By keeping the voice and data communications in one device and the computing and graphics in another, there are a certain number of advantages. You can replace your PDA without having to replace your phone, for example.

Cell Phone and Notebook or Tablet

Just as the cell phone can provide data services for a PDA, it can also do so for a notebook or tablet computer. There are no popular notebook or tablet equivalents of the Smart Phone. You could never hold the notebook or tablet to your ear to talk. It seems that as long as you need to make phone calls, there will also be at least a separate handset that needs to be carried around with these larger devices.

DEVICE MANAGEMENT

As you can see there are variety of portable devices from which to choose. Each has a characteristic set of strengths and weaknesses. Some are more expensive than others, and some may be more aesthetically pleasing than others. This diversity is fine since different people in your workforce have different needs. What is optimal for one set of employees will not necessarily be optimal for another.

It is also worth noting that the variety is not likely to go away any time soon. The technology is still changing very quickly, and the market has not yet settled on standards. Since handheld computers are constantly evolving, somewhere along the way you are likely to make some changes to the class of device being used as well as the brands you prefer.

Needless to say, you will have to deal with a diverse set of portable computing devices. At any given point in time, these devices will be spread out geographically. To help manage the complexity, you will need a robust set of tools and procedures.

One concern you may have is that applications have to be rewritten to accommodate the different form factors. However, this is not such a big issue. As we shall see in Chapter 7, a wireless application gateway can minimize much of the complexity by re-formatting application output according to the device being used.

Another thing to remember is that you will have to implement the proper procedures to quickly replace lost or stolen devices. This means that standard configurations should be put into place so that when a replacement is delivered, the new device is configured in exactly the same way as the one it replaces.

Backup procedures will have to be put in place to minimize loss of data when a device is lost or stolen. There are a variety of other circumstances where you will need that backup. For example, some portable devices have to be reset from time to time, causing data loss. Data might also be lost when batteries go dead.

Once your user base starts to get large, you will need an easy way to check on which versions of software are running on each device. You will need a way of updating software applications and data files without a lot of user intervention.

PORTABLE DEVICES AND THE MOBILE ENTERPRISE

In Chapter 3, we considered the four classes of employees that could most benefit from mobile technology today. Let's look at which devices are best for each of these kinds of employees.

Salespeople

Salespeople generally need devices that work well indoors. For those salespeople who have short visits with clients, a long boot-up time can pose problems. Another consideration is whether or not a big screen interferes with conversation between your salespeople and their clients.

If there is a very limited amount of data that the salesperson needs to access real time, a data-enabled cell phone might do the trick. However, in most cases, a salesperson needs to perform more than one query and view several lines of results. This is why a PDA is probably the portable computing device of choice for those salespeople for whom client visits are short in duration.

You should be mindful of the way the PDA looks coming out of the vest pocket of a salesperson. The appearance should be consistent with the message you are trying to convey. For example, somebody dressed conservatively should not pull out a PDA that looks like it was designed for a teenager. On the other hand, if you are selling products for teenagers, the youthful look might work quite well.

When the salesperson is using a PDA, a good way to enable network access is through a Bluetooth-enabled cell phone. The salesperson can leave the phone in his or her vest pocket and just operate the PDA, which automatically controls the cell phone to establish network communication. This looks a bit like magic when seen for the first time.

For those salespeople who tend to have long visits with clients, a notebook computer might be more appropriate. Boot-up time is less of a problem in this case, and the conversation is likely to get into some detail, requiring a large database of information on hand and a large screen for shared viewing. A notebook computer is also ideal for giving presentations.

Service Employees

Service people frequently need to read a lot of documents. Screen size and disk space are important for this purpose. Here a tablet computer or a notebook might be the most appropriate device.

In the case where the service person works in a rough environment where things tend to get knocked around a bit, a ruggedized device will be necessary. Workers may need to read data outdoors, so the display needs to allow viewing under sunlight.

For those service employees who do not have to read a lot of documentation on their portable device, screen size and disk space are of lesser concern. All other things being equal, you might consider cell phones, PDAs, or Smart Phones.

For those cases where the service employee needs to receive dispatch messages, you will need a device that can receive an alert. Cell phones and Smart Phones are quite good for this. An SMS message can be pushed to the phone to signal a dispatch message. The message could contain the address of the next site and a little bit of information on the problem. For this same case, you might also consider a PDA with a communications card that allows direct access to the wireless network.

Consultants

Consultants have some of the same needs as the salespeople selling high volume/low value products. They need a powerful device, and they have time to wait for it to boot up.

Usually consultants do not need real-time access to enterprise information. It is sufficient for them to get downloads from time to time. For example, they may have to exchange some email, or they may want to find out more on a particular subject, but they rarely need an immediate response.

Notebooks, PDAs, and Smart Phones are probably the right kinds of devices for your consultants. Aesthetics and fashion are important here. Usually, consultants should appear to be on the leading edge, so you should look for devices that provide such an image.

Traveling Professionals

Email, calendar, and notes are the most important functions for the traveling professional. In many cases, a long boot-up time can be a problem. When you are running around from place to place you do not have time to sit down and wait for a notebook computer to boot up.

PDAs and Smart Phones have enough power to allow the traveling professional to send and receive email, update his or her schedule, and to take a few notes. Of course, there are some limitations. For example, email attachments are either filtered out, or they are presented differently on the PDA than they would be on a notebook or desktop computer.

If mail messages are really small, and very little data input is required to respond to mail, a cell phone might even work. A step up from this would be the cell phone equipped with a small keyboard.

SUMMARY

There is a great deal of variation in the kinds of portable computing devices being sold today. This causes a lot of confusion among buyers. The good news is that we can start to make sense of it all by classifying the devices and arranging them in order of richness of features. For the mobile professional, the five categories of devices that are most important can be listed in increasing order of functionality: *cell phones, PDAs, Smart Phones, tablet computers,* and *notebooks.*

Depending on the job function, one kind of device is probably more appropriate than the others. There are some guidelines for making these choices, but it will really come down to the specific needs of your company. Also consider the personal preferences of the end-users. Aesthetics and fashion should not be left out of the selection process.

Smart Phones are an example of an all-in-one device. They are both PDAs and cell phones. While this hybrid is appealing to many people, they are not everybody's cup of tea. Many people prefer using two separate devices—one as a PDA and the other as a phone. The form-factor of the hybrid device is a compromise, making it awkward to use. Furthermore, the hybrids may not perform different functions as well as those devices that are designed to do few things well.

Several companies make rugged versions of some of these devices. If you need computers to operate in extreme weather conditions or other hazardous environments, there are several products that might be of interest to you.

As you plan to mobilize your enterprise, you will have to have an infrastructure and procedures for managing all of the different devices that will be out in the field. These devices need to be kept up to date and they need to be backed up. Users should not have to be technical themselves. All of the device management procedures should ease the job of the user, not make it still more difficult.

Wireless Network Technologies

The magic of wireless networks is an absolute requirement for any 21st century workforce. Radio transmission will put critical information in the hands of customer-facing employees; and it will allow anybody who is away from company premises to perform some key tasks as if he or she were in the office. Over time, wireless technology will probably be used in ways we cannot even think of now.

I wish I could just tell you it works without your having to worry about the details. Just plug it into the wall, flip on the switch, and *voila,* it does its job like magic. But unfortunately this is not yet the case. Anybody involved in mobilizing their enterprise has to have a good working knowledge of the basic principles of wireless communications and of the standards upon which today's mobile networks are built. When it comes time to shop around for the products and solutions necessary for the mobile enterprise, a little proficiency with the key buzzwords will serve you well.

My goal is to provide you with the understanding you need in this area. We will start out by going over some of the fundamentals. These are the things that will hold true no matter which standard or protocol we are talking about. With this foundation, we will then get into how some of these principals and technologies are used in wireless networks today.

TIPS ON TERMINOLOGY

Perhaps the most difficult part of understanding wireless voice and data technology is simply coming to grips with the vocabulary. The industry is notorious for mixing terms and quickly changing their meanings. Before we get too far into our discussion on wireless networks, let's clarify some of the terms that sometimes cause confusion.

Frequency and Wavelength

In this chapter we talk about radio frequencies, which are measured in units called Hertz. One Hertz is equal to one cycle per second. That is, a signal whose frequency is one Hertz moves through its different states in 1 second. Such a signal can be graphed against time, as shown in Figure 6–1.

A 1 Hertz signal is not too interesting for us. We are more interested in the signals that cycle at a much higher rate. To talk about these higher frequency signals we will need to recall three Greek prefixes: *kilo, mega,* and *giga.* Reminders of their meanings, along with indications of how they are used here, are shown in Table 6–1.

TABLE 6–1   Units for Measuring Frequency

Prefix	Usage	Meaning
kilo	KHz	One thousand cycles per second
mega	MHz	One million cycles per second
giga	GHz	One billion cycles per second

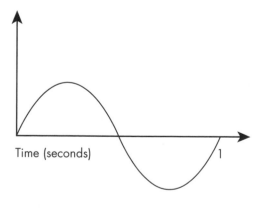

FIGURE 6–1   1 Hertz.

Frequency and wavelength are related by the formula: *frequency times wavelength equals the speed of light.* To get a feel for this formula, take another look at Figure 6–1. If we were to graph that signal over distance instead of time, the 1-second interval would be shown as 186,000 miles. In other words, that 1-Hertz signal has a wavelength of 186,000 miles!

Bands and Spectrum

The term *band* is used to refer to a range of frequencies. Unfortunately, this term is thrown around rather loosely, causing some confusion. Here are four common uses of the word band:

1. The range of frequencies is given. For example, one can refer to the *824–849 MHz band.*

2. One of the frequencies is given. For example, one can refer to the *1900 MHz band.* This is understood to mean the range of frequencies from 1850–1990 MHz, which is a well-known block of frequencies allocated for use in the United States.

3. A range is given, but it does not really mean *all* of the frequencies in that range. For example, one might refer to the *800–900 MHz band,* when it is understood that actually there are two important noncontiguous bands between 800 and 900 MHz that are used for cellular licenses in the United States. In this case, the reference is actually to those two noncontiguous bands.

4. The name of its intended use is given. For example, we frequently refer to the *cellular band*, which are the two noncontiguous ranges of frequencies (824–849 MHz and 869–894 MHz) allocated for cellular networks.

To confuse matters even further, the word *spectrum* is also used to refer to a range of frequencies.

Cellular and PCS

Now that we got some of the simple terms out of the way, let's turn our attention to some of the more confusing terminology. One of the big points of confusion is around the terms *cellular* and *Personal Communications System* (PCS). The *Federal Communications Commission* (FCC) has used these two terms to distinguish between two different frequency ranges, from which it grants licenses to network operators. The so-called cellular band lies within 800–900 MHz; the so-called PCS band lies within 1850–1990 MHz.

The word *cellular* was first used to refer to a network model in which the network is made up of a set of contiguous radio coverage areas. Such a model is drawn as a honeycomb. Each of the radio coverage areas is called a *cell*, like the cells in a honeycomb.

The cellular model was first put into commercial use when the FCC granted the licenses in the 800–900 MHz band. These licenses were originally referred to as cellular licenses. Several years later, when it became clear that more bandwidth would be needed, the FCC allocated another block of frequencies with the intent that operators would make use of new digital technology to provide a flexible set of services only possible through digital. This set of services was called personal communications services, because they personalized telephone communications. For example, a subscriber would have a telephone number at which he or she could always be reached. This was a great idea, and this and many other services were made available through competing network standards operating in the PCS band.

These network standards also use the cellular model, so they can be called cellular networks. Furthermore, these same standards that were first put to use in the PCS band have since been put to use in the cellular band by operators holding cellular licenses. The result is, there is not much left to distinguish between cellular and PCS other than in reference to the two different frequency bands allocated at different times by the FCC.

In addition to this use of the term *cellular*, we will also see the term *cellular* used in reference to the network model based on groups of radio coverage areas. Cellular has become the generic name for mobile telephone networks.

TDMA and CDMA

Another point of confusion is in the distinction between an air interface and a network standard. An air interface is the communication between the network antennas and the handset. This includes well-defined rules on how information is transmitted and received, and how the airwaves are shared to maximize the number of calls that can be handled simultaneously. This sharing is accomplished through multiplexing techniques. Later in this chapter we discuss three such techniques: *Frequency Division Multiple Access* (FDMA), *Time Division Multiple Access* (TDMA), and *Code Division Multiple Access* (CDMA).

A wireless network standard includes the definition of an air interface; but it also includes a lot of other things, such as call set-up procedures, authentication procedures, and interfaces to a public landline network.

Unfortunately, the terms TDMA and CDMA are frequently used in reference to two popular wireless network standards. These are IS-136 (TDMA) and IS-95 (CDMA). IS-136 uses TDMA as its multiplexing technique. However, TDMA is also used in other network standards, such as *Global System for Mobile Communication* (GSM). Likewise, IS-95 uses CDMA as its multiplexing technique, and there is nothing to say that other network standards cannot also use CDMA as part of the air interface. In fact, a variant of CDMA, *wideband CDMA* (W-CDMA), is used as the air interface for 3G standards.

In this chapter, when referring to the multiplexing techniques, I use the terms TDMA and CDMA. When referring to the wireless network standards, I will call out the standard names in parenthesis—TDMA (IS-136) and CDMA (IS-95).

FUNDAMENTALS OF RADIO SIGNALING

Wireless voice and data networks operate using radio frequencies to transmit signals from the network to a receiving device and vice versa. Radio frequencies are a form of electromagnetic radiation (EMR), which is the transmission of energy in waves that have both electric and magnetic fields.

Electromagnetic Radiation

We all know and love at least one form of electromagnetic radiation: visible light. Anybody who listens to the radio, watches television, warms up leftovers in the microwave, or opens their garage door with a remote control takes advantage of other forms of electromagnetic radiation as well.

These various forms of electromagnetic radiation differ only in frequency and power. And they all travel at the same break-neck speed of light, which is about 186,000 miles per second. Figure 6–2 shows various forms of electromagnetic radiation and where they lie with respect to one another.

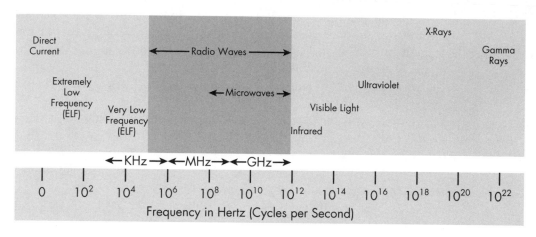

FIGURE 6–2   Various forms of electromagnetic radiation.

Radio Frequencies

Radio frequencies lie in the range from 100 KHz to 300 GHz. Within this range, a further distinction is made for the range of frequencies from 300 MHz to 300 GHz, which are called *microwaves*. At the far left you see the electromagnetic frequencies generated by direct current and emanating from various electric appliances, including your computer. On the right side we see where electromagnetic radiation starts to get harmful—in forms like ultraviolet radiation, x-rays, and gamma rays.

Zooming in on the area of our interest, Table 6–2 shows some of the ways in which radio frequencies are being used today.

TABLE 6–2   Some Uses of Radio Frequencies Today

Application	Spectrum
AM radio	535–1605 KHz
VHF TV	54–72, 76–88, 174–216 MHz
FM radio	88–108 MHz
UHF TV	512–806 MHz
Cellular	824–849, 869–894 MHz
Specialized Mobile Radio (SMR): Mobitex and ARDIS	806–824 MHz, 851–869 MHz, 896–901 MHz, 935–940 MHz
PCS	1850–1910 MHz, 1930–1990 MHz
802.11b, Bluetooth	2.4 GHz
802.11a, HiperLAN2	5 GHz

Some of these terms may be new to you. Others, such as radio and TV are very familiar to you and do not need to be discussed here. We will cover all the other terms in this chapter.

Signal Propagation and Disturbances

Like all electromagnetic radiation, radio signals spread out as they travel. In doing so, they lose intensity over distance. This *path loss* is exactly the same effect we witness when looking at a flashlight or car headlights shone in the dark. The farther the signal travels from the source of transmission, the more it fades.

Interference is also an issue. It is hard to see a flashlight or car headlights in the light of day, because of all the other light bouncing around. The same principal applies to radio signaling. If there are other sources of transmission on the same frequency, and especially if those sources are transmitting at higher power, it becomes very difficult for the receiver to pick out the signal in which it is interested.

Radio signals tend to bounce off most obstacles, and especially big ones like mountains, buildings, and even cars. The effect of this is that multiple copies of a signal will reach the receiver—those that traveled directly from the transmitter, and those that bounced around a bit before making their way to the receiving device. This phenomenon is called *multipath*.

Remember that the shortest path between two points is a straight line, so the first copy of the signal to reach the receiver is the one that has not bounced around—or maybe the one that bounced around the least. Subsequent arrivals of the signal cause interference that has to be dealt with through complex processing.

Increasing Frequency

As frequency increases, the wavelength gets shorter, thus allowing more information to be encoded in a given amount of time. However, a drawback is higher frequency signals fade quicker. For our purposes, we can assume doubling the frequency halves the distance the signal can travel. This is unfortunate, given our ever-increasing hunger for more bandwidth. But by applying more power, we can compensate and boost a high frequency signal to a greater distance.

Another thing that increases with frequency is the complexity of the transmitting and receiving equipment. There is no free lunch here. Greater data rates cost more power and require more complex equipment.

In some cases this kind of problem can work itself out very nicely. For example, in the United States, PCS operators were initially at a disadvantage to cellular operators, because PCS licenses are at twice the frequency of cellular licenses. All things being equal, this would require more transmission equipment to cover a given area. However, at the same time, the subscriber base increased, thus requiring cellular operators to increase the number of cells just to support the higher subscriber densities. The playing field was thus leveled.

Another thing that happens when the frequency increases is that the need for *line of sight* (LoS) increases. As the term implies, line of sight means that there are no obstacles between the transmitter and the receiver, so if you had a powerful enough telescope at the receiving end, you could see the transmitter.

Modulation

Information can be sent from a transmitter to a receiver by means of a regular signal, which takes the form of a sinusoidal wave. This baseline signal is called the *carrier*, and data is encoded by changing (*modulating*) certain of its characteristics. There are three different characteristics of the carrier that can be changed: its amplitude, its frequency, and its phase. If the receiver is tuned in to the carrier wave, it will notice the changes the transmitter makes to these three characteristics, and will interpret such changes as information. The different modulation techniques are shown in Figure 6–3.

Amplitude modulation (AM) involves changing the strength or amplitude of the signal. As you have probably already guessed, this is the technique used for AM radio. Unfortunately, channel interference affects the strength of the signal as it makes its way toward the receiver. This results in things like bursts of static, which you have probably suffered while listening to AM radio.

Frequency modulation (FM), on the other hand, is all about changing the frequency of the signal. This technique is used for FM radio, and when it was introduced it was a major improvement in commercial radio. When this kind of modulation is used, interference has a lesser effect on the signal.

Phase modulation (PM) is the technique whereby the phase of the carrier is changed. That is, a change is made to where the signal starts. Since phase changes are discontinuous, it is much more difficult to encode analog signals using PM. However, PM is quite well suited for digital signaling.

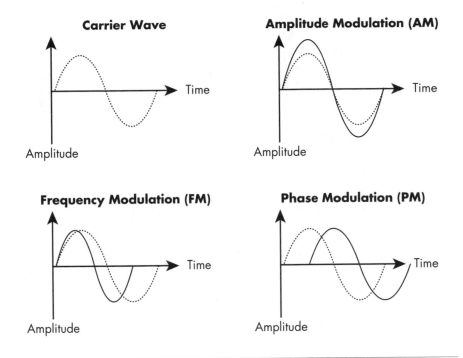

FIGURE 6–3   Modulation techniques.

Analog versus Digital

In analog systems, information is directly and linearly encoded onto the carrier by modulating the carrier's frequency (FM). All points on the signal count, therefore, all of the various disturbances that stand between the transmitter and the receiver—such as path loss, interference, and multipath—produce a noticeable degradation in the quality of the communication. Generally, the farther the receiver is from the transmitter, the more the signal is modified, and the poorer the quality of the call.

The basis for digital signaling, on the other hand, is to encode discreet values—ones and zeros—onto the carrier. When voice is digitally encoded, it can be compressed, and then transmitted faster than the person can speak. This frees up network capacity and allows more calls to be handled at a time. Also, when the signal is digitally encoded, more sophisticated multiplexing techniques can be employed, which further increases the capacity of the network to handle calls. Since the information is encoded as ones and zeros, corrections can be made for the various disturbances in the air channel by "rounding" to one or zero. Consequently, digital phones have less to do to filter out noise, resulting in a phone that is smaller, less complex, and with a longer battery life. Finally, security can be enhanced through stronger authentication of the handset using digital encryption.

Although analog is still used extensively in the United States, digital is clearly the way forward. Box 6–1 summarizes the reasons digital signaling is the way to go.

Box 6–1   Why Use Digital Signaling?

Digital signaling offers the following advantages:
- Accommodation of a greater number of subscribers
- Superior voice quality
- More reliable data services
- Smaller, less complex phones
- Longer battery life
- Enhanced security through digital encryption

It is highly likely that in the long term all networks will be based on digital signaling techniques.

Multiplexing

Several techniques are exploited in today's wireless networks to maximize the use of the limited radio frequencies, while at the same time keeping calls from interfering with one another. The challenge is to optimize the number of calls that can be handled simultaneously, while still maintaining good call quality in the process. Hats off to the innovators who have developed the methods at our disposal today. These methods are called *multiplexing*.

Three different kinds of multiplexing are widely used in wireless networks today. These are *frequency division multiple access* (FDMA), *time division multiple access* (TDMA), and *code division multiple access* (CDMA). The former can be used in analog or digital networks; the latter two require digital signaling.

FDMA

Frequency division multiple access, or FDMA, works by assigning frequency ranges to channels at the time of call setup. These ranges are reserved to the assigned channel for the duration of the call. Figure 6–4 shows three calls separated by FDMA.

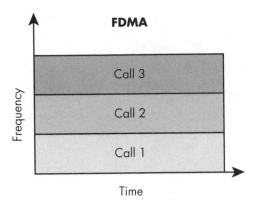

FIGURE 6–4 Frequency division multiple access.

Since frequency is limited, the use of FDMA by itself imposes a strict limit on the number of calls that can be handled simultaneously.

TDMA

Time division multiple access (TDMA), which is employed within an FDMA system, allows digital networks to handle more calls by assigning time slots within a frequency range to each channel at the time of call setup. Digital signaling goes hand and hand with voice compression. The result is speech can be transmitted faster than it can be spoken, so some time is freed up on the network. This extra time can be used to allow other conversations to take place in the same frequency range. Figure 6–5 shows nine calls separated by TDMA.

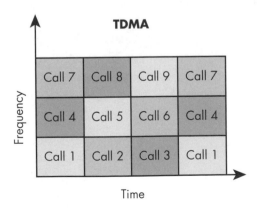

FIGURE 6–5 Time division multiple access.

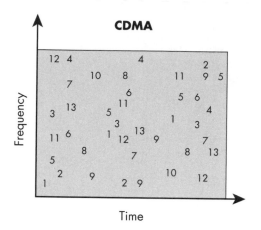

FIGURE 6–6 Code division multiple access.

In a TDMA system, each handset transmits and receives only during the time slot assigned it for a given call in progress.

CDMA

Code division multiple access (CDMA) operates using a principal called *spread spectrum*. Under this scheme, each channel may use all of the available frequency at the same time. For each of the channels, the signal is encoded using a unique tag or code, which one may think of as a kind of multiplier. The receiving end uses the same code to extract only the signal it is allowed to hear. Figure 6–6 shows several calls separated by CDMA.

One interesting aspect of this technique is that if there is interference in a given frequency range, it can be largely overcome since the signal is spread out over other frequencies as well. It is widely agreed that CDMA is the most efficient of the three methods of multiplexing. In fact, wideband CDMA, a further refinement of the original techniques, is to be used going forward in 3G networks.

CIRCUIT SWITCHING VERSUS PACKET SWITCHING

In communication networks, there is a distinction between circuit switching and packet switching. Circuit switching was originally developed to accommodate voice. Packet switching, on the other hand, was conceived with data in mind.

Voice Communications

Mobile telephone networks were originally designed to provide voice communication services. Therefore, to be successful a network had to accommodate the characteristics of human conversation. For example, in speaking we expect minimal delay. If you say something and it takes the other person several seconds to hear what you said, natural conversation cannot take place. We also expect a steady flow, that is, the network cannot send a bunch of stuff at once, stop for a while, then send some more. Instead, it has to transmit speech at a constant rate. One last characteristic of conversation that is important is that we expect both sides to be able to speak at once. What kind of conversation would there be if one side could not interrupt the other?

In network terms these three features would be referred to as *low latency*, *streaming*, and *full duplex*, respectively. Up until recently, they were provided exclusively through *circuits* in the network. The concept of routing such circuits through a network is referred to as *circuit switching*. When a call is set up, resources are reserved in both directions, and regardless of whether any speaking occurs, nobody else can use those resources. In terms of radio communications between the handset and the network, a circuit takes up a range of frequencies or a time slot, depending on what kind of multiplexing is being used. But in either case, unless both parties in a conversation are extremely talkative, airwaves and network resources are underutilized.

Data Communications

By contrast, data communications require a different set of features. A little latency can be tolerated, and the network can be "bursty." That is, the network can send a bunch of stuff, stop for a while, and then send more stuff. However, data communications require higher reliability. If you lose data, that loss has to be detected, and the data has to be resent. This is not the case with voice communications. If you lose a little information during a conversation, the problem is solved when the person on the other side of the line says, "What?" and the speaker repeats what was said.

Since data is something of an afterthought to the designers of mobile telephone networks, until recently, data services have usually been provided as an overlay. For example, data may be transmitted over a regular voice circuit using a specialized modem. This is known as *circuit switched data* (CSD), and its major drawbacks are that a call has to be set up to start the communication, the call has to be terminated to end the communication, and in between, network resources are usually wasted. The setup and termination cause some delay, and the wasted resources have to be paid for by somebody.

Another way that data communications have been overlaid onto voice networks is by borrowing time from the signaling channels to provide messaging services. The primary example of this is the *short messaging service* (SMS).

The *always-on* data services you may have heard of are provided through *packet switching*, which is a technique that differs from circuit switching in that data is sent in small, independent chunks or *packets*. Each of these packets has a *header*, which contains addressing information allowing the network to route the packet to the other end. There are different ways of sending packets so that various users can share frequency ranges and time slots while avoiding contention. In any case, the result is that when packet switching is used to provide data communication services, the airwaves and network resources are utilized more efficiently.

Voice over Packet

Thanks again to those clever engineers and their everlasting quest to make possible the impossible, there are now ways of using packet switching to provide voice services more efficiently. In addition to addressing information contained in packet headers, there are other parameters used to communicate information to network routers so that they handle each packet according to the requirements of the particular service demanded by the user. To provide streaming services, such as voice or video, packet headers contain *quality of service* (QoS) parameters telling routers things like how quickly the data contained in the packet needs to get to the other side. Using QoS parameters, networks can provide voice communications over packet services by having the routers minimize delay and provide a steady stream for voice packets. As mentioned above, another aspect of the voice service is that the network has the luxury of dropping a packet or two without ruining the conversation.

Packet switching is a more flexible technique, allowing for better use of airwaves and network resources and at the same time providing a richer set of communications services. In fact, the transition to full packet switching is one of the important aspects of 3G networks.

LICENSED VERSUS UNLICENSED SPECTRUM

Cellular

Since bandwidth, like real estate, is a limited resource, it has to be rationed. This is done through government licensing; and in the United States, the government body that takes care of this is the Federal Communications Commission (FCC). In 1981, the FCC began licensing commercial cellular spectrum, which lies in the 800–900 MHz band. For these purposes, the commission defined 734 *cellular geographic statistical areas* (CGAs), of which 306 are *metropolitan statistical areas* (MSAs), 428 are *rural statistical areas* (RSAs), and one is reserved for the Gulf of Mexico.

PCS

In 1995 the commission allocated new spectrum blocks for higher bandwidth cellular communications. Networks operating in these frequencies are referred to as *personal communications systems* (PCS). The spectrum allocated for PCS lies around 1900 MHz. Here the FCC granted licenses on different geographic blocks, which were actually defined by Rand McNally & Company. The two types of areas are *major trading areas* (MTAs), which include multiple cities or states, and *basic trading areas* (BTAs), which include only one metropolitan area. There are 51 MTAs and 493 BTAs.

Specialized Mobile Radio (SMR)

The FCC also licenses 26.5 MHz of spectrum in the 800 and 900 MHz bands for use in *specialized mobile radio* (SMR). These licenses were sold in a piecemeal fashion on a tower-by-tower basis. Many of the SMR licenses were bought up by Nextel, which proceeded to build a nationwide network around them. Note that while both cellular licenses and SMR licenses are in the 800–900 MHz bands, as shown in Table 6–2, they do not occupy the same frequencies within that range. Therefore, there is no interference between the two. The primary use for SMR has traditionally been for dispatch services, which differ from mobile voice communications in that these services require both one-to-one and one-to-many communications, and they generally do not require interconnection with the public fixed-line telephone network. However, in recent years enterprising individuals have devised ways of using the 26.5 MHz of SMR spectrum more efficiently, and they are now able to provide traditional voice services. This puts Nextel in competition with cellular and PCS operators.

SMR licenses are also used for the Mobitex and ARDIS networks, which are used by Palm™ devices and RIM BlackBerry pagers. These neworks will be discussed later in this chapter.

3G

The FCC is currently trying to figure out where it can allocate spectrum for use in 3G networks. There are some issues around what the World Radio Conference 2000 (WRC-2000) has identified as bands to be used for world-wide 3G services (806–960 MHz, 1710–1885 MHz, and 2500–2690 MHz) and what is available for use in the United States. What will probably happen is the United States will not be consistent with the global 3G standard, and we will continue to use multiband phones for global roaming.

Unlicensed Frequency: Industrial, Scientific, and Medical (ISM)

Such are the complications of rationing something as precious as radio frequencies. Fortunately, not all bands are subject to licensing. This unlicensed spectrum is sometimes referred to as *industrial, scientific, and medical* (ISM) spectrum.

Generally these are bands that lie in higher frequency ranges where signals do not travel as far unless they are pushed along by high power. Equipment transmitting at unlicensed frequencies still needs to be certified for conformance to power regulations, the goal being to prevent interference, which would be caused by transmission over a great distance.

This certification is much easier on manufacturers. But what happens with unlicensed spectrum is some of the popular bands get used for different purposes, and interference does become an issue. For example, Bluetooth and 802.11b (wireless LAN) both use frequencies around 2.4 GHz; and because of this, the two interfere with one another. Other uses of the 2.4 GHz band include garage door openers, microwave ovens, and some cordless phones. These are also potential sources of interference for 802.11b and Bluetooth networks.

THE CELLULAR MODEL

Up until the 1970s mobile telephony was based on a single, centrally located, high-powered radio transmitter that served an area about 50 miles in diameter. Only a small number of calls could be handled at a time; and special numbering schemes were employed, so that placing a call between a mobile network and a fixed-line network (or vice versa) required special dialing. Microprocessors used in phones had to reach a certain level of sophistication before the phone could receive orders from a base station and then switch communication from one network antenna to another without dropping a call.

By the mid-1970s, Bell Labs had completed work on a new model that improved mobile telephony in several ways. This new concept first took shape in the standard called *advanced mobile phone system* (AMPS), which is described later in this chapter. For now, let's explore the cellular model in isolation. It provides the framework for most wireless telephone networks today, regardless of the standard being used. In this model a network is made up of a confederation of radio coverage areas, called *cells*.

It was not until the early 1980s that the FCC finally cleared the way for deployment of commercial cellular networks. The primary reason for the delay was the FCC wanted to set up a scheme that fosters competition. The commission settled on dividing the country into geographic coverage areas and issuing two licenses in each of these areas, so that the public could choose between two different service providers.

Cells

Each cell has its own set of transmitters and receivers—one or more omnidirectional antennas located at the center of the cell or one or more directional antennas, which may be placed in different parts of the cell, including the edges. The directional antennas sitting at the edges can be used to cut down on interference between cells. An antenna that acts as a transmitter and a receiver is called a *transceiver*. A cell's antennas, along with the computing systems that control them, are collectively referred to as a *base station*.

We frequently see a honeycomb pattern used to represent cellular networks, but in fact, this is simply because it is more convenient to draw them as hexagons (see Figure 6–7). In reality, the coverage area of a cell is shaped more like a circle than a hexagon. While a cell phone is turned on, the cellular network continuously measures the strength of the signal from the handset to all antennas that are close enough to detect the signal. The cell where the signal is heard the loudest is the cell that handles the subscriber at that instance. All other things being equal, if you travel in a circle around an omnidirectional antenna, the signal strength will be the same at all points. Even with a directional antenna, the coverage patterns will look more like arcs than edges on a hexagon.

An individual cell might be as small as a building, or it could be as big as 20 miles across. The size and design of the cell are determined by all sorts of things, including population densities, landscapes, and man-made obstacles. On the one hand, it is desirable to make the cells small to cut down on the

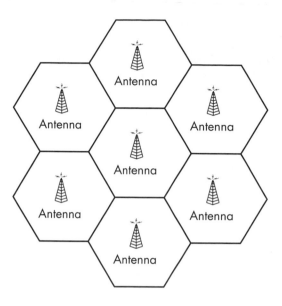

FIGURE 6–7   The cellular model (omnidirectional antennas).

amount of power required to transmit signals. On the other hand, smaller cells require more antennas and more of other types of network equipment. Furthermore, extra real estate is required to seat the antennas and the additional equipment.

Handoff/Handover

When a subscriber moves from one cell to another, the network notices a transition in which antenna receives the signal the best, and it performs a procedure called *handoff* (also called *handover*), which results in passing the responsibility for handling that subscriber to the new cell. In some systems, it is actually the phone that measures signal strength from various antennas, and the phone reports these measurements to the network, which then initiates the handoff. In either case, these sophisticated techniques require cooperation from several components in the network, as well as from the phone; and just like magic, it is all done transparently to the user. Calls in progress continue as if nothing happened.

Complex algorithms are employed to avoid unnecessary handoffs. Can you imagine the nightmare of a user walking along the border between two cells, if such algorithms were not used? The conversation would switch back and forth between two cells, causing inefficient use of network resources and of the handset itself. With so much switching between cells, the subscriber would probably detect dramatic degradation in the quality of the call.

Roaming

When the subscriber turns on the cell phone, a database in the network, called the home location registry (HLR), is updated to record the fact that the subscriber is now reachable. If the subscriber is in an area covered by a different network operator, the visiting location registry (VLR) of the foreign network is updated, and it notifies the HLR of the subscriber's home network so that the subscriber can be reached. In this case, the subscriber is said to be *roaming*.

The key difference between roaming and movement between cells within a single network is that roaming involves movement from a network operated by one company to that operated by another company. In the United States, it is often the case that these different networks are using different standards and they may also be using different frequency bands. In order for a phone to allow a subscriber to move between such networks, the handset has to be *dual-mode* and/or *dual-band*.

Dual-Mode/Dual-Band

A phone is said to be dual mode if it handles two different protocols or standards. A common case of this would be a phone that operates in a TDMA (IS-136) network and can switch to operating in an AMPS network. Later in this chapter you will see why this is relatively easy to do.

A phone is said to be dual band if it is able to operate in two different frequency bands. A common case of this is a phone that operates in the cellular frequencies (800–900 MHz) and also in the PCS frequencies (1850–1990 MHz). Another common case, which is used by intercontinental roamers, is the phone that can interoperate with GSM networks using different bands, for example, those used in Europe and those used in the United States.

Aside from the concerns around changing protocols and/or frequencies, there are several other issues that have to be considered to accommodate roaming. One of these is that process nearest and dearest to the hearts of all network operators: billing subscribers. A standard called IS-41 provides guidelines for how roaming should be handled.

Network Standards Using the Cellular Model

The cellular model is the basis for all mobile telephone network standards we will discuss in the rest of this chapter. A list of these network standards, the frequency bands in which they operate, and the names of some of the big operators using the standard are shown in Table 6–3.

TABLE 6–3   Networks Using the Cellular Model

Standard	Frequency Band	Operators
AMPS	Cellular	AT&T Wireless, Cingular Wireless
TDMA (IS-136)	Cellular and PCS	AT&T Wireless, Cingular Wireless
GSM	PCS	VoiceStream, AT&T Wireless, Cingular Wireless
CDMA (IS-95)	Cellular and PCS	Sprint PCS, Verizon Wireless

As you will see, there are some key differences between these network standards. For example, they use different multiplexing techniques, they have different ways of reusing frequency, and they have different ways of performing handoff/handover.

AMPS

The first widely used cellular networks were based on analog signaling. In the United States these networks used a standard called *Advanced Mobile Phone Service* (AMPS), which was developed in Bell Laboratories in the mid-1970s. AMPS began commercial deployment in the early 1980s and various versions are still used throughout North America as well as in Latin America, Eastern Europe, Australia, and parts of Asia.

In the United States, AMPS operates within the 800–900 MHz radio band. In any given area, two different operators are granted licenses, and each can use half of the 824–849 MHz range for receiving signals, and half of the 869–894 MHz range for transmitting.

Maximizing Frequency Use

Calls are separated through FDMA, with each channel using 30 KHz of the spectrum. The channels from the network to the handset are called *forward* channels; and those from the handset to the network are called *reverse* channels. To understand how many channels are available to any given operator, just take half of the 25 MHz available in each direction (each half goes to one of the two operators granted a license) and divide that by 30 KHz. The result is 416 two-way radio channels available to each operator.

Call setup occurs through the use of 21 separate control channels. Once a call is set up through the control channels, a pair of forward and reverse channels is allocated.

To maximize the use of the available spectrum, frequency channels are reused between noncontiguous cells. The cells of a network are divided into clusters, such that each cell of a cluster uses a distinct set of frequencies that do not interfere with radio activity in adjacent cells. The pattern of frequency use is then repeated in adjacent clusters. The number of cells in a cluster (N) is governed by the distance-to-reuse ratio (d/r). The configuration shown in Figure 6–8 assumes a cluster with N = 7.

The advantage of this frequency reuse is that each of the clusters has a 416 two-way channel capacity. The 21 control channels come out of those 416 two-way channels, thus leaving room for 395 two-way channels, which is the number of calls that can be handled simultaneously within a cluster of cells in an AMPS network.

During communication between a cell phone and the network, the power level is adjusted to the minimum required at the time. This is done to cut down on interference and to preserve precious battery power. This technique also makes it possible to have cells of varying sizes. Indeed, in areas where

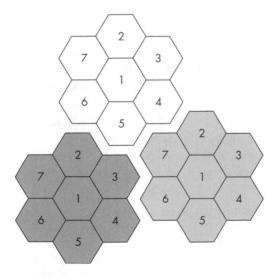

FIGURE 6–8 Frequency reuse in AMPS networks (N=7).

subscriber density is relatively high, cells are split into smaller units with special care being taken to maintain the same d/r ratio.

AMPS Data Services

There are two ways in which data transmission is offered over AMPS networks. These are through the services of *circuit switched data* (CSD) and *cellular digital packet data* (CDPD). Let's discuss them in more detail.

CSD

Circuit switched data is just a fancy way of saying that a voice circuit is used to transmit data. Since voice circuits in an AMPS network are analog, it is possible to use modems directly over a voice circuit. However, you will not get the same data rate you would over a fixed-line phone network. This is due to disturbances in the air interface. Remember that the word *modem* is short for modulator/demodulator. As the name implies, the modem transmits information by modulating a carrier signal. One of the characteristics of the signal that is modulated is its amplitude—a characteristic that may fluctuate unpredictably as a result of disturbances in the airwaves. The receiving end may misinterpret such changes in amplitude as data values.

   To overcome these issues, special communications protocols have been developed. Three such protocols that are widely used today are MNP 10, ETC, and MNP 10 EC. In order to use these protocols, compatible modems have to be on the handset side and on the network side. You will therefore have to check with the network operator for details on where they offer CSD services.

CDPD

Like CSD, cellular digital packet data (CDPD) uses voice circuits to transmit data. However, instead of tying up a circuit as is done with CSD, CDPD *borrows* circuits when they are not busy. This technique allows efficient use of network resources. However, it requires special equipment on the network side, so you cannot count on it being available everywhere there is voice service. The coverage area will be limited to those places where the network operator has made the investment to make CDPD available.

AMPS for the Mobile Enterprise

The value of AMPS for the mobile enterprise is that the coverage area is still relatively extensive. However, not all of the data services are available everywhere there is voice coverage. CDPD requires extra network equipment, and operators may not view this extra equipment as a worthwhile investment for certain markets.

TDMA (IS-136)

In order to accommodate more subscribers, digital systems were devised and deployed in the early 1990s. As mentioned previously, when voice is digitized it can be compressed, freeing up resources that can be used by other callers.

Digital AMPS (D-AMPS)

The first digital systems deployed in the United States were built on top of the existing AMPS networks. This overlay is called Digital AMPS (D-AMPS), and it is sometimes also referred to by the name of the standard in which it is defined, IS-54. D-AMPS makes use of the time freed up through voice compression by assigning three separate time slots to each of the 30-KHz radio channels.

Each of these time slots represents a separate channel used for separate calls. That is, TDMA is used on top of the FDMA already in use for the analog network. As is shown in Figure 6–9, this upgrade to an AMPS system immediately triples the call capacity.

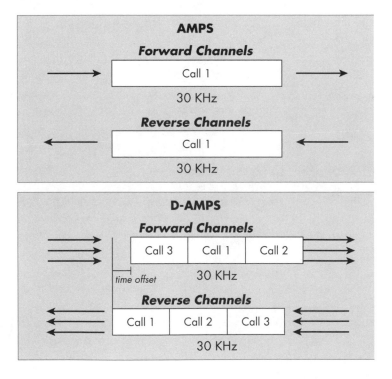

FIGURE 6–9 Increased call capacity through D-AMPS.

Note that in the D-AMPS system, the time slots in the forward channel are slightly offset from the time slots in the reverse channels. Furthermore, there is no overlap between the forward and reverse time slots for a given call. These two timing features were built into the system with the complexity of the handset in mind. If a handset had to receive and transmit simultaneously, extra components would be required.

From D-AMPS to TDMA (IS-136)

A further improvement on D-AMPS is the so-called TDMA standard, IS-136. The primary enhancement brought on by the TDMA (IS-136) network standard was the introduction of the *Digital Control Channel* (DCCH), which allows a lot of neat features to be implemented, including caller ID, voice mail message waiting indicator, text paging, normal paging, and advanced fraud protection.

One important feature of TDMA (IS-136) and D-AMPS is the ease with which a *dual-mode* phone can be designed. Recall from our earlier discussion that dual-mode phones operate with two different network standards and thereby allow roaming into areas where the wireless phone service is implemented using a different standard. Since AMPS networks still offer extensive coverage in the United States, it is important for dual-mode phones to operate using the AMPS standard. This greatly increases the roaming area. Because TDMA and D-AMPS are overlays onto the AMPS networks, it is relatively easy to develop a phone that works with the digital standards, and also has the ability to switch to AMPS.

TDMA (IS-136) Data Services

There are three ways in which data services can be offered over a TDMA (IS-136) network. These are *circuit switched data* (CSD), *short message service* (SMS), and *enhanced data rates for global evolution* (EDGE) services.

CSD

It is not possible to use a regular analog modem on a digital system. The circuits use a coding scheme designed for the characteristics of voice conversation. However, there are special modems that can be used to transmit data over TDMA (IS-136) voice circuits. The idea is the same as CSD used for AMPS networks. That is, a call is established, data transmission occurs using the circuit, and then the call is terminated. The only difference is in the type of modem used to encode the data.

In the case where the TDMA (IS-136) network is operating in the cellular band, remember that the phone should be able to switch to analog mode. By switching to analog mode the phone can use the same CSD service described above for AMPS.

SMS

Most telephone networks actually consist of two networks: one for subscriber communications and the other for communications between network components. The latter is a messaging-based network that allows the various components to work together to do things like set up and terminate calls, debit a prepaid account, look up an 800 number, and find a roaming subscriber. In wireless phone networks, this same messaging network is used to allow subscribers to send short messages to one another. This idea was originally conceived by the architects of the GSM standard, but it has since been put to use in TDMA (IS-136) and CDMA (IS-95) networks as well.

In TDMA (IS-136) networks, SMS messages are 256 bytes in length. Two types of services are provided: broadcast SMS and unicast SMS. Through broadcast SMS the same message is sent to all subscribers in a coverage area. This is useful for things like weather and traffic alerts or advertisements from the network operator. Unicast SMS is more interesting to us. This is the service whereby messages are sent to a single subscriber.

SMS messages are sent in *push* mode. That is as opposed to *pull* mode where the subscriber initiates the dialog and *asks* for messages. Since SMS messages are pushed, SMS is useful for sending alerts. SMS may also be used as originally intended, that is, for sending short messages.

EDGE

Enhanced Data Rates for Global Evolution (EDGE) is similar to *General Packet Radio Service* (GPRS), which will be described in the section on GSM. The difference is that EDGE is able to squeeze more bandwidth out of the same frequencies by using more elaborate *phase modulation* (PM) techniques. EDGE represents a path to 3G for TDMA (IS-136) networks.

EDGE services have not yet been rolled out. Once they have been deployed, you can expect a fast, always-on data service. Theoretically, data rates of up to 384 kbps will be possible with EDGE. However, you should be skeptical of the first generation of EDGE-enabled handsets. Extra processing will be required, and it may take a generation or two before the handsets do this efficiently.

TDMA (IS-136) for the Mobile Enterprise

The value of TDMA (IS-136) for the mobile enterprise is the wide coverage area. Remember that dual-mode TDMA (IS-136) phones are relatively easy to design, so it is easy to get coverage where there is AMPS coverage.

EDGE promises a very fast data service. If the reality approaches these promises, you should look for ways of making use of EDGE for your mobile enterprise in the future.

GSM

As was the case in the United States, the first generation of cellular telephone networks in Europe were analog. However, whereas in the United States there was one dominant standard for analog cellular (AMPS), in Europe there were a variety of incompatible analog standards used in different countries.

In spite of the roaming limitations resulting from this incompatibility, mobile telephony had become popular in Europe. With the growth in the number of subscribers, the limitations of analog became clear. It was widely accepted that digital would be the way of the future.

Having experienced the disadvantages of incompatible networks, in 1982 several European operators agreed to develop a common digital standard. Remember that in Europe at that time almost all telephone networks were state-owned monopolies. They had already developed an organization for standardizing various aspects of telephony. This organization was called the Council of European PTTs (CEPT). It was through CEPT that operators commenced discussion on the new digital wireless standard, which it baptized *Groupe Special Mobile* (GSM). The meaning of this acronym has since changed; it now stands for *Global System for Mobile Communications*.

CEPT designated 900 MHz as the band in which GSM would operate. Since then, two more versions of the standard were introduced to provide GSM services in the more recently licensed bands. These versions are called GSM1800 (primarily used in Europe) and GSM1900 (primarily used in the United States).

GSM uses TDMA to separate calls. The time slots occur within channels that occupy 200 KHz of bandwidth. There are eight such time slots per channel. GSM achieves 8 to 16 times the call capacity of AMPS systems.

Subscriber Identity Module (SIM)

One of the important aspects of GSM is the *subscriber identity module* (SIM), which is a small card that is inserted into the phone. This card is a *smart card,* or a small computer just like those you may have seen on credit cards in many European countries. A SIM holds all of the information that defines a subscription. If you take your SIM out of your phone and put it into another phone, the second phone will then receive calls on your phone number.

One useful feature of the SIM is that it holds a *certificate*, or a code that uniquely identifies that card. Essentially this is the same idea behind the credit card. When a credit card is swiped through a card reader, the merchant is assured of the identity of that card. This, along with the customer signature, which uniquely identifies the person, is enough assurance to complete a financial transaction. This latter concept is known as *cardholder presence.*

For your GSM phone to be used to purchase goods, something has to be done to verify cardholder presence. For example, a handwritten signature on the handset, a password, or biometrics (scanning your eye or reading your fingerprint) might serve as proof that you are who you say you are. Credit card issuers, handset manufactures, and GSM operators are working together to devise an acceptable means for verifying cardholder presence through GSM handsets.

GSM Data Services

There are three ways in which data services are currently offered through GSM networks. These are *circuit switched data* (CSD), *short message service* (SMS), and *general packet radio services* (GPRS).

CSD

As is the case with TDMA (IS-136), an analog modem cannot be used to provide data services on a GSM voice circuit. However, appropriately equipped phones offer data and fax services over a voice line. Under normal conditions, the data transmission rate will be around 9.6 kbps. Using special adapters or software data compression, you can improve on this significantly.

SMS

Short Messaging Service (SMS) was first devised for GSM networks. As described in the section on TDMA (IS-136), SMS borrows capacity from the network control channels to allow users to send short messages. On GSM networks, SMS messages can be up to 160 characters long.

SMS has become very popular in Europe. It is widely used by teenagers, and a kind of shorthand has evolved allowing users to say more per message. European operators are extremely happy to be getting this extra source of revenue, and they encourage its use by publishing vocabularies of the shorthand.

Many European businesspeople also use SMS. While this has its limitations, it is useful for things like alerts or scheduling meetings.

GPRS

General Packet Radio Service (GPRS) is a packet network overlay for GSM networks. It requires upgrades to antennas and it requires two extra components in the network: the *Serving GPRS Support Node* (SGSN) and the *Gateway GPRS Support Node* (GGSN). GPRS is to be deployed in two phases, with the first phase covering a maximum data rate of up to 57.6 kbps. GPRS represents the path toward 3G for GSM networks.

GPRS is still in its initial phase and needs time to develop further. Widespread coverage is not yet available, and the first generation of handsets supporting GPRS is a disappointment. A lot of extra processing is required for the handset to support GPRS. This makes the handset more complex and it drains the battery faster.

We can expect this to improve in the future. However, be prudent in selecting GPRS for the short term. Make sure that there is coverage where you need it, and make sure the handsets you choose provide the performance you need.

EDGE is a relatively easy upgrade from GPRS. It is simply a matter of replacing components at the base station. Handsets also have to be replaced to go from GPRS to EDGE.

GSM for the Mobile Enterprise

GSM service is just now starting to be widely available in the United States, making it a viable option for the mobile enterprise. SMS can be used for exchanging short messages and CSD can be used for larger exchanges.

GPRS promises to be a reasonably fast data service once it is fully rolled out and once good GPRS-enabled handsets become available. You should keep an eye on the progress and look for GPRS service in the geographies you need it.

CDMA (IS-95)

You will remember from discussions earlier in this chapter that there are principally three multiplexing techniques used in mobile telephone networks today. These are FDMA, TDMA, and CDMA. Let's now turn our attention to CDMA, and to the network standard in which it was first used: IS-95.

Frequency Hopping Spread Spectrum (FHSS)

CDMA works by allowing each transmitter to spread its signal out over all of the available frequency. This idea is called *spread spectrum*, and it was first conceived in the 1940s. One type of spread spectrum communications is *frequency hopping*, in which the transmitter "hops" around between frequencies in a manner determined by a code. The receiver knows this code and is therefore able to tune in to the different frequencies in the correct sequence and pick out what the transmitter is sending. The full name of this technique is *frequency hopping spread spectrum* (FHSS). Figure 6–10 shows how a particular call might look graphed by frequency over time when FHSS is used.

FHSS was used by the military in the early 1950s to reduce the effects of jamming and noise, and perhaps more importantly, to make eavesdropping very difficult. Since the signal is constantly switching frequencies, exposure to jamming or noise is reduced to those instances when the signal happens to

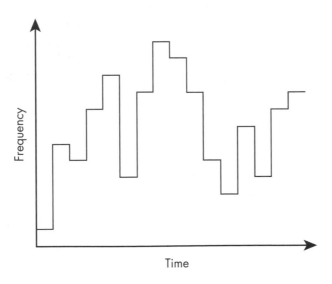

FIGURE 6–10   Frequency hopping spread spectrum (FHSS).

be on the frequencies where these disturbances are occurring. Successful eavesdropping can only be accomplished by those with knowledge of the hopping sequence. Imagine the size of the computer that would be required to try all possible hopping combinations in order to listen in on a call for which the code is not known!

The American company Qualcomm refined these techniques and adapted them for use in public wireless phone networks. The result is called *code division multiple access* (CDMA). Qualcomm holds patents on the underlying technology, and therefore receives licensing fees wherever it is used.

Synchronization and power management are critical aspects of CDMA. The transmitting and receiving ends must be synchronized in order for them to hop about the frequencies in step with one another. Power management is necessary to prevent one signal from overriding others, that is, the base station must receive all signals at the same level.

This turns out to be quite a tricky thing to manage. Synchronization and power management are performed by a steady flow of commands from the base station to the handset. To interpret and act on these commands, fairly sophisticated processing is required in the handset. For this reason, CDMA could only be made commercially available with recent advances in CPU technology.

CDMA is frequently explained through a cocktail party analogy. Imagine a cocktail party where several conversations are occurring. Two people talking to one another are able to filter out the other conversations, which are just background noise as far as they are concerned. However, if some of the other talking gets too loud, it becomes harder to make out the conversation of interest. A variation of that analogy is to imagine the different conversations are being held in different languages. This brings out the aspect of CDMA whereby the transmitter and the receiver are the only two parties who know the hopping sequence for their particular communication.

Since all available frequency can be used by all transmitters at the same time, networks using CDMA do not have to employ frequency reuse schemes to avoid interference. Instead, CDMA allows contiguous cells to use the same frequencies. To get a feel for what an advantage this is, compare frequency reuse schemes of other cellular networks (Figure 6–8), with the way frequencies would be allocated if CDMA were used in the same set of cells, as shown in Figure 6–11.

Another interesting feature of CDMA (IS-95) is the so-called *soft handoff*. When a subscriber moves from one cell to another, a new channel is allocated in the new cell before the channel from the previous cell is dropped. This is in contrast to the handoff procedures in AMPS, D-AMPS, TDMA (IS-136), and GSM. In these other systems, the first channel must be dropped before a new

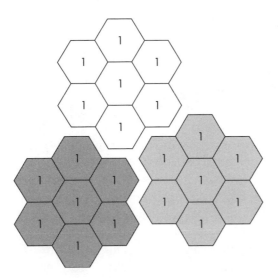

FIGURE 6–11   CDMA reuses the same frequencies in adjacent cells.

one can be taken on. As you can imagine, the soft handoff feature of CDMA (IS-95) results in fewer lost calls while a subscriber is moving about.

CDMA (IS-95) was first put to use in the PCS band (1850–1990 MHz). However, since then operators holding cellular licenses have recognized its benefits and have put it to use as an overlay on AMPS networks in the cellular band (800–900 MHz).

Data Services

There are three types of data services offered by CDMA (IS-95) networks. These are *circuit switched data* (CSD), *short messaging service* (SMS), and *cdma2000 1xRTT*.

CSD

As with TDMA (IS-136), CDMA (IS-95) networks can provide a data service over a voice circuit. On an appropriately equipped handset, data rates of 14.4 kbps can be achieved.

SMS

Like TDMA (IS-136) and GSM networks, CDMA (IS-95) networks provide a *short messaging service* (SMS). CDMA (IS-95) supports up to 255 characters per message. CDMA (IS-95) SMS supports several features not supported by TDMA (IS-136) and GSM networks, including:

- An urgent message indicator, which identifies a message as urgent.
- Message acknowledgment, which allows the sender to see that the message was received.
- An off-hook service, which notifies the subscriber that there is a message while he or she is on the phone.

cdma2000 1xRTT

The 1xRTT standard was developed in 1999 specifically for use in CDMA (IS-95) networks. Theoretically, data rates of up to 144 kbps can be achieved using this protocol in a mobile environment. However, in current implementations you can expect data rates to average between 28 and 80 kbps.

1xRTT is implemented as a significant upgrade to CDMA (IS-95) networks. Such an upgrade represents a path toward 3G for these networks, much as GPRS represents a path toward 3G for GSM networks.

So far this service has been deployed and is being used in South Korea. In the United States, Sprint PCS and Verizon are rolling it out.

CDMA for the Mobile Enterprise

In the long run, 1xRTT will be of great benefit to the mobile enterprise. For the time being, however, it is not widely available. As CDMA 1xRTT does become available in the areas where you need data services, you should look for ways to make it a part of your mobile enterprise. This service will provide your mobile employees with a very fast data rate, allowing them to access the critical information they need.

DATA NETWORKS

Cellular networks are not the only systems providing wireless data services. There are also several networks that were developed strictly for data transmission. Some of these started out as paging networks. Others were developed to allow minimal remote access to company computers.

The two data network systems most important to the mobile enterprise are *Mobitex* and *ARDIS*. These use two different protocols that were developed several years ago and have since been put to use to allow personal digital assistants (PDAs) access to Internet services.

Mobitex

In a joint effort during the early 1980s, Ericsson and Swedish Telecom Radio developed a communication standard called Mobitex. In the mid-1990s other manufacturers were invited to join in the evolution of Mobitex and to develop equipment using it. The largest Mobitex operator in the United States is Cingular Interactive (formerly Bellsouth Wireless Data). The Cingular Interactive network operates in SMR bands.

Mobitex is a packet-switched network with packets reaching a maximum of 512 bytes long. Bit rates of 8 kbps and 19.2 kbps are offered. Palm™ devices and the RIM BlackBerry two-way pager both use Mobitex. One of the advantages of Mobitex is that the coverage area is more extensive than many of the data services offered by cellular operators.

ARDIS

Around 1990 Motorola and IBM developed a data communication protocol to allow IBM employees to access mainframes. This standard, DataTAC, was implemented in a network called *Advanced Radio Data Information Service* (ARDIS). ARDIS offers data rates up to 19.2 kbps and operates in SMR bands.

American Mobile Satellite (AMSC) acquired ARDIS in 1998 and the resulting company was renamed Motient. The ARDIS and satellite network were integrated to provide coverage through rural and metropolitan areas. This combined network provides services such as fleet tracking over vast geographic areas.

The RIM BlackBerry pager uses the Motient network to provide messaging services. This has been very successful so far, but more complex services will be required by the mobile enterprise in the future.

Data Networks for the Mobile Enterprise

In the long run, the mobile enterprise will be better off using the data services offered through cellular networks. Such services will eventually offer the greatest coverage area and the highest bandwidth. However, in the short term, if all you need are simple data services, Mobitex and ARDIS may be the way to go. Just remember not to build too much around these networks, as you will likely have to make a switch somewhere down the line.

BLUETOOTH

In 1998 a group of companies including Ericsson, Nokia, IBM, Toshiba, and Intel started work on a standard to allow different types of mobile devices to

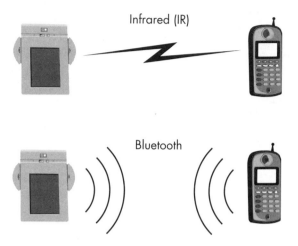

FIGURE 6–12   Infrared versus Bluetooth.

easily interconnect. This technology was given the name *Bluetooth* from the nickname of the 10th-century Danish King Harald Bluetooth.

Another RF technology that has been used for this same purpose is *infrared* (IR). However, the problem with IR is that it requires line-of-sight. That is, you have to aim two devices at one another. Bluetooth does not have this constraint. Operating in the unlicensed 2.4 GHz band, it is based on omnidirectional radio transmission. This distinction is shown in Figure 6–12.

Bluetooth has a range of 10 meters or 100 meters, depending on the power class of the devices in communication. Because of the omnidirectional nature of the radio transmission, one device may communicate with several others simultaneously. Devices act as either master or slave, with the master being able to form a *piconet* with up to seven active slave devices.

When two Bluetooth devices communicate for the first time, a pairing procedure occurs. As a result of this procedure, a secret link key is generated. This link key is used for authentication and encryption during future interactions. It is important to remember, by the way, that authentication is of the device, not of the user. For this reason, the mobile enterprise should make sure that the device itself is secured with a password, and that in that addition, sufficient application layer security is in place to authenticate the user. Remember that small devices tend to get lost and stolen, and you would not want to compromise the security of your enterprise data.

Part of the Bluetooth specification includes protocols for telephony control. The designers had in mind the scenario where one device controls a telephone to gain network access (Figure 6–13). This is exactly what we need.

FIGURE 6–13 Bluetooth for cellular access.

Bluetooth for the Mobile Enterprise

Bluetooth is a great way of connecting your PDA or laptop to your cell phone to gain access to a cellular network. In this way, the data device does not have to be enabled for network access on its own. The cell phone will provide you with that service. You can do all of this leaving your cell phone comfortably in your pocket or briefcase.

WIRELESS LANs

As the term implies, a wireless LAN is a local area network (LAN) implemented using wireless technology. By nature these networks operate at low power (to avoid interference), and at a relatively high frequency (to provide high data rates). It is usually assumed that the users of wireless LANs are moving about from time to time, but not at high speeds. The industry term for this is *pedestrian wireless*, which is to distinguish from both *vehicular wireless* (where the user may be driving a car) and *fixed wireless* (where the user does not move at all). The faster a user is moving, the more difficult it is to provide fast and reliable data service. Cellular networks, by the way, are a case of vehicular wireless. That is, they are designed with the assumption that the user may be moving about in a vehicle. This is usually acceptable for voice transmission, but it cuts down on the quality of data transmission.

Like a cellular system, a wireless LAN is a confederation of antenna systems acting together to form a network. Also like cellular systems, wireless LANs provide a feature that allows users to move about without losing their connection. In wireless LAN terminology this feature is called *roaming*, whereas, in cellular networks the same feature is called *handoff* (or *handover*). Remember that when we are talking about cellular systems, the term *roaming* specifically refers to the movement between networks run by different operators.

Cellular networks cover wide areas, using up a range of frequencies over a large distance. In order to prevent monopolies, and to protect the public interest, government bodies regulate cellular networks. As discussed earlier in this chapter, one of the aspects of this government regulation is that the frequency is licensed.

The frequencies chosen for use by wireless LANs are not licensed, since the intent is for these systems to cover small areas that are usually owned by the same entity that operates the network. For example, companies would use a wireless LAN within their own buildings and for use by their employees. Another usage would be in a *hot spot*, which is some facility open to the public, and where wireless LAN access is provided. The owner of the facility typically does this at a profit. In some cases they make their money by charging users for the access time on a subscription basis. In other cases, the access is free, and is used as a way of attracting customers to come in and pay for something else. Examples of hot spots would be hotels, airports, shopping centers, sports bars, cafes, restaurants, and convention centers.

It is also possible to use a confederation of wireless LANs to form a wide area network. This would work well in cities, for example. However, as of this writing, no company is offering such a service on a wide scale. If this kind of arrangement does become widespread, the FCC will probably step up regulation to prevent regional monopolies.

The three popular wireless LAN standards are 802.11, HiperLAN, and HomeRF. Of the three, the one that is most interesting to us is 802.11, since it is by far the most widely used in hot spots and company offices.

Background on 802.11

The 802.11 standards were developed by the Institute for Electrical and Electronics Engineers (IEEE). This work began in 1990, and the standard is still evolving today. The first version is simply called 802.11. The second, and most recent, complete version is called 802.11b. The third version, which strangely enough is called 802.11a, has been completed recently. While products supporting 802.11a are now starting to hit the market, most analysts do not expect 802.11a to displace 802.11b until the year 2004.

802.11b supports data rates of 5.5 and 11 Mbps. It operates in the 2.4 GHz band using *direct-sequence spread spectrum* (DSSS) for the air interface (aka the physical layer). As the name implies, DSSS is a class of spread spectrum signaling. Remember that FHSS, which was covered in the discussions on CDMA and Bluetooth, is another class of spread spectrum signaling.

The distinguishing feature of DSSS is the use of a *chipping code*, which spreads the same data over multiple frequencies. This redundancy increases the chances that the receiver can recover data in the event of an error in transmission. The choice of DSSS for the physical layer was taken with data services in mind. Remember that reliable transmission is much more important for data services than for voice services.

802.11b offers an *independent configuration,* whereby two stations connect to one another directly. A second configuration offered is called an *infrastructure configuration.* In an infrastructure configuration, stations communicate with one or more *access points* (APs), which are connected to a wired LAN. These different types of usage are depicted in Figure 6–14.

An infrastructure configuration is made up of cells, which are called *basic service sets* (BSS). Each BSS is controlled by an AP. A station connects to the network by first acquiring synchronization information. It does this by either probing for a nearby AP (a procedure called *active scanning*) or by listening for beacons that are periodically transmitted by APs (a procedure called *passive scanning*). Once synchronization is achieved, the station and

Independent Configuration

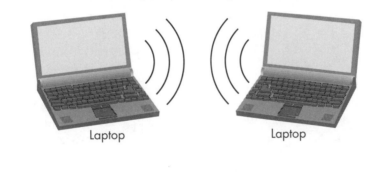

Laptop   Laptop

Infrastructure Configuration

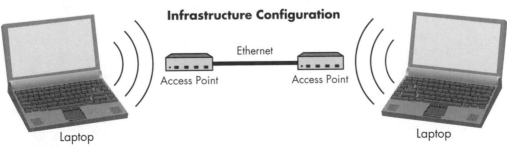

Ethernet

Access Point   Access Point

Laptop   Laptop

FIGURE 6–14 Two configurations for 802.11b.

the AP authenticate one another through an exchange of passwords. When trust is established, a process called *association* occurs, whereby the station and the AP exchange information about capabilities. Finally, data exchange commences.

As mentioned previously, in 802.11b nomenclature, *roaming* is the process that occurs when a station moves from one BSS to another without losing the network connection. There is a good bit of variation between the implementation of 802.11b in equipment from different vendors. The result of this is that roaming between networks using differently branded APs may not work.

Security is an issue with 802.11b, and with wireless LANs in general. Remember that even if you are using the wireless LAN within the confines of your office, somebody could be eavesdropping from the company parking lot. If you are sharing the office building with another company, the same problem exists.

The solution is to use a *virtual private network (VPN)*, which you may already be using to dial in to the company intranet from hotels and home offices. A complication with this is that when a VPN is being used, roaming becomes a problem. That is, every time a user moves into another BSS, he or she has to reauthenticate with the VPN. From the user's point of view, this can be quite disruptive and can interfere with the behavior of the application being used at the time.

The good news is that several companies have come up with solutions to this problem. For example, HP markets a solution called OpenRoaming. Part of the software runs on the client side (PDA or laptop), and part of it runs on a server in the company network. Using OpenRoaming, employees can use VPN and still roam. OpenRoaming also allows users to walk outside of the company premises and transparently switch to using a GPRS network.

Some of the improvements we can expect to see in 802.11a are in higher data rates and better *quality of service* (QoS). 802.11a promises data rates of up to 54 Mbps, operating in the 5 GHz spectrum. Higher power levels will be able to push a signal up to 48 kilometers. This long-distance usage is expected to serve as a bridge between two wireless LANs. It will also be interesting to see if 802.11a starts to compete with cell phone networks for wide area access to data services.

We do not need to be concerned with 802.11a for the time being. The components are currently too expensive, and there is already a lot of momentum around 802.11b. It is safe to bank on 802.11b now, as most of the initial 802.11a products will be backward compatible with 802.11b. This is a smart move on the part of the manufacturers, because it ensures interoperability with existing infrastructure. You may recall that this is similar to the way 100 Mbps Ethernet products were introduced into the market. Most products were backward compatible with 10 Mbps Ethernet to allow them to operate in existing networks.

802.11 for the Mobile Enterprise

We are mostly interested in wireless networks that provide a wide area of coverage. These are the networks that will help you get your employees out of the office and in front of the customer where they belong. In the near term, wireless LANs will not help us much at the customer site. You cannot build your business processes around the assumption that your customers will have an 802.11b network installed. Even if they did, would you require your employees to ask their customers if they could use the customer's wireless LAN?

One thing you should consider, though, is equipping your mobile professionals with 802.11b-enabled notebook computers and PDAs for use in the various hot spots they will happen into during the course of business travel. This will enable them to use their email and perform other office tasks while in airports, hotels, convention centers, and so on. In the near term, however, you cannot expect widescale availability. First of all, market penetration is still low. Second, if you subscribe to a service using one network provider, you cannot access the services of another. For the time being, you will have to plot out the likely paths of your mobile employees and subscribe to access at strategic points along the way.

It could be argued that wireless LANs installed in company offices allow visiting employees to get connected more easily while at any company site. This is certainly a nice thing to have. But at best it only saves the visiting employee a few minutes. After all, how long does it take to plug in a computer and reboot? The time saved probably would not justify a wireless LAN by itself.

Where a wireless LAN does have good business value is in places where employees walk around the company premises as part of their job, and where data retrieval or update is an integral part of the job process. For example, a wireless LAN in a hospital allows doctors to go from patient to patient carrying around a PDA to access patient records and to make updates as necessary. Factory workers, retail salespeople, and hotel employees are other job functions where business value can be derived using a wireless LAN.

LOCATION TECHNOLOGY

A fundamental aspect of mobile telephony and data services is just what the name implies—mobility. That is, the user can move about and still have voice and data access. It would be ideal to be able to provide services to the user based on where he or she is at the time. This notion has not escaped network operators and content providers. In fact, they are working toward providing such services.

We can alk about location technology in terms of its two distinct parts:

• *Location determination* is the process by which the subscriber's coordinates are determined. On a fixed-line network it is easy to know where the subscriber is: he or she is at he other end of the line. On a wireless network, the only thing that can be easily determined is which cell the user is in. However, techniques have recently been developed to narrow down the subscriber's location.

• *Location-based services* are the applications that make use of the subscriber's coordinates by applying knowledge of the geographic area. To do this well, applications must have a database of information that can be retrieved by location.

Let's take a closer look and see what these two aspects of location technology mean to the mobile enterprise.

Location Determination

It turns out that federal regulation is a key driver for wireless network operators to implement algorithms for determining the position of a handset.

Enhanced 911 (E-911)

One of the main reasons people use cell phones in the United States is for security. They like to be reachable in case of an emergency. They also like to be able to call for help in an emergency situation. A problem with calling for help is that when a subscriber dials 911, the network cannot pass information about the location of the subscriber to the *public safety answering point* (PSAP). This makes it difficult to dispatch emergency personnel.

To remedy this problem, the FCC issued the Enhanced 911 (E-911) mandate. This edict requires operators to develop the capabilities to provide location information to PSAPs in two phases.

The Phase I requirement was that operators communicate the telephone number of the originator of the 911 call and the location of the cell site handling the call to the PSAP. Implementation of this requirement started on April 1, 1998. Since then, operators have been required to implement this fea-

	67% of calls	95% of calls
Handset-based ALI	50 meters	150 meters
Network-based ALI	100 meters	300 meters

FIGURE 6–15   Phase II E911 Requirements.

ture within six months of a request by a designated PSAP. To make use of this information, work is also required at the PSAP. As of today, due to funding constraints, many PSAPs have still not developed the necessary capabilities, and they therefore have not requested this feature from the operators. The result is that this feature is not yet implemented everywhere.

Implementation of Phase II began on October 1, 2001. The Phase II requirements are that operators implement *automatic location identification* (ALI), which provides a much higher degree of accuracy than simply the cell site location. The accuracy requirements are different based on whether ALI is handset based or network based. The specific rules are shown in Figure 6–15.

Handset-based ALI is implemented using a *Global Positioning System* (GPS). Network-based ALI can be carried out in a variety of ways. Most of the network operators have opted for the technique called *Enhance Observed Time Difference* (E-OTD). This is the only network-based ALI we discuss here.

The E-911 mandate is actually a blessing in disguise for operators. While it requires additional investment, in the case of network-based ALI, the operator is in the unique position of knowing where the subscriber is. This is information the operator may be able to sell to content providers wanting to provide location-based services. Operators will also be able to sell location information to enterprises who want to use location-based services to improve employee productivity.

We can only hope that location information will not be abused, and that the civil liberties of the subscriber will be protected. This will be the subject of debate in the coming years. Stay tuned to see where this leads.

Algorithms to Determine Location

To give you a better understanding of how location is determined let's discuss the two techniques that most operators in the United States are planning to implement. The first technique, *Assisted Global Positioning System* (A-GPS), is handset based. The second technique, *Enhanced Observed Time Difference* (E-OTD), is network based.

A-GPS. GPS is a satellite-based system that is capable of determining the location of a handset to within a few meters. However, a drawback to the use of GPS in telephone handsets is the line-of-sight requirement. Because GPS requires line-of-sight between the satellite systems and the handset, it cannot be used inside buildings or when the user is standing under a tree.

A solution to this is *Assisted GPS* (A-GPS), in which the network assists the handset in determining location. The network keeps track of location readings delivered by the handset. When the handset cannot receive the satellite signal, the network uses these past readings to estimate the current location.

E-OTD. *Enhanced Observed Time Difference* (E-OTD) is a technique whereby the handset measures the arrival times of signals coming from at least three base stations. The handset is aware of the location of each base station. By comparing the difference in arrival times of the signals coming from each of these base stations, the handset is able to determine its location within 50 to 125 meters.

Location-Based Services

Given the coordinates of a handset, special services might be provided to the subscriber. For example, an application might give users directions based on where they are at the time. Another application is to assist companies in tracking their delivery trucks. One final example is an application that notifies the subscriber of an event occurring in the vicinity of where he or she is at the time.

Such applications require geographical information. For example, if a restaurant is only 200 meters from you, but there is a river between you and it, the application should not suggest you try that restaurant.

Location for the Mobile Enterprise

The mobile enterprise might use location-based services for a variety of reasons. For example, by knowing where each field engineer is, a dispatching algorithm can select engineers based on proximity to the trouble spot. Tracking delivery vehicles is another useful service for the mobile enterprise. Finally, location-based services could be used to help mobile professionals find a customer site, a restaurant, or a hotel.

The problem is it will be several years before networks provide location information extensively. For the time being, you will have to map out where you need such services and check on their availability.

Where it is absolutely necessary to use location-based services over wide geographic areas, consider using a GPS system that is independent of the handset and the wireless network. Such a solution will require a high degree of customization, but it could turn out to be a key differentiator for your company.

SUMMARY

We have just covered some very complex topics in a small amount of space. Entire books have been written about several of the things we went over in just a few paragraphs. But the goal here was not to make you an expert on wireless networks. Rather, the goal was to provide you with the working knowledge you will need to evaluate products being offered to help mobilize your enterprise. If you are interested in learning more about wireless networks, a list of recommended reading is provided in Appendix B.

In selecting mobile solutions for your enterprise you will have to carefully consider the various network options available in the places you need them. You should also do some planning based on the likely evolution of these network services. To plot out coverage areas, it might help to look at some of the online coverage maps. Appendix A lists Web sites of several network operators; most of them include network coverage maps.

Remember also that data transmission services may not be necessary in your case. Some alternatives are synchronization (requiring little or no data transmission) and voice interfaces (which gives you network coverage anywhere you can use your cell phone).

In no case will a data application resolve the need for the mobile professional to make phone calls. If you can assume your mobile worker has a cell phone, you might consider as part of your mobile solution having the data device control the cell phone via a Bluetooth interface. In this way, you use the communication functions of the phone thereby reducing the requirements of the data device.

You should also consider equipping your mobile professionals with 802.11b-enabled data devices, since this can cut down on some of the time wasted during business travel. Careful consideration should be given to where you need 802.11b services most. A subscription to the services of one chain of hot spots is unlikely to get you service at hot spots operated by different companies.

Location-based services might be considered on an as-needed basis. Eventually these services will be very useful, but today this technology is in its infancy and the initial applications might prove to be a disappointment to you. Be very careful in selecting location-based applications for the time being.

C H A P T E R   7

Wireless Application Gateways

In order to mobilize an enterprise, a special platform is needed to take care of the peculiarities of wireless networks and small devices on the one hand, and enterprise applications on the other. All traffic passed between the enterprise and mobile workers will be routed through this kind of system.

These new platforms are commonly referred to as *wireless application gateways* (WAGs), a term coined by the research advisory firm Gartner. On the one side, WAGs interface with enterprise applications to extract data and post updates. On the other side, the WAG will repackage application data to make it readable on a portable computing device. The best of the wireless application gateways will also support an entirely different application flow—one that makes sense for customer-facing employees.

It is important to understand what is required of a wireless application gateway, and how some of the ones on the market today work. In the process of mobilizing your enterprise you are likely to have to evaluate different WAGs to determine which one is best for you.

JOINING THREE WORLDS

Let's take a generic look at some of the technical challenges that have to be addressed in order to mobilize your enterprise. Hopefully this will shed some light on how the different pieces fit together to make a solution.

The mobile enterprise is made possible by joining three different worlds: wireless networks, Internet, and enterprise applications. As you can see in Figure 7–1, these three worlds have very different characteristics:

- *Wireless networks* have high latency (takes longer for a bit to get from one place to another), low bandwidth, and high bit error rates. Also in the world of wireless networks, sessions are less stable. This is for several reasons. One is that you might step into an area susceptible to radio interference. Another reason is that the battery on the device might run out during a session.

  An equally significant aspect of the wireless world is the diversity of handheld devices being used. Input mechanisms, display characteristics, processing power, and memory capacity differ on the various devices.

- The *Internet* makes use of a rich suite of protocols and applications that expect certain network characteristics. These applications also expect certain types of client computers. We want to take advantage of the Internet infrastructure and all the software and services that have been developed around it. However, we have to take special measures to interface the Internet with the wireless world, where network characteristics are different, and where there is great diversity in client computers.

- *Enterprise applications* manage the information we are trying to make available to our mobile professionals. The trouble is they are not always integrated in ways that make sense for customer-facing employees.

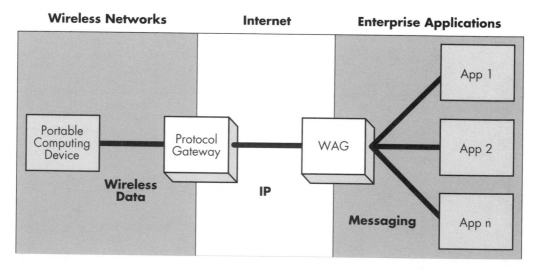

FIGURE 7–1 Joining three worlds.

These applications were built to interface with desktop clients with large screens and keyboards, and high-bandwidth connections. The world of enterprise applications has already been integrated with the world of the Internet. Now we have to bridge this world and that of wireless networks, where the screens are small, keyboards are awkward or nonexistent, and the connections are slow.

We can speak in generic terms about the components needed to join the three worlds. These are not components in the sense of being one integrated piece of software or hardware. In fact, there are a variety of configurations that are possible—and many involve several software and hardware modules.

These are components in terms of performing an integrated set of functions. The components and the functions they perform are:

- *Protocol gateway* is needed to convert from wireless data protocols to Internet protocols. For example, if you are using a CDPD data service (see Chapter 6), the network operator has a specialized gateway to bridge the wireless protocol to IP. Likewise, if you are using GPRS, data traffic passes through a gateway interfacing the wireless data with Internet.

  Even when the wireless data protocol supports IP directly, there still needs to be some kind of gateway between the wireless network and the fixed-line Internet. Many of the communications parameters have to be different on the wireless side to compensate for the high latency, low bandwidth, and high bit error rate. Those same parameters will not be used on the Internet side. The job of the protocol gateway is to serve as interpreter between the two sides.

  The protocol gateway may also have to manage a split session, that is, there might be a session from the device to the gateway on the one side, and one from the gateway to the WAG on the other side. The protocol gateway bridges the two sessions.

  We will not pay too much attention to the protocol gateway. In most cases, it sits on the operator network, and its function is transparent to you as the customer. I will include the protocol gateway in the discussion on data exchange models, and then we will focus exclusively on the wireless application gateway.

- *Wireless application gateway (WAG)* is needed to manage application content and set up presentation of output for smaller devices. There are a lot of other things that have to be done by the WAG. We explore those things later in this chapter.

Between the parts shown in Figure 7–1, data is passed in different ways. What I have shown is sort of an apples-to-oranges comparison; in fact, IP may be present in all three of the exchanges. Also, one cannot talk about IP and messaging as being on the same level of communications. The point is to emphasize the most prominent aspect of the data exchanges:

- *Wireless data* is the data service offered by your wireless network provider. This might be CDPD, CSD, GPRS, 1xRTT, or some of the other technologies discussed in Chapter 6.

- *IP* is the underlying protocol used on the Internet. In fact, there is a suite of protocols around IP. We do not need to go into details on these protocols. You can just assume that where I refer to IP, I am referencing the entire set of protocols that are available on the Internet.

- *Messaging* is the paradigm most widely used to allow enterprise applications to exchange data. This is usually accomplished through middleware that creates a *message bus*. The ways in which applications may exchange data on this bus include *publish/subscribe* and *request/reply*.

  With publish/subscribe, applications subscribe to a data channel. When one application has data to send, it "publishes," that is, the data is broadcast to all those who have subscribed.

  Using a request/reply system on a message bus, applications explicitly "ask" for data from one another by issuing a *request*. The *response* contains the data that was requested, or an error indicator if the data is not found.

DATA EXCHANGE MODELS

Let's take a look at four data exchange models to get a better feel for data flows between the device and the enterprise. The kinds of exchanges we will look at are prefetch and aggregate, on-demand, push, and synchronize. These exchanges are not mutually exclusive. For example, you might push data that was prefetched.

Prefetch and Aggregate

In some cases it makes sense to prefetch data and aggregate it on the mobility platform. When a request comes from the device, it is serviced from the data already sitting on the WAG. This improves response time. Figure 7–2 shows how prefetch and aggregate works:

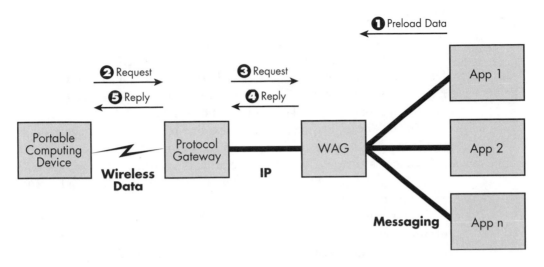

FIGURE 7–2 Generic view of prefetch and aggregate.

1. On a regular basis, perhaps every night, data is fetched from back-end applications and loaded onto the WAG. The WAG might reorganize the data in a way that makes sense in the context of a specific business process. Another way of saying this is that the data might be put into *business objects* to be used by the mobile professional.

2. When a user performs some action, the application on the portable computing device makes a request, which is packaged in whichever wireless data protocol is being used—1xRTT, GPRS, CSD, and so on. (See Chapter 6 for more on these protocols.)

3. The protocol gateway repackages the message into Internet Protocol (IP) packets.

4. The wireless application gateway fulfills the request by itself and sends the reply to the protocol gateway.

5. In the reverse direction the protocol gateway repackages what it gets on the Internet side and puts it into the format required for the wireless side.

The prefetch and aggregate model works best in cases where the time it takes to fetch back-end data and put it into business objects exceeds what can be tolerated for response time. This model also assumes the data being prefetched is relatively nonvolatile, that is, the data is not expected to be obsolete by the time it is sent to the user.

On-Demand

The most common usage model is the "on-demand" model (Figure 7–3). In this case, the mobility platform does not collect data beforehand. Instead it fetches the data from back-end applications as needed. It may also have to reorganize the data into the business objects needed for mobile applications. For the on-demand case, all of this is done on the fly.

The difference between this case and that of prefetch and aggregate is that in this case, the wireless application gateway makes requests to back-end applications as needed. There are several ways in which this request can be made. I describe the more popular options later in this chapter when I discuss *enterprise application integration* (EAI).

Because the WAG requests data from back-end applications as needed, the user is presented *fresher* data. In the case where the data is prefetched and aggregated on the WAG, there is a possibility that the data becomes obsolete or irrelevant between the time of the prefetch and of the user request.

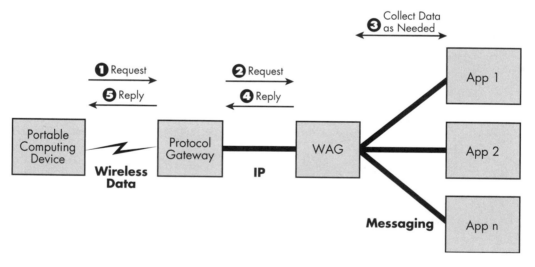

FIGURE 7–3   Generic view of on-demand.

Push

In the push model, data is sent to the portable computing device without a request coming from the device. This case is exactly what is needed for dispatch or to alert you that a new email has arrived. Figure 7–4 shows a generic model for how this would work.

The steps that are taken in this case are:

1. An event occurs. For example, an email message arrives or it becomes a certain time and an alarm goes off. Events may also be human or application generated, for example, a dispatch notice.
   The WAG may be set up to detect the event directly. Alternatively, a back-end application might detect the event and send an alert to the WAG.

2. The WAG *pushes* a message to the protocol gateway.

3. The protocol gateway repackages data in the other examples. Note that there may be an address translation at the protocol gateway. For example, the Internet world might view the portable device as having an IP address, but the wireless network needs to address the device with a phone number.

The WAG must be able to handle the case where the portable computing device is not available at the time of the alert. To do this the WAG should

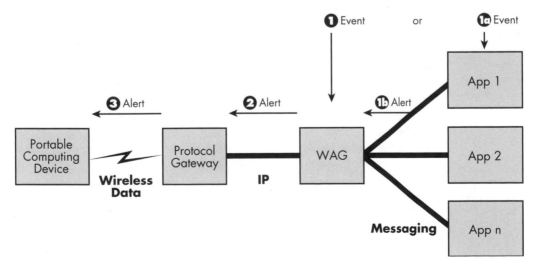

FIGURE 7–4   Generic view of push.

include a mechanism to queue alerts for subsequent delivery attempts. If several attempts fail, and the alert is high priority, there should be an alternative delivery path. For example, the WAG might try the user's cell phone first. After several failed attempts to send the alert to the cell phone, the WAG might then send a message in the form of a fax to an administrative assistant at the office.

Synchronization

In cases where real-time access is not needed, it is better to provide users offline access to applications. That is, they work using data stored on the device. To do this synchronization must be used. This is the process by which data on the device is brought up to date with changes made on the enterprise side. The synchronization process usually also propagates updates in the other direction, that is, enterprise applications are updated according to changes that were made on the device.

Although synchronization is best accomplished over a high-bandwidth fixed-line connection, it may also occur where a reliable, high-bandwidth wireless service is available.

Synchronization works as shown in Figure 7–5:

1. The WAG checks for differences between what is on the portable computing device and what is on the enterprise side. In order to check what is on the enterprise side, the WAG usually queries one or more applications and puts together the results according to the way it is viewed by the device.

2. If updates are needed on either the portable computing device, the enterprise side, or both, the WAG makes the updates. Once again the WAG has to reorganize the data as it is seen by the enterprise applications.

The synchronization model has additional complexities involving conflict resolution. If more than one mobile professional updates the same data, a decision has to be made as to whose change is kept. The same is true for the case where a mobile professional updates information that is also updated by somebody using the back-end applications directly.

Conflict resolution is usually a question of policy. The WAG should offer a way of configuring how conflicts are handled according to the policy you wish to implement. Your policy might include a prioritization of users, so that the updates of one class of users take precedence over those of another class.

The worst policy is to just take updates as they occur through synchronization. Remember that two different users may make updates in a certain order while in the field, but they may synchronize in the opposite order. For

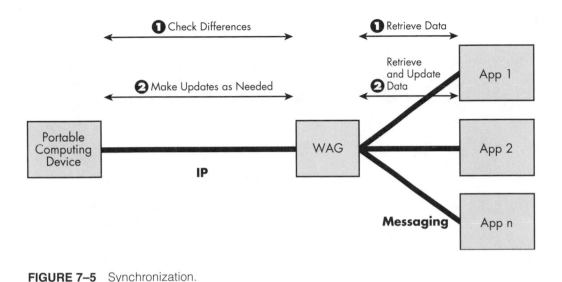

FIGURE 7–5 Synchronization.

example, Joe reads a meter at 10:00, and Sally reads the same meter at 11:00. If both note the reading on their portable computing device, and then Joe synchronizes after Sally, it is Joe's update that is kept.

THIN CLIENT/THICK CLIENT

There are two extreme computing paradigms that can be employed to help the mobile worker. On one hand, applications can run entirely on the server side with the device performing only display and data capture functions. In this case, the device is said to be a *thin client*, because it is running very little of the application software. Since the device is acting like a dumb terminal, this model assumes the presence of a really good wireless data service.

The other extreme is where all application logic runs on the device and requests are made to the server from time to time to retrieve data not already stored on the device. In this case, the device is said to be a thick client. Where a thick-client model is used, synchronization plays a greater role. Not only does data need to be refreshed on the device, the updates on the device must be posted to the server so the rest of the company can benefit from the changes.

In between these two paradigms are all sorts of shades of gray. Innovative caching schemes might be employed. For example, the WAG might predict what data the user will need and push that data to the device when bandwidth permits.

UNDERLYING TECHNOLOGIES

We now turn our attention to the wireless application gateway. Let's start out with a discussion on some of the technology on which many WAGs are built. Much of this is already used to develop and run robust Web sites. Many WAG vendors have seen the benefits of applying these same technologies to the mobility paradigm.

J2EE™

Java™ was invented by Sun Microsystems, but ever since 1998 it has been evolved and specified by a consortium of companies working through a process called the Java Community Process. Anybody may freely use the standards and refer to their products as being compliant with the standards.

There is also a certification process to determine the degree with which products adhere to the standards and the degree to which software is portable across Java platforms. This certification process is managed by Sun Microsystems, and there is a licensing fee for selling software that has been certified. Sun also retains ownership of many of the brands and trademarks, and a licensing fee applies to some of the names associated with the standards. One should never be fooled by the prospect of getting something for free. There is always a catch.

Java 2 specifications were released in 1998. Three target platforms, or *editions*, were identified as part of this release. These are:

* *Java 2 Standard Edition (J2SE)*™, which is a standard set of tools and APIs for writing and deploying Java applets and applications. I will say no more about this platform, as only the other two editions are important to the mobile enterprise.

* *Java 2 Micro Edition (J2ME)*™, which is a platform for mobile devices. This works nicely for thick client devices. I discuss J2ME in a separate section.

* *Java 2 Enterprise Edition (J2EE)*™, which is designed to provide a common platform that takes care of many of the technical details that have to be performed by all applications. By using such a platform application developers no longer have to reinvent some of the common tasks, such as transaction management, data communications, and security. The J2EE environment performs these tasks for the applications.

Many WAGs are based on J2EE. There are at least three reasons for this. First of all, J2EE makes it easier for developers to implement the logic needed to transform content from one markup language to another. Second, by providing features for the encapsulation of business logic in reusable components, J2EE is also generally attractive as an environment in which to develop and run business applications. Finally, application servers are generally based on J2EE. Application servers are the foundation for most web platforms. Forward-looking WAG vendors have recognized the need to base their gateways on application servers as well, and for the same reasons: scalability and high availability.

The J2EE application model consists of components, containers, and connectors:

- *Components* are pieces of reusable business logic written by application developers. Given a set of preprogrammed components that perform some of the fundamental business processing, developers can assemble the components into an application.
- *Containers* enclose components. They take care of some of the common tasks so components do not have to. These tasks include transaction management, communication with client computers, and security for the components.
  Containers also provide standard APIs to components, APIs such as Java Message Service (JMS) for back-end integration and Java Database Connectivity (JDBC) for database access. This unifies the programming model and simplifies the job of writing a component.
- *Connectors* define an API that allows J2EE software to plug into existing applications, such as the large enterprise applications of our interest.

Application developers implement components. System vendors implement containers and connectors.

In the next few subsections I give an overview of the aspects of J2EE that are most relevant to understanding WAGs. These are Java servlets, JavaServer Pages (JSPs), Enterprise JavaBeans (EJBs), Java Database Connectivity (JDBC), and Java Messaging Services (JMS).

Java Servlets

Web pages may be static, or they may be dynamic. Static Web pages are completely defined before any request is made, that is, they do not change for each request. Dynamic Web pages, on the other hand, contain data values that can only be known after a request is processed. For this reason, dynamic pages are generated for each request.

The first generation of Web technology used a common gateway interface (CGI) script to generate dynamic Web pages. Under this scheme, the web server invokes a CGI script to handle a request. The script accesses databases and other resources and returns results in the form of a Web page.

Subsequently, other ways were developed to generate dynamic Web pages. Netscape developed a scheme called the Netscape server application programming interface (NSAPI), which was a way for Netscape Web servers to invoke procedures dynamically. From an opposing camp, Microsoft developed Internet Server API (ISAPI).

The Java model uses *servlets* to generate dynamic Web pages. The difference between the Java model and the other methods discussed above is that the Java servlets are designed to run on any Java platform, that is, they are machine and OS independent.

Like all other J2EE components, servlets are executed in a container provided by the J2EE platform vendor. Among other things, the container takes care of the HTTP communications with the client, and it takes care of access to various resources, such as databases.

JavaServer Pages

JavaServer Pages (JSPs) can also be used to generate dynamic content. A JSP is a page that contains both a static definition of how the page is to be formatted and Java code, which is interpreted by the Web server to generate dynamic content. This is analogous to Microsoft's Active Server Page (ASP) technology.

JSPs are especially useful in performing content transformation. When a request is made, the code is executed to format the page based on the type of device making the request. For example, if the device is a WAP-enabled phone, WML is generated.

Enterprise JavaBeans

Enterprise JavaBeans (EJBs) provide a model for the development of distributed object-oriented business applications. This model is based on reusable sets of data and operations on that data. There are three types of beans:

- *Session beans* represent a set of actions to be performed during a session with one client. They generally perform a series of tasks in the context of a transaction. Session beans may be stateful, retaining information between transactions within a client session. Session beans may also be stateless, losing all information after a transaction is completed.

- *Entity beans* represent persistent resources, such as databases, customers, and prices. These beans live as long as the resource they represent.

- *Message-driven beans* represent a single message. They can be used in association with Java Message Service (JMS) to represent messages passed between two loosely coupled applications.

Application developers can write their own set of EJBs for their particular business. Different applications can then make use of the same beans.

Java Database Connectivity

Java Database Connectivity (JDBC) provides a uniform interface to different relational databases. JDBC is the Java counterpart to Microsoft's ODBC. The difference is that JDBC is platform independent.

Since Java Virtual Machines (JVMs) are available for all major computing platforms, platform-independent database applications can be written using JDBC.

Java Messaging Service

Java Messaging Service (JMS) provides a standard interface to messaging middleware. This middleware creates messaging buses that use models such as publish and subscribe and request/demand. We will see more on this later in the chapter as part of the discussion of the WAG functional reference model.

Many enterprise applications are already connected to messaging services as a way of exchanging data. JMS is therefore one way to interface with enterprise applications.

J2ME™

Java 2 Micro Edition (J2ME), one of the three Java 2 editions, is targeted for use on portable computing devices characterized by reduced memory, battery operation, network connectivity, and restricted displays. These devices include smart cards, cell phones, PDAs, and set-top boxes.

The J2ME platform consists of virtual machines and core APIs. *Profiles* are defined for particular types of devices. These profiles include a specification of the Java Virtual Machine required to support the device and a set of runtime libraries for the device.

In Chapter 5 I discussed some of the operating systems running on the popular PDAs. A J2ME platform might run on top of the operating system, providing a runtime environment for offline applications. If you are running a thin client, you will certainly not need such a runtime environment. However, for thicker clients, that is, cases where a lot of offline processing is performed on the device, J2ME might make sense.

A WAG might store a set of Java applications that are downloaded to devices as needed. The application could then run in offline mode most of the time, connecting only when data exchange is needed. The primary function of the WAG in this case might be to download applications.

Avoid being fooled into thinking that Java applications that run on one class of device can run in the same way on a different class of device. Different virtual machines and runtime libraries are needed for cell phones than for PDAs. Therefore, cross-platform portability will not be achieved across different kinds of devices.

Extensible Markup Language

The World Wide Web Consortium (W3C) develops protocols to ensure interoperability on the World Wide Web. This organization specifies HTML, XML, and several other technologies I discuss here.

In 1998, the W3C published the specifications for eXtensible Markup Language (XML), which is a meta-language, that is, it is a language for defining other markup languages. XML provides syntax for using *tags* (words enclosed in "<" and ">") and *attributes* (name = value), but it does not define semantics. The semantics are up to the applications using the XML document.

The *document type definition* (DTD) language can be used to define semantics. This language allows developers to specify which tags and attributes are allowed in a given document type.

Application developers can define the meaning of the tags and attributes within a given *name space*, which is a fancy term that refers to the scope of a definition. Within a private name space, developers can define whatever they want.

XML makes a clear distinction between data representation and data presentation. Data is represented in XML documents in a structure described through document type definitions (DTDs) or through XML schema definitions (XSD). The presentation of the document can be defined through stylesheets using an extensible stylesheet language (XSL).

Applications use XML processors to read a document. To interpret an XML document according to the rules in a stylesheet, an XSL processor may be used.

XML Processors

An XML processor is a software module that reads an XML document and provides applications access to the content and structure of that document. So that applications can use different XML processors without having to undergo a lot of change, some standards have been defined around how XML processors read a document and how they represent the content and structure of a document to applications.

Two of these standards are DOM and SAX. The W3C specifies DOM. SAX, on the other hand, is a de facto standard that works around some of the problems with DOM.

Document Object Model

The Document Object Model (DOM) defines an in-memory representation of an XML document as well as the application interface that allows applications to traverse the in-memory representation and make modifications. DOM is based on a tree structure representing the document. The W3C specifies DOM for use with HTML and XML.

Simple Application Programming Interface for XML

Applications using DOM have to load an entire XML document into memory before they can do anything with it. This poses a problem when documents are large and/or when the application is running on a constrained platform, such as a handheld device.

In order to overcome this problem, developers came up with an alternative called Simple API for XML (SAX). Using SAX, an XML processor can call custom event handlers to process each element as soon as it is read in. This method is not specified by any standards organization, but it has become quite popular and can be considered a de facto standard.

Extensible Stylesheet Language

The Extensible Stylesheet Language (XSL) provides a way of transforming a source document to another format. Stylesheets contain template rules, which define output structures to apply to a given part of the source document. An XSL processor parses an XML document matching elements of the document to template rules from the stylesheet. When it finds a match, the rules are applied. As shown in Figure 7–6, this mechanism can be used to transform the output of an application into a format that can be used by many cell phones.

Many WAGs perform content transformation in this way. However, as we shall see later in a more detailed discussion on content transformation, even this system can get quite complicated as the number of supported devices grows.

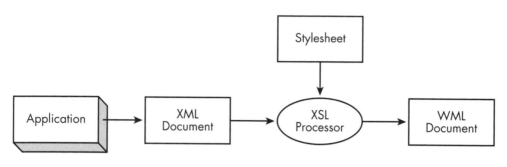

FIGURE 7–6   Content transformation.

Other Markup Languages

Markup languages provide a way to specify data along with some information about that data. Document authors used traditional markup languages to indicate how they wanted their data to be presented. This solved the problem whereby different applications presented the same document in different ways.

The idea of markup languages has been around since the 1960s when IBM developed the *generalized markup language* (GML) for use on mainframes. Others were using similar ideas at the time. But the sheer size of IBM lent weight to all of its efforts, and GML was no exception.

In the 1970s, the American National Standards Institute (ANSI) developed the first standardized markup language. This was called *standardized general markup language* (SGML). Like XML, SGML is actually a metalanguage that can be used in a DTD to define another markup language. For example, the famous *hypertext markup language* (HTML) can be defined using SGML.

HyperText Markup Language

Up until now, HTML has been the markup language used to define Web pages. It is relatively simple, and it provides a way of letting users jump to related documents through a mouse click. One can browse the Internet by traversing a stream of related ideas, in much the same way as we think. One idea leads to another, and so on.

HTML has also allowed document authors to specify how the data is to be presented independently of the application doing the presentation. Needless to say, these are powerful notions that have revolutionized communications. HTML put a nice interface on the Internet and it allowed people who do not even know each other to link ideas by linking Web pages.

However, as we shall see below in the section on xHTML, there are some major drawbacks to HTML. These drawbacks have been recognized, and the W3C has addressed them in xHTML, an evolution out of HTML.

Wireless Markup Language

To allow a limited form of Web browsing on cell phones, the WAP forum specified *wireless markup language* (WML). This markup language, which was never adopted by the W3C, has features that allow batch downloads of pages, different persistence models, and stripped-down content.

Using Java ServerPages, it is not too hard to automate a transformation from HTML content to WML. This is done through a process called *transcoding*, which I describe later in this document. However, it is not so easy to go in the opposite direction, from WML to HTML, when programmers make use of the different WML persistence models. This changes the lifetime of variables, which could lead to strange program behavior if the transformation is not done with a great deal of care.

Compact HTML

Originally specified by NTT DoCoMo, and later adopted by W3C, compact HTML (c-HTML) is another way of providing limited Web browsing on constrained devices, such as cell phones. NTT DoCoMo uses this markup language in its hugely successful i-Mode, which started out in Japan and is being deployed in other countries.

Whereas WML forces a different programming model than HTML, c-HTML uses the same model as HTML. Because c-HTML is more closely tied to HTML, going back and forth between HTML and c-HTML is a much easier process.

Extensible HyperText Markup Language

There are two problems with HTML that have made it hard to develop robust applications around it. These are:

- HTML documents are not well formed; that is, there is room for ambiguity in the way a document is written.
- Extensions cannot be added; that is, if a vendor wants to add tags to perform some extra functionality, other applications will choke on the HTML document.

To solve these problems, and to align HTML with XML, the W3C defined *extensible hypertext markup language* (xHTML). Because xHTML documents are well formed, XML processors can parse them.

Voice XML

AT&T, IBM, Lucent Technologies, and Motorola developed VoiceXML, which is an XML-based markup language for representing speech. W3C has now taken on this markup language as a standard.

Some WAGs offer a voice interface, a useful alternative to a purely data interface. One advantage of a voice-driven application is that you can access the application anywhere you have cell phone coverage. Another advantage is that you do not need a data device.

Application Servers

Application servers are platforms on which mission-critical Web applications are built. More often than not, these platforms are based on J2EE. They are built to maximize reusability, to be scalable, and to be robust. There are many companies selling application servers, including BEA, HP, IBM, Sun, Sybase, and Oracle.

Load Balancing and High Availability

Application servers are usually arranged in a cluster to handle a large amount of traffic. A load balancer sits in front of the cluster and passes out requests to the different application servers in a way that distributes the workload as evenly as possible. Figure 7–7 shows how this works.

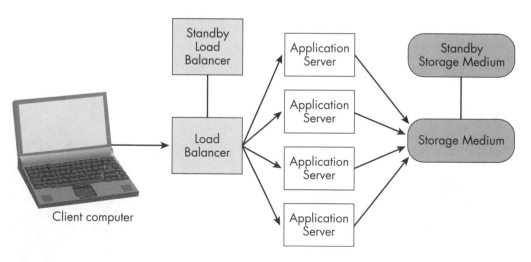

FIGURE 7–7   Cluster of application servers.

This cluster arrangement has the additional benefit of being highly available. If one application server goes down, the others will probably continue to function. The load balancer distributes traffic without regard to open sessions, that is, one application server might handle the first request of a session, then another might take the second request, and so on.

In order for this to work properly, the application servers have to share information on the state of ongoing sessions. Again, this has a nice advantage that when one server goes down, all other servers know the state of all open sessions—and any one of them can pick up the session on the next request.

In order to achieve true high availability, the load balancer and the state information have to also be duplicated. Otherwise, the whole cluster goes down if either of these two fails. Cluster components that are not duplicated are known as *single points of failure*. If a single point of failure goes down, that part of the system no longer functions, and the entire service might cease to function.

Storage area network (SAN) technology provides a single logical interface to a redundant storage medium. Using this technology, an application server in a cluster can write state information to a logical shared disk. All peer application servers can read the state information from this same logical shared disk.

WAGs and Application Servers

Forward-looking WAG vendors are basing their platforms on application servers to achieve scalability and robustness. Today, as most mobile enterprises do not yet have a large user base, one might not notice if a wireless application gateway does not scale well. However, once the floodgates open, the scalable and robust platforms will stand alone as winners.

WAG FUNCTIONAL REFERENCE MODEL

Let's now take a look at the kinds of functions a WAG might perform. This discussion will be around the reference model shown in Figure 7–8. This model is not an architecture; that is, the functions that are shown next to one another do not necessarily sit next to one another in an implementation. Rather, this model puts functions in logical groups to help us think through requirements.

Most vendors will not offer all of the features shown here—and maybe you do not want them all anyway. In any case, the reference model will serve as a framework for thinking through which products provide which features and which features are important to you.

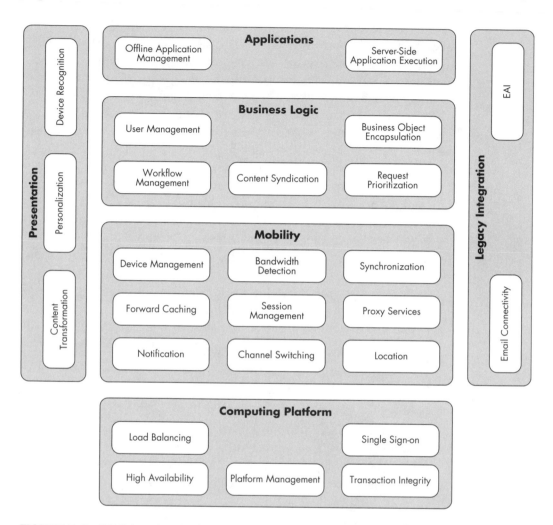

FIGURE 7–8 WAG functional reference model.

Vendors may not group these functions in the same way I am presenting them. They may also use different terms. The industry is still too young to settle on standard terminology—and even with mature technology, different vendors and authors will sometimes use different terms.

The groupings and the terms used are not important. What is important is that you understand the definitions of these functions, and that you get a clear understanding of which ones are offered by your vendor.

Throughout this process you should think in terms of which features are important to you in your unique case. In Chapter 11 I will take you through a process that can help you match the solution to the particular business problems you are trying to solve.

Presentation

An important function of the WAG is to present data in a way that is tailored for specific devices. Data is taken from back-end systems in a format that cannot be used by small devices. The wireless application gateway must therefore transform the content into a format the device understands. For incoming data, the WAG may also have to perform a reverse transformation to remove any device-specific formatting.

The separation of application processing and presentation is essential in a world where there are so many different kinds of devices. One cannot expect each application, or each part of the platform, to have to know about all of the different kinds of devices being used. This is a very complicated task—and after all, the applications and the other parts of the platform already have enough work to do.

Device Recognition

The WAG must be able to recognize the type of device involved in an exchange. It needs to know the hardware that is being used and the browser. This information will then be used to format output accordingly.

The W3C specifies a framework called *Composite Capabilities/Preferences Profile* (CC/PP), which can be used to communicate device characteristics as well as personal preferences. The WAP forum specifies a different way called User Agent profile (UAProf).

CC/PP is loosely defined and has not yet been used on a large scale. Members of the WAP forum actually developed UAProf because they found CC/PP lacking.

The Composite Capabilities part of the CC/PP name is the part where the capabilities of the device are indicated. Taking a step further, the user may also have personal preferences, which are indicated in the Personal Profile part of CC/PP.

Personalization

The WAG may also allow individual users to specify preferences in how data is presented. In this case, the presentation is specifically formatted not only for the device and browser, but also for the individual. CC/PP and UAProf also allow users to express personal preferences.

Portable computing devices are generally used by only one person. Because of this, and because these devices have limited human interfaces, the importance of personalizing the interface is all the more pronounced.

Content Transformation

The presentation function of the WAG has to fit content to specific devices and users. This process, known as content transformation, can be performed in many different ways.

The first way of transforming content was by picking out fields from existing HTML pages and putting the values into a different markup language. This is a nice stopgap that makes use of existing Web content written for HTML. This technique is called *transcoding* or *screen scraping*. Users can usually configure a transcoding platform to indicate which fields are to be taken from the HTML page and where they are to be placed in the new document. Usually this is done through a graphical user interface. This configuration process results in Java servlets and/or JSPs. When a request comes in, the servlet or JSP is invoked to perform the transformation.

One problem with transcoding is the processing time involved in converting each document in this way. As your system becomes more popular among users, you may run into problems scaling up if transcoding is being used.

Another problem is that the source HTML page is likely to change over time. If the platform is looking for fields in certain positions, or if it is looking for specific tags, it may not find them. When transcoding is used, one must keep track of when source pages are changed. Even when the pages are coming from company-internal applications, this could become a daunting task over time.

Perhaps the biggest problem with transcoding is that it forces the mobile worker to follow the logic of an application designed for fixed-line access. The order in which pages are presented and the flow of the application cannot be easily tailored for the mobile worker when transcoding is being used. As we shall see in Chapter 8, different logic is needed for the business processes of the mobile professional.

A step above transcoding involves the use of XSL and XML. A stylesheet is built for each device indicating how data is to be presented on that device. The back-end applications must provide output in XML. The data from the XML documents is formatted for the device according to the stylesheet.

A variation on this method is to model each device according to its features, such as the display size and browser type. Component style guides are developed for each device feature, and the components are assembled according to the device. This method achieves a degree of reusability, simplifying programming and configuration.

Servlets and/or JSPs may be used here as well. When a request comes in the servlet or JSP invokes an XSL Transformer (XSLT), which performs the transformation according to the style sheet, the XSLT then passes the device-specific output back to the servlet or JSP.

Applications

Ultimately, the WAG is a platform on which applications are managed and run. Applications may be run offline; that is, they may be run on the device when there is no data connection. Applications may also run on the WAG with frequent data exchanges between the device and the WAG.

Many WAGs offer a development environment. In some cases, an application written using the development environment of one vendor can be run on the WAG of another. But usually this is not the case. Even when standards such as J2EE are used, not enough work has been done to standardize the way mobile applications are developed and run. The industry is not yet mature enough. However, this will certainly come in the not-too-distant future.

Offline Application Management

Where the user has a thick client the WAG may download entire applications to the device as needed. In this case, one of the jobs of the WAG is to manage application versions. When the device is running an old version of an application, the latest version may be downloaded. This should not be done without the user's consent—and it is usually better done as part of a synchronization process when the device is connected through a fixed line.

Server-Side Application Execution

The WAG may also offer a runtime environment for applications. The applications make use of the services of the platform—they do not have to be concerned with many of the details of mobility, fault tolerance, security, and so on. All of that is taken care of by the WAG.

In this way, developers can concentrate their efforts on understanding business processes and writing applications that make these processes more efficient. If the business process layer is present, and if the necessary business objects have been modeled, an application can be written by putting together a collection of reusable components.

Business Logic

A WAG may package business logic that is used by many applications. By separating the functions that are to be reused from those that are application dependent, modifications can be isolated and application developers do not have to reinvent the wheel for each new application.

User Management

A wireless application gateway should include functions for managing users. This can include the capability to classify users in terms of their job roles. By classifying users in this way, different application logic can be served up according to the job role or roles the user performs. WAGs may also limit access to certain functions based on the user's job role(s).

Some WAGs have their own user database. Others use Lightweight Directory Access Protocol (LDAP) to read and update profile information from some other source within the enterprise. This minimizes duplication of data that is needed by several applications within the enterprise.

Workflow Management

A workflow engine can be used to track forms and data through a series of steps. This engine can take as input a process model that reflects how work is done.

For example, a wholesale salesperson might go to a retail outlet and check inventory. She will note the inventory of the products her company sells. This information is uploaded, thereby completing one task. The process model dictates that the next stop for this information is the warehouse. The workflow engine then automatically passes a form to the warehouse so that the stock can be immediately pulled. When the stock is pulled, the second task is complete. The process model says that the third step is for a delivery truck to pick up the load and bring it to the retail outlet. The workflow engine notifies the driver that the stock is ready and gives him the address of the retail outlet. When delivery occurs, the workflow engine is notified and the process is complete.

Content Syndication

Businesses frequently have a need to pull content from external sources and make that content available to mobile employees. For example, a news feed targeting certain industries and business functions might be useful. Pharmaceutical companies will want their sales reps to have access to the latest news on drug approvals.

Request Prioritization

A business may want to prioritize requests, so that higher priority requests are processed quicker. Prioritization may be based on a number of attributes. For example, the type of request may dictate the priority. Workers with certain job functions may have their requests processed before other workers. It may even make sense to prioritize based on the individual making the request.

The WAG may offer a way of configuring priorities. The runtime environment works to make sure those priorities are honored.

Business Object Encapsulation

Companies have a number of data structures and operations on those structures that are commonly used. These structures and the associated operations make up a business object. These objects reflect some business process, such as invoice generation, order generation, price lookup, and so on. The business objects can be prepackaged on the WAG so that they can be reused by different applications. One nice way of doing this is through enterprise java beans (EJBs), which are mentioned earlier in this chapter.

When an application includes logic for generating invoices, it does not have to be written into the application. Instead, the developer can include the business object and invoke it as needed.

Mobility

Wireless application gateways will include a set of functions that are specific to mobility. These are the functions that bridge the gap to the wireless world.

Device Management

There will be a large number of mobile devices out in the field. The mobile platform has to provision those devices; that is, it has to set them up with an initial configuration. It also has to track software and data changes so that each device is in a known state.

Functions for backing up the devices should also be provided. If a user loses his device, he will need to quickly obtain another one with an identical configuration.

Forward Caching

Some WAGs will try to figure out what the user is likely to do next and push the data needed for those tasks to the device in advance. The smarter WAGs will push the data according to how much bandwidth is available.

Notification

It is often necessary to notify a mobile professional of an event. For example, she might need to know that email has arrived, that a price list has changed, or that it is her turn to perform some task as part of a workflow process. Notification may also be sent to an application on the device without the user knowing about it. In any case, the WAG should have the capability to push messages to the device and/or the user.

The data may be pushed in several ways. It could be pushed using SMS or GPRS (see Chapter 6), it might be pushed through a paging service, it could take the form of a phone call or an email message, or it can be pushed as a fax transmission.

Some WAGs will offer a configurable set of push options and some rules to dictate the order in which options are tried. For example, an SMS message may be tried first, then if that is not acknowledged within a certain amount of time, a fax may be sent. The user might indicate a preference for push mechanisms depending on the time of day. For example, a user may indicate that she will be near a certain fax machine at a given time of day. At this time the WAG knows to alert the user through a fax message.

Notification might also be based on location. If the WAG knows that the user is in a certain place, it might push information relevant to the area. Location may be one of the parameters used to define notification rules.

Channel Switching

Some WAGs offer the ability to maintain a session as the user switches devices and/or networks. A user might start out using a WAP phone and then switch to a desktop computer. The WAG tracks this change and allows the session to be continued in some form on the desktop computer. A similar procedure is to have the WAG send output to a different device. For example, a worker may be using a PDA to input details of a contract. Then on the user's request, the contract is sent to a nearby fax machine.

Another popular example where channel switching might be used is to switch from a voice interface to a data interface. A field technician might start a session with a voice interface, capturing information on a job just performed. Then the session would have to switch to a data device to allow the user to upload a signature.

One example where channel switching enables workers to move from one network to another is the case where a mobile professional uses GPRS while away from the office and 802.11b while inside the office. While the user is moving around, he is able to use the same application in both environments without logging off or rebooting. This is because the WAG detects the change in networks and adapts to the different characteristics.

Session Management

The Web paradigm is based on independent exchanges of data between a client and a server. Nothing is tracked between subsequent exchanges. Using *cookies*, a session can be established. A cookie contains information on the session and is passed back and forth between the client and the Web server.

When smaller devices are being used over low-bandwidth connections, it may not be feasible for standard cookies to be used. Instead the WAG may have to hold the cookie on behalf of the device. An abbreviated cookie is passed between the device and the WAG to identify the session. The cookie held by the WAG contains the full information on session state.

There are other considerations that need to be taken into account to manage sessions over a wireless connection. Since the medium is inherently unstable, the wireless application gateway has to allow for sessions to be paused and resumed. However, a session cannot be paused indefinitely. The WAG must terminate a session after some configurable amount of time has elapsed.

Bandwidth Detection

The WAG may try to determine the bandwidth of a connection so that other parts of the platform can throttle data accordingly. It may even monitor the bandwidth during the session. The WAG should at least have knowledge of the wireless data service being used. The platform may act differently according to the characteristics of the data service. For example, it might reduce the complexity of graphical output if the network is relatively slow.

Location

Location-based services may be enabled by the WAG. Functions might be included to query a network for the coordinates of a user. As discussed in Chapter 6, there are several ways in which a network might determine the location of a handset.

Alternatively, the WAG may determine the user's position without the network's help. If a GPS receiver is attached to the portable device, software on the device might upload coordinates to the WAG. GPS can determine location to a high degree of accuracy. However, it does not work inside buildings and it is expensive.

Regardless of how the wireless application gateway obtains coordinates, it can either offer a set of location-based services as part of the platform, or make the coordinates available to applications that run on the platform. Such services and applications might include providing optimized driving directions to a field worker, listing nearby restaurants and hotels, or tracking the whereabouts of company vehicles.

Proxy Services

The WAG may serve as a proxy for large data objects that are passed around during Web sessions. I mentioned how this might be done with cookies. It might also have to be done for URLs. For example, the client may use abbreviated URLs, with the WAG holding the full-sized URLs on behalf of the client.

The WAG may offload some of the processing that would normally occur on the device. Complex computation might occur on the WAG, with the result being passed back to the device. This is especially needed when the device being used is a cell phone.

Synchronization

Wireless technology will never be as fast and as stable as fixed-line connections. Even though we will certainly see great improvements in wireless services in the near future, we will see even greater improvements in fixed-line services. For this reason, it will always be desirable to have a fixed-line channel to the portable computing device from time to time.

As it stands today, not only is it desirable to have fixed-line synchronization capability, it is downright necessary. The thick-client model absolutely requires synchronization; and synchronization is also required for all but the thinnest clients that have no on-device memory whatsoever.

Synchronization of enterprise application data usually requires knowledge of the business objects. You cannot just synchronize at a database level. The synchronization process must take into account the semantics behind the data.

The WAG must employ some mechanism for dealing with conflicts. If two mobile professionals update the same data, whose update is kept? The same question can be asked for the case where somebody updates the data on the enterprise side and somebody else updates the same data on a mobile device.

The people operating the wireless platform will have to understand the policy for dealing with conflict. There should be some mechanism for manual override and *compensation* (an "undo" of a previously committed transaction) or *rollback* (an "undo" of a currently open, noncommitted transaction).

Computing Platform

The WAG is supported by an underlying computing platform. This computing platform provides the robustness needed for business-critical software systems, such as those that deliver critical information to your mobile workforce.

Load Balancing

If you intend to mobilize a large workforce, you will need a WAG that operates in a clustered configuration. The load of incoming requests will have to be distributed among those computers. The best way for a WAG vendor to accomplish a load-balancing architecture is to base the WAG on an application server that runs in a cluster.

Load balancing may or may not involve even distribution of the load. Some of the computers may have different capabilities—or some may be performing tasks other than handling requests. The load should be distributed in a way that maximizes system throughput (the amount of time it takes to handle one request) and capacity (the number of requests that can be handled simultaneously).

High Availability

High availability requires redundant systems. When one system goes down, the other one takes over. Such a system costs at least twice as much as a nonredundant system. High availability systems are also more complicated to develop and operate. You should carefully think through how much downtime you can put up with, and get a system that guarantees that and not much more.

Transaction Integrity

In many cases, mobile applications will tie into back-end systems and perform complex transactions that take several steps to complete. If some component of the system goes down in the middle of such a transaction, the data might be left in an unusable state.

The WAG should offer services for backing out of incomplete transactions. If it does not, somebody has to take care of this task. Otherwise, you run the risk of leaving some of your critical data in a state that is unusable to your enterprise applications.

The mobile enterprise is very much dependent on wireless networks, where sessions are inherently unstable. The risk of crashing in the middle of a transaction is much higher than it is in the case where a session is run over a fixed-line network. This makes features for guaranteeing transaction integrity all the more important.

Single Sign-On

Many of the enterprise applications that will be used for mobile applications require a user sign on. It would be very annoying for the mobile professional to have to log on to each of these systems individually. Most WAGs offer a single sign-on capability where the user signs on to the WAG and the WAG signs on to the enterprise applications on behalf of the user.

This capability can also be coupled with resource pooling of EAI interfaces to optimize performance and minimize resource demands associated with large wireless user communities. Rather than having an interface connection to a back-end application for each wireless user, each connection can be shared by several users. In this way, large numbers of simultaneous wireless users can be supported using fewer back-end resources.

Platform Management

A robust computing platform should include management functions. For example, the platform should monitor the performance of the whole system and alert system operators to any problems. Errors should be logged in a way that helps operators troubleshoot problems. Mechanisms should be provided to shut the WAG down gracefully and to restart it.

Legacy Integration

Wireless application gateways have to provide a way to interface with enterprise applications, such as enterprise resource planning (ERP), customer relationship management (CRM), supply chain management (SCM), knowledge management (KM), and email systems. Information must be obtained from these applications, and there must be a way to post updates back to them.

Enterprise Application Integration

Enterprise application integration (EAI) can be accomplished in several ways. First of all, most application vendors provide an API that can be used to interface with their applications. The WAG would use the API to get information and to post updates.

There are also many third-party vendors that sell prepackaged connectors to enterprise applications. This software is usually integrated with messaging middleware. The middleware provides a *messaging bus*, over which applications can request data from one another and send data to each other.

Enterprise applications may also provide XML output. Knowing the XML schema for the particular application, the WAG can obtain data through this interface. There is a lot of work going on now to standardize the ways in which applications use XML to exchange data.

Another approach is to simply pick out fields from the Web interface of an enterprise application. The WAG could just use transcoding to take some of the fields off Web pages and format them for mobile devices. This is not a good way to operate in the long run. First of all, it forces the mobile user to follow the same application flow as would be presented through the Web interface. This usually does not make sense in the context of the business processes of a mobile worker. Second, this approach inherits all the problems of transcoding. It is not scalable, and managing application changes is complex.

Some WAGs will interface directly with a database management system. This is usually a bad idea, since it is usually not sufficient just to know the database layout. It is more often necessary to understand the semantics behind the data. Without knowing how the different fields in different parts of the database are used by the application, you run the risk of making updates that render the data useless. For this reason, it is far better to interface with business applications that work on a semantic level.

Email Connectivity

There are two major email systems that a given WAG is likely to interface with. These are Microsoft Exchange and IBM Lotus Domino. These email backbones offer APIs that the WAG uses to pick up messages to deliver to the device. Using the notification functionality, a wireless application gateway may push messages to the device as they arrive in the user's mailbox.

Some wireless platforms, such as the RIM Mail Redirector, push a portion of each message to the device. If the user wants to view more, the device then fetches another chunk of the message.

The wireless application gateway should also offer a way of synchronizing email. This should present intuitive behavior to the user. For example, if the user deletes a message on the portable device, the synchronization process should cause the message to be deleted on the enterprise side.

Attachments present certain problems. Either the attachment is left on the server and not sent to the device at all, or the attachment is sent to the device in a format that the WAG knows the particular device is capable of handling. Either way, the user might be surprised by the way attachments are handled. It is probably best just to wait to read the attachment once back on a full-sized computer.

Email systems also provide personal information management (PIM), which includes address books and calendar functionality. These useful features should also be provided on the handheld device through the service of the wireless application gateway.

APPLICATION DEVELOPMENT

Wireless application gateways typically offer a set of tools to enable development of mobile applications. Together these tools form a development environment that usually includes a graphical user interface to make it easy to design the high-level logic of the application. Other tasks facilitated by these platforms are the definition of device capabilities and integration with legacy applications. A device emulator is usually provided so that developers can see how their application looks when run on different devices.

Given two J2EE-based WAGs, it should be possible to develop an application on one WAG and run it on the other, without having to make too many modifications.

SUMMARY

Wireless application gateways are the centerpiece of the mobile enterprise. Different vendors have implemented WAGs in different ways. Most are based on J2EE and use XML technology as a way to exchange data independently of presentation format.

Regardless of how they are implemented they all have roughly the same set of functions to perform. You should take a look at the possible functions and pick out the ones you need. This will help you choose a WAG for your enterprise.

At a minimum, WAGs should perform legacy integration, content transformation, and synchronization. These are the basic functions needed to provide data to the mobile workforce on portable computing devices.

Enterprise Applications

Portable computing devices provide the mobile worker with an important tool for viewing and updating information. Wireless networks allow us to transmit data to those mobile devices. Wireless application gateways manage the interface between wireless networks and back-end applications. These three classes of technology provide a channel between the enterprise and the mobile worker. In doing so, they take us half way to the magic of friction-free sales and service.

The next challenge is figuring out what information you want to make available to your mobile workers and how you get at that information. How effectively you do this will make the difference between a workforce that is *out*standing in the field and one that is *out* standing in the field.

It is important to understand enterprise applications and how they can be used to provide your mobile workers with critical information in a timely manner. Let's start out by taking a look at how business software has evolved, paying special attention to the trends that enable enterprise applications to reach out and help the mobile workforce.

THE EVOLUTION OF BUSINESS APPLICATIONS

By the 1960s, most large companies were using computers. To get anything out of them, a select set of employees had to be trained in programming these machines. Nobody had a computer science degree back then. The people trained to do the programming had a variety of backgrounds. Many were educated in finance, accounting, or mathematics. They usually had an in-depth understanding of some of the business processes of their company.

As the processing and storage capabilities of computers increased, so did the level of abstraction at which the computer programmer could work. Higher level programming languages became possible, programming tools were developed, and commonly needed tasks were packaged for reuse by other programmers. All these things allowed the computer programmer to spend more time modeling complex business processes and getting the computer to move away from pure number crunching to perform tasks for just about everybody in the enterprise.

Needless to say, software magic has come a long way in the last 40 years. Over this time span we can pick out three interesting trends to examine:

- *Business process automation.* By understanding which business processes got automated, and when they were automated, we can get an idea about which processes might be automated next.

- *Software development, packaging, and integration.* Our mobile workers will need access to a variety of sources of information. We need to understand how well the back-end applications are integrated and what tools are at our disposal to do any additional integration that might be necessary to help mobile workers. Taking a look at the trends that have led us to the level of integration experienced by most enterprises today will help us in this regard.

- *Presentation of application output.* Traditionally application developers have designed their software with a particular user interface in mind. This influences the behavior of the application. Examining trends in how applications output information to users will help us see where these applications might take us in the future.

By taking a look at these developments we can get a better understanding of how enterprise applications have come to their current state, and we will see the manner in which they are heading toward mobility in the very near future.

Business Process Automation

In the beginning computers were very difficult to program. High-level programming languages were nonexistent, there were almost no tools to help the programmer, there was very little memory to play around with, and few people were trained in programming. However, companies made big investments in computers because they were seen as a way of improving those business processes that were most prone to human error. People are just not made for number crunching—computers are.

The first business applications performed tasks such as payroll, general ledger, accounts receivable, accounts payable, and fixed assets. This was quite natural. It did not take a complicated program to get the computer to do these things, and these were the tasks humans did poorly. What a relief it must have been to know that payroll would be done the same way every pay period! Once this process was automated, the people who used to perform the tedious task could be put on something more interesting.

Then around the 1970s, many businesses started using computers to perform human resources (HR) tasks. Computers could store databases of information on employees and produce reports as needed. This information was previously stored on paper and filed away in large rooms.

By the 1980s most of the so-called back-office processes had been automated. Business applications performed invoicing, order management, finance, accounting, human resources, and loan processing.

One interesting set of applications that sprung up during this time were *expert systems*, which were fed a lot of information on a given topic. These systems would cross-reference various information, and attempt to draw inferences from what was taken in. Big efforts were also made in the areas of Artificial Intelligence (AI) and Natural Language Processing (NLP) during this time. The interesting thing here is that there was an attempt to use computers to make sense of large quantities of information. This represented a move away from pure number crunching.

In the 1990s applications were developed to automate the so-called front-office tasks. Software was put to use to perform market analysis, sales funnel tracking, and sales forecasting. Customer relationship management (CRM) software suites provided an integrated set of applications to perform these kinds of tasks.

Also during the 1990s collaborative applications became popular. These were applications that are distributed among several companies in partnership to automate intercompany processes such as supply chain management (SCM). Corporate email systems also became widespread in the 1990s.

Now in the 2000s we will see a trend toward automation of business processes of employees who spend a lot of time at the customer site. These employees will have access to the enterprise applications no matter where they are. You can count on a new suite of applications that will be specifically tailored to improving the efficiency of these employees.

Box 8–1 summarizes the trend in business process automation. This trend has taken us from the back office to the front office—and now it looks like it will take us to automation of activities at the customer office. We might call the suites of applications that do this *customer-office applications*.

Box 8–1   The Trend in Business Process Automation

The trend in business processes automation has progressed in this order:

1. **Back-office processes** were the first to get automated. This is where the biggest bang for the buck could be achieved with relatively simple programming and a lot of number crunching.
2. **Front-office processes** were automated next. These tasks help out with sales and service activities, but do little to nothing to help the salesperson or service worker who is actually with the customer.
3. **Customer-office processes** are the next set of processes that will be automated. This is the work that has to be performed in the presence of the customer at his or her office.

Software Development, Packaging, and Integration

In the 1960s, there was no prepackaged software. Companies either developed the systems themselves or they outsourced the software work to a computer-consulting firm, such as Electronic Data Systems (EDS). Either way, software was custom built for each individual company.

In the 1970s, many companies sprung up to provide prepackaged software. In one case, a group of people left IBM Germany to start a company called SAP. The first area of focus of SAP was in developing human resource (HR) applications. As we shall see later in this chapter, and in Chapter 12, SAP is now an important company for the mobile enterprise.

By the 1980s, most companies were running a variety of stand-alone applications, each of which performed a different set of functions. For example, the financial applications were separate from the distribution applications. But frequently these two applications needed the same data. Up until that time the same data had to be entered more than once, or some elaborate schemes had to be used to transfer data from one application to another in batch mode. One problem with batch processing was the delay in getting data from one system to the other.

For this reason, the *ordre-du-jour* became integrated suites of enterprise applications that would work off the same data. The first scheme for doing this was called enterprise resource planning (ERP). The idea was to have all of the back-office applications running off the same database. In this way the different departments in a company would no longer have their own versions of the same information.

Different companies produced ERP suites. Some were great at one set of back-office functions, but not so good in another area. Also other integrated application suites became available to perform other tasks. Customer relationship management (CRM) performed front-office tasks. Supply chain management (SCM) performed supply chain tasks, interfacing with supply chain partners.

To integrate the different application suites it became necessary to allow software from different vendors to exchange information in real time. Several ways of accomplishing this have evolved, including the following:

- *Application-programming interfaces (APIs)* provide third-party software developers with an interface to enterprise applications. By using an API provided by the enterprise application vendor, the third-party developer can write an application to retrieve and update the business objects managed by the enterprise application.

- *Object request brokers (ORBs)* provide a run-time model whereby *objects* can be exported by one application and used by others. An object is a set of data and the operations on that data. One hopes that the object corresponds to some self-contained abstraction, such as *employee*, *invoice*, or *sales funnel*.

- *Message-oriented middleware (MoM)* is software that sits between two or more applications, allowing them to pass messages between one another. Messages might be sent from one application to another or from one application to several others.

The methods and tools used for this kind of integration are now commonly referred to as enterprise application integration (EAI). We discuss this further in a section below.

Box 8–2 summarizes the trend in software development, packaging, and integration.

Box 8–2 The Trend in Software Development, Packaging, and Integration

The trend in software development, packaging, and integration has progressed in this order:

1. **Customized software** was the only choice in the beginning. If businesses wanted the computer to do something for them, they had to either develop the software themselves or outsource the development. In either case, the resulting software was unique.

2. **Prepackaged applications that stand alone** were the next evolutionary step. These were applications that could be bought off the shelf. However, each application performed a specific set of tasks and it ran off its own version of company data.

3. **Integrated application suites** was a step forward in that a set of applications could be delivered to help a company in a variety of business activities. These applications shared data.

4. **Standard middleware for interfacing applications of different vendors** is now being used to allow different business applications to share data and work together to automate complex tasks.

Presentation of Application Output

In the early days, output from just about any computer application was in the form of a huge printout on ugly computer paper. This was not at all interactive. Programs had to run in batch mode, crunching lots of numbers for a long period of time and spitting out all the answers at the end.

Then "dumb" terminals became the way of interfacing with a computer. These were terminals that had almost no processing power themselves, but they provided a text-based interface to allow people to interact with computer applications.

By the late 1980s, the economics of computing were such that a pretty sophisticated computer could be put on the desks of most employees. Local area networks (LANs) allowed these workstations to communicate with one another. However, it was still important to consolidate business applications—and especially the business data these applications manipulated. Therefore, applications that concerned several people had to be run on some central computer. Care had to be taken to ensure the integrity of the data as large numbers of users read and write that data. The paradigm that sprung out of this is called client/server. ERP was the first application suite that made big use of the client/server model.

Then in the mid- to late-1990s Internet access was open to just about anybody. Virtually every medium to large company set up a corporate *intranet* during this time. Virtually every company had a website that could be accessed by the outside world, and could be used to advertise products, sell products, or generally to provide information.

Most software vendors that survived this period did so in part because they made their important applications accessible from a Web browser. This is true of all of the vendors of large enterprise application suites—that is, those software vendors we will discuss in this book.

In case you have not noticed, let me tell you that the world just does not sit still anymore. We are in the midst of another major change in the way people use computer applications. People are starting to carry around small computers that have some way of connecting to the rest of the electronic world.

This may be through desktop synchronization for the time being, but increasingly people will connect through wireless networks.

This brings about some major changes in how application output is presented and in the actual behavior of applications. Up until the Internet revolution it could usually be assumed that applications were being used on the company premises. This lends itself to automation of back-office business processes, such as finance, accounting, order management, and human resource management. With the Internet, it became much easier for mobile professionals to access company applications from a hotel room. This allowed salespeople to prepare for the next day's meetings, or it allowed them to write a report on what they did that same day. Such usage cries out for the automation of front-office business processes, such as sales funnel management or opportunity management.

Now with people holding computers in their hand as they are talking to the customer, we can expect the automation of a new set of business processes. These are the processes that take place at the customer office.

Box 8–3 summarizes the trend in application presentation. This trend takes us from introversion to extraversion. That is, how an application can be used has driven decisions as to what applications are to be used for. When applications could only be used on the company premises, the business processes that were automated were those tasks one performs while on the company premises. When the Internet allowed some remote access to business applications, more externally oriented business processes were automated. Now technology puts you right in front of your customer. You can now automate the activities of customer-facing employees.

Box 8–3 Trend in Presentation of Application Output

Presentation of application output has evolved through the following steps:
1. **Printouts** provided the first medium over which computers could give people answers. Very little interaction was possible.
2. **Dumb terminals** were an improvement in that applications could be more interactive.
3. **Client/server** configurations were such that users had an actual computer on their desk. That computer communicated with a server, which stored shared data and ran shared applications. The client computer could perform some of the processing that was specific to the individual user.
4. **Internet/Web browser** allows access to company applications over an Internet or intranet. The application assumes very little about the computer being used on the client side. The Web browser provides a common environment for the application to interface with the user.

5. **Mobile devices** will now be a commonly used tool for interfacing with enterprise applications. Applications will take into account that the user may be away from company premises. Presentation of the output is complicated by the small size of these devices, and by the large variation in the current generation of mobile devices.

All Roads Lead to the Customer Office

If we take the three trends together we can see how more and more sophisticated business processes are being automated, how the level of integration of different applications is increasing, and how we are moving toward making application output available to the mobile worker on a small handheld device.

Another way of looking at it is shown in Figure 8–1 where we see the trend from inward focused use of software to that which is more outward focused. The effect on the balance sheet moves from one being strictly cost cutting to one that is both cost cutting and revenue generating. The trends move from *back-office* applications to *front-office* applications. Then they take us to the point where we are now: *customer-office*. After all, that is where your employees should be spending most of their time. We need to make them more effective while they are there. And we can only do so through tight integration with the back-office and front-office applications that are already installed and running.

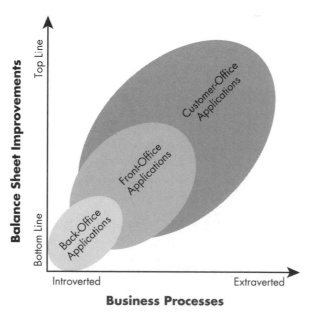

FIGURE 8–1 Front-office, back-office, and customer-office.

We might also think of Internet storefront applications as being customer-office applications. They put your company right in front of the customer in his or her own office. While these applications are extremely important, they are not the focus of this book. Here we are interested in helping *your* employees while they are at *your* customer site. After all, human interaction will not disappear from business. Customers still want to make eye contact with real people from your company. We do not want technology to depersonalize our business. In fact, we want quite the opposite. We want technology to help us get at critical information in customer-office situations. Such information contributes to personal interaction by providing your customers with seamless movement between the different channels your company provides for customer interaction. In other words, if your customer orders something on the Web, you want your salesperson who happens along 2 minutes later to be able to say something about that order.

The sizes of the ellipses shown in Figure 8–1 are not in proportion with the size of the software package or the relative costs of the solutions. What is shown is the balance sheet effect and the internal versus external focus of these classes of applications. The figure also shows how these different classes of applications are integrated. Front-office applications have to be integrated with back-office applications. Similarly, customer-office applications will have to be integrated with both front-office and back-office applications. Mobile workers need to retrieve all three kinds of information, and they will also have updates to make to those three sources.

In the next several sections we will look at the various enterprise application suites that are used in companies today. Our primary area of interest is in how these enterprise applications will help the mobile worker.

ENTERPRISE RESOURCE PLANNING (ERP)

An enterprise resource planning (ERP) package is an integrated suite of applications that address the following back-office activities:

- Finance
- Manufacturing
- Purchasing
- Distribution
- Human resources

ERP packages run off one enterprise-wide database in such a way as to minimize data duplication.

ERP was originally supposed to be off the shelf. However, in reality it could take a company three to five years to get a full ERP system up and running. This was for several reasons. First of all, most companies already had legacy applications that held a lot of critical data. Each combination of legacy applications was different, so installation and configuration of ERP was different for each company. Second, there are certain industry-specific tasks that had to be taken into account. Manufacturing companies, for example, have no need for insurance claims processing applications. The third reason for the difficulty is that every company is organized differently, so cross-company collaboration works differently from company to company. One final reason ERP systems have been difficult to get running is that accounting and tax laws are different from country to country, so the financial applications have to be adjusted accordingly.

Because of the hidden costs associated with lengthy ERP implementations, in recent years ERP has developed a bad reputation. This, and the recent paradigm shift to the Internet model, caused all of the major vendors of these packages to distance themselves from the term "ERP." In fact, none of these vendors now claims to be an ERP vendor. Their software suites are now generally called e-business suites to reflect their adoption of the Internet paradigm. In this book, I use the term ERP because that is what these suites were called when you bought them, and the intent of this book is to help you get the most out of your legacy applications. You have made the investment; here is a chance to extend the benefits through mobility.

Despite the unexpected difficulties in getting an ERP system running, enterprises have benefited from such packages in at least the following ways:

• Decreased inventories
• Faster financial closings
• Real-time information from live databases
• Intra-organization communication and collaboration

ERP systems provide functions in the areas of finance, manufacturing, purchasing, distribution, and human resources. While these are back-office activities, some of the modules are useful for customer-office business processes. The kinds of functions that might be offered by your ERP system, and that might be useful for customer-office activities, are:

• *Pricing*: to allow a salesperson to quote prices while at the customer site.
• *Order entry*: to allow a salesperson to enter an order while at the customer site.

- *Order management*: to allow a salesperson to check on the status of an order while at the customer site.

- *Parts ordering*: to allow a field engineer to order parts while at the customer site.

- *Inventory management*: to allow a salesperson to check on the availability of products, and to fill orders from multiple locations.

- *Timekeeping*: to allow field engineers and consultants to enter the amount of time they spent on a project.

- *Invoicing*: to allow a salesperson or a field engineer to generate an invoice for products or services.

The leading ERP vendors are SAP, Oracle, PeopleSoft, Baan, and J.D. Edwards. All of these companies are adding mobile features to their offerings.

SUPPLY CHAIN MANAGEMENT (SCM)

Supply chain management (SCM) software suites allow different companies to synchronize their activities along a supply chain. This involves collaborative planning and execution across several companies to coordinate the movement of goods from different sources, through the supply chain, and along to the final customer. By optimizing this process so that materials are only moved when needed, inventory is kept to a minimum and efficiencies are gained. Because products do not have to be fully configured until they are ordered, another benefit of SCM is that a wider variety of configurations can be offered to the final customer.

To promise a product to a customer, a salesperson has to know if the product is available. This may require some automatic check to see if the product or its components are available from a supply chain partner. It is also useful for the salesperson to be able to check on the feasibility of various product configurations. The salesperson should be able to see how profitable one configuration is versus another or how profitably a product can be delivered on one date versus another. SCM suites provide all of this functionality.

To help the mobile worker we are interested in the following SCM functions:

- *Available-to-promise (ATP)*, which scans the different supply locations—both yours and your partners'—to determine current and in-process stock.

- *Capable-to-promise (CTP)*, which checks to see if a product can be built by checking all combinations of manufacturing lines and stages.

- *Profitable-to-promise (PTP)*, which selects least-cost order fulfillment options based on predefined rules.

- *Monitor and control orders* to allow a salesperson to detect exceptions in order fulfillment.

The leading SCM vendors are i2 Technologies, SAP, Oracle, PeopleSoft, and Manugistics. These companies are all working mobility into their offerings.

CUSTOMER RELATIONSHIP MANAGEMENT (CRM)

Customer relationship management (CRM) is an integrated set of front-office applications designed to help companies understand their customers. The applications that make up a CRM suite provide functionality to help in marketing, sales, customer service, and partner relationship management. They take a company through the different elements of a customer life cycle, which can be broken down to five phases: targeting, acquisition, retention, growth, and service.

The different ways in which a company and its customers interact are referred to as channels. By recording data taken from each of the channels and integrating that data, the company can gain a 360-degree view of its customers. A lot can be learned about the efficiency of customer interaction as well. For example, a company can analyze the relative effectiveness of each of the channels in terms of cost and profitability. By collecting as much information as possible about customers, more effective marketing campaigns can be launched.

The following is a list of just a few of the benefits derived from CRM:

- Salespeople are more effective because they go into a customer visit with a better understanding of the customer.
- Management gets better visibility into the sales pipeline.
- The accuracy of sales forecasting is improved.
- Marketing campaigns are more effective because they are based on a better understanding of the customers.
- Customer loyalty and retention is improved because customers are served better.
- Missed opportunities can be identified and dealt with as appropriate.

We are particularly interested in the parts of CRM dealing with sales, service, and marketing activities. The sales and services applications will help mobile professionals. The marketing functions will be enhanced by the extra data entered by mobile professionals.

The CRM functions that should be made available to the mobile workforce are:

- *Opportunity management*: to view and update the list of sales opportunities in the pipeline. Details of each opportunity include the amount of the expected purchase, the probability of winning the deal, the current stage of the sales cycle, and the expected close date.

- *Contact management*: to allow sales and service workers to track and profile customer contacts.

- *Activity management*: to help sales and service people organize complex tasks and schedules and assign actions to other people on the team.

- *Quote and order generation*: to allow salespeople to quote prices and take orders. This might include the ability to provide quotes on complex configurations.

- *List management*: to identify and target deals ready to close in the current month.

- *Lead management*: to capture leads from various channels and to define business rules to rate and qualify the leads.

- *Customer information*: to allow salespeople to review customer information, including the products that are installed, outstanding service requests, and payment history.

- *Expense reporting*: to allow mobile professionals to enter travel expenses as they are incurred.

The CRM functions made available to sales and service professionals should generally allow both viewing and updating. Unless your customer-facing employees are entering data, you are losing out on an important source of information about your customers. If you equip your sales and service people with the tools needed to enter updates about what they learn during their customer interactions, you can dramatically enhance the quality of your CRM data. This benefits other parts of the company, including the marketing department.

Leading vendors of CRM software are Siebel, SAP, Oracle, PeopleSoft, and E.piphany. All of these vendors offer tools to help in integration with ERP and other applications. Each of these vendors provides mobile modules to put CRM in the hands of the mobile professional.

ENTERPRISE APPLICATION INTEGRATION (EAI)

Enterprise application integration (EAI) is a catchall term that refers to the integration of business processes and applications across organizations. This may be organizations within the same company when back-office and front-office business processes are being integrated. It may also be organizations from different companies, when, for example, supply chain integration is involved. In either case, a set of technologies, methodologies, and tools are required to perform the task.

Do you remember the dream of integrated application suites that brought about ERP systems in the 1980s? Many of our problems were resolved through this shift in the way business applications were integrated. However, the issues of integration still exist at a different level. Now we are faced with integrating business processes. Even when this involves the integration of software applications from the same vendor, it can be a complicated task. The problem is that the different business processes may not lend themselves to natural integration points. For example, the credit checking process may not be easily integrated with some supply chain activities. However, where these operations involve the same company, certain data on that other company needs to be shared between the two separate business applications.

Despite vendor claims of being able to deliver an 80% off-the-shelf EAI package, the reality is that at best about 30% of an EAI effort is indeed off the shelf. The rest must be customized to your business. The fact is, your business processes, your choice of legacy applications, and your integration points are unique. There are also choices in the model of integration. For example, integration can be through a nightly batch process, it could be triggered by an event (such as an update to a shared business object), or it could occur on a real-time, as-needed basis. The choice you make in how you integrate your applications will also determine the nature and level of difficulty of your next integration exercise.

Some of the tools that help in EAI are application programming interfaces (APIs), object request brokers (ORBs), and messaging-oriented middleware (MoM). Some level of standardization can be achieved through the use of extensible markup language (XML). As we saw in Chapter 7, XML is foundation technology allowing data to be exchanged as well as *data* on the data. That is, a description of what the data represents is sent along with the data. This is a big step forward, but there still has to be agreement on parameters between applications exchanging data.

One of the key things to remember about EAI is that you want to isolate changes. For example, as you update your ERP systems, you do not want to have to change the integration points, and you certainly do not want to have to change your CRM system. This is something to keep in mind when making choices about how EAI is implemented.

In mobilizing your enterprise you will be automating a new set of business processes—customer-office processes. This will require integration with existing front-office and back-office business processes and applications. For this reason, EAI will be a critical aspect of your activity.

It may be the case that you have already integrated your CRM system to the appropriate back-office systems. In this case, you may only need to access CRM modules to get everything you need for your mobile workforce. Congratulations on having done your homework early! You will see the payoff when you start automating your customer-office tasks.

KNOWLEDGE MANAGEMENT (KM)

In order to manage large quantities of information—and to make some sense of that information—a class of systems called knowledge management (KM) has been developed. Knowledge management (KM) is an umbrella term referring to various systems that address the following problems:

* *Information silos* result when different people and organizations in a company do not share knowledge. Most of the time the problem is that there simply are no easy ways to share what you know. In other words, when it is difficult or impossible to share information, information will not be shared. If, on the other hand, tools exist to allow employees to easily submit their learnings to a repository or easily retrieve the learnings of other people, sharing will occur. KM systems generally provide these tools.

* *Information overload* results when too much information is thrown at employees, when information is poorly cataloged, or when the quality of the information is questionable. By cataloging corporate knowledge and offering methods for filtering that knowledge, KM systems address this problem.

* *Loss of corporate memory* occurs when people leave the company and take their brains with them. The problem again is that when there is no easy way to capture knowledge, that knowledge does not get captured. Corporate memory can be retained to some extent through the use of KM systems.

Elements of KM Systems

There are several ways of solving these problems; and indeed, KM is something of an umbrella term for a variety of solutions. One type of KM system is the enterprise information portal (EIP). Through a Web interface users can enter new information, administer the information store, and retrieve information. Alternatively, a knowledge management system might be a standalone document management (DM) system, wherein all information is stored in the form of a document. KM systems may also make up a part of other enterprise application suites. For example, many CRM vendors provide business intelligence (BI) modules that allow companies to analyze information taken in and stored in the CRM system.

Typically a knowledge management system will consist of the following elements:

- *Capture mechanisms* to take knowledge in. This could be an active process where the author of a document checks a new version of his or her document into the system. Alternatively, this could be a passive process whereby the system *profiles* some area of interest and stores what it learns. A pertinent example of this would be the system that recognizes which products are frequently purchased together. This connection is useful to a salesperson, because it might help him or her propose the sale of one product given an interest in the other. This *cross-sale* proposition is based on a *learned* correlation of two or more products.

- *Cataloging features* to group information in a sensible manner. In many cases a subject-specific *taxonomy* is developed. This allows different pieces of information to be related according to the vocabulary of that particular subject.

- *Storage* of the knowledge in a central repository, so that each bit of information is stored only once. Version control features must also be in place, as documents and other representations of information evolve as more is learned.

- *Access control* to make sure only those users with correct permissions can access corporate knowledge. Certain employees have rights to update certain information; others can only view it.

- *Retrieval features* to make it easy for those seeking knowledge to easily find it and view it, or listen to it, whichever the case may be. Retrieval features include search engines and some capacity to present the results in an appropriate format.

Choosing the Right Scope for KM

One of the complications in knowledge management is that information is communicated and stored in different forms—e.g., as a document, as a picture, as an audio file, or as a video. Having the information in all of these different formats makes capturing, cataloging, and retrieval more difficult. A system cannot pick information out of a picture in the same way it would pick information out of a document.

Another complication lies in how and where the information is stored. You do not want to ignore information that is already stored somewhere, or information that is *owned* by a different system. For example, the natural home of much corporate knowledge is in ERP, CRM, email, and news feeds. Therefore, a good KM system must have a way of indexing links to that other information. Furthermore, if you really get down to it, your best source of information is the human beings in your company. A comprehensive KM system should include a mechanism for tracking and cataloging expertise within the company.

A third area of complexity is in ensuring the quality of information. Consider the problem of verifying subject matter expertise. If an employee claims to be an expert in a subject matter, should the system just believe him or her? Probably not. For this reason, some KM systems attempt to judge expertise through a rating system.

These three problems go away if you minimize the scope of your KM system. That is, if you expect your KM system to collect and store *all* of the information that your enterprise possesses, the result will be a big flop. If, on the other hand, you limit your KM system to some subject area or some closed user group, you can probably get a lot out of it. For example, a good knowledge management system can enhance the productivity of your service engineers, cataloging problem-solving information and best practices. The system could also track employee expertise, so that for a given subject area it is known that a certain set of employees are experts.

If you equip your service engineers with a smart phone (the phone/PDA combination discussed in Chapter 5), you could provide a click-to-dial feature whereby the engineer indicates the nature of a problem. The KM system returns a list of people who have solved similar problems in the past. If the engineer clicks on one of them, the smart phone initiates a phone call to that person. Alternatively, instant messaging (IM) or email might be used in a similar manner. After all, if the person you need to contact is so good at fixing problems, he or she is probably too busy working on some problem to be able to answer your phone call. A fancier version of the same solution would include proximity and busy indicators next to each expert in the list. These would indicate where each expert is (or if they are close to you) and whether or not they are busy at the current time.

Workflow

Workflow is usually associated with knowledge management, and especially document management, because documents are frequently passed through different phases. For example, an insurance claims document has to undergo an initial validity check. From that point, it might be passed to a claims processor who modifies the document or adds an attachment, then it might go to the claims adjuster, and so on.

Workflow may also be important for the mobile worker in cases where the mobile worker is performing a task that is part of a larger process. A good example of this is the utility meter reader who updates the meter count and causes a document to be passed to the next stage of processing—billing. It is worthwhile thinking about how workflow is relevant to your business, and how it would be applied to your mobile workforce.

KM for the Mobile Enterprise

Knowledge management is an essential element of the mobile enterprise. Salespeople, service workers, consultants, and traveling employees all need to access corporate *knowledge*. Specifically, the functions of KM that we want to make available to mobile workers are:

- *Document retrieval*: to allow the mobile worker to look up and view sales or technical documents.
- *Collaboration*: to allow mobile workers to share information on problem solving.
- *Expertise tracking*: to allow the mobile worker to find and access company experts in a timely manner.
- *Learning*: to allow mobile workers to access training tools while sitting around an airport or in a hotel room.
- *Knowledge capture*: to provide mobile workers with an easy way to input new knowledge, so that the rest of the company can learn from the experiences of the mobile worker.

I want to put special emphasis on this last point. Remember that your mobile workers are the ones who know the outside world best. If you are not learning from them, you are probably making decisions based on internally generated myths. For this reason, it is essential that customer-facing employees possess tools that allow them to feed what they learn back to the rest of the company. Since these individuals may not see any immediate value in sharing this information, it is essential that these tools be easy—and maybe even fun—to use. Do not wrap a clumsy user interface around a task that few people want to perform anyway.

EMAIL

No mobile professional should be without email access. Over the last 10 years email has become an essential business tool. The mobile worker should not be deprived of such a powerful tool just because he or she is moving about trying to drum up business for the company.

All of the leading vendors of email systems—Microsoft, IBM, and Openwave—have worked mobility into their offerings. Furthermore, third-party vendors have developed software to extract email from different systems and present it on the mobile device. In addition, there are some email systems that have been specifically designed for mobility. For example, Research In Motion (RIM) has developed an email system for use with their BlackBerry pager. Several network operators offer email services. Many of these services are made possible through software from the company Openwave.

It is worth noting that there are a few aspects of the mobile environment that make the email experience different from that which you would get while at the desktop. Some of those differences are:

- *Network presence* can be detected so the sender can know whether or not the recipient has his or her device turned on. It can usually be assumed that if the small device is turned on, it is also within reach of the user.

- *Instant messaging (IM)* can make use of the network presence information. We may also see some use of location information so that one can send an instant message to a colleague known to be in the vicinity.

- *Unified messaging (UM)* is done a little differently. On the one hand, your data device may also be a telephone. In this case, voice mail and email can be provided on the same device. On the other hand, it is more difficult to send different kinds of media over a wireless network and present it on a small device.

- *Attachments* may not be workable on a small mobile device. This is because the small device usually does not have the same presentation capabilities as a desktop system.

Personal Information Management (PIM)

In addition to messaging, the leading email systems offer personal information management (PIM), which allows users to store contact information. Contact management is also provided through CRM, but you may want to keep the CRM contacts separate from other contacts. For example, the CRM system could be used to track customer contacts; whereas, the PIM functions through the email system could be used to track company contacts.

Collaboration

Email systems also offer tools to allow collaborative work. This could be in the form of shared databases relating to a common subject matter, or it could be in the form of newsgroups. These functions can help your mobile worker find information on a given subject. It is also useful to allow your mobile workers to feed new information into these work groups.

Remember, the mobile worker is an important source of information. Unfortunately, up until now, technology has not allowed mobile workers to easily submit their learnings to the rest of the company. Now is the time to take advantage of new technology to make this possible.

ADDITIONAL APPLICATIONS

Several other applications should be considered for the mobile worker. We discuss some of them here.

Time and Expense

Mobile workers usually have to fill out expense reports and they might also have to account for their time. Nothing is more annoying to a mobile professional than having to go into the office after a long trip to fill out an expense report. Let them do it while they are on the road waiting for an airplane or sitting in a hotel.

Applications enabling input of this information may be part of your ERP and/or CRM systems. It may also be a separate application. In any case, you should consider equipping your workers with software that allows them to do their expense reports and account for their time while on the road.

News

News applications can allow personalized news feeds. Headlines, and maybe even entire articles, pertaining to an area of interest can be downloaded to the mobile device at the time of synchronization (discussed below). In addition, your mobile solution might also include functionality to allow employees to fetch more details on a particular subject in real time using wireless data services.

News is usually very popular among mobile professionals. Reading through interesting articles can ease the boredom of business travel. In many cases, the information contributes to your company's intellectual capital, and is therefore of value to the company.

Alerts

Alert engines can be used by the enterprise to notify mobile professionals of events they need to know about. These engines can usually be configured per employee so that each person indicates what he or she needs to be alerted to. For example, an executive might need to be notified of a deal closing, of specific customer issues, or of the crossing of some financial threshold.

It is usually possible to configure the system to try contacting the employee through different means depending on the day of the week, the time of day, and so on. Most systems will also allow configurations so that one means is tried first and then other kinds of notifications are sent. For example, in the afternoon, the desktop client might be tried first. If the alert is not acknowledged, the system will then try to send the alert to a cell phone.

DESKTOP SYNCHRONIZATION (DETACHABLE/DISCONNECTED)

Every mobile enterprise solution should include some desktop synchronization. This will help move large quantities of data to and from mobile devices. It may also be used instead of wireless data services in cases where real-time data is not needed, and where it is not cumbersome for mobile employees to perform synchronization. Desktop synchronization is also sometimes called *detachable* or *disconnected* mode. Because synchronization is best done with some knowledge of enterprise application logic, we will discuss it in this chapter.

Synchronization can be accomplished by:

- *Prefetching Web pages.* This works well when the application consists of a static set of Web pages. Of course not many applications fit this description, but one that does is a news feed. This kind of synchronization is relatively simple. Because of this, and because news is usually a popular item with mobile workers, it is recommended that you consider using this kind of synchronization to provide a mobile news feed.

- *Synchronizing a smaller, mobile version of a database with the larger database sitting behind company walls.* This works well when your mobile application really needs most of the fields and records in the database. Otherwise, the synchronization winds up downloading way too much to the mobile device. Not only does this take up more space than necessary, it may cause problems in cases where updates are made to this data on the mobile device and then synchronization occurs at a later point. By the time the synchronization is performed, somebody else may have made updates to data that you did not even want to have on your device. But because you had that data on your device, and because you are posting updates, the synchronization software may not know how to distinguish between what you changed and what you did not change. Furthermore, it may not know how to relate your changes to those of the other workers posting updates. This kind of synchronization may be provided by the vendor of the database management system (DBMS) being used.

- *Synchronizing business objects.* The difference between synchronizing business objects and synchronizing the database is that in the former case, the synchronization logic takes into account the data abstractions used by the mobile application. Therefore, the synchronization process can download only those data structures that the mobile application uses. This kind of synchronization requires knowledge of the application. For this reason, it is usually best performed through software delivered by the vendor of the enterprise application being used. Frequently, however, the customer-office applications will be composed on a wireless application gateway interfacing with several enterprise applications. In this case, the best source of synchronization logic will be the vendor of the WAG.

- *Synchronizing email and PIM.* At the time of synchronization you can download messages in your inbox to your mobile device. Likewise, you can also upload messages that you composed on your mobile device so they can be sent. This kind of synchronization has been a part of any viable email system for a while now, as this has long been required for laptop usage.

ENTERPRISE APPLICATIONS FOR THE MOBILE WORKFORCE

It is worth noting that some things, such as contact information, pricing, and customer lists, can be taken from more than one system. We should also note that there is variation in what is offered in the application suites from different vendors. Your particular set of enterprise applications will probably be unique, so you will have to take a close look at how you can get at the information you need in your unique situation.

In any case, do not understate the task of integrating your mobile solution with legacy applications. This may very well be the hardest part of mobilizing your enterprise. This is very tricky business. Some vendors will make it sound easy; usually this is an honest mistake. These vendors might be long on wireless expertise, but short on skills in the integration of legacy applications. In Chapter 11 we examine the different kinds of companies selling solutions for the mobile enterprise, and we bring out the relative strengths and weaknesses of each class of company. This will help you pick out the different angles from which each company will approach you. As is the case with any human being or group of human beings, companies are prejudiced by their own history and core competencies.

One of the easy ways of getting at data from the back-end applications is to pick out the HTML fields from application output. However, one problem with this approach is that when the HTML page layout changes, you have to make a change to the mobile front-end configuration. If, on the other hand, the back-end application produces output in xHTML or XML, change to the legacy application is more isolated. Beware though that in this latter case, initial setup may be more difficult. This is because when xHTML or XML are used, the fields needed by the mobile worker may have to be "tagged." In this case, a change will be required to the output of the legacy application.

The first generation of customer-office applications is going to consist of customized configurations of different legacy applications. Over time, however, the industry will settle down on some standard processes, and we will see prepackaged applications designed to help sales and service people as they are interfacing with customers.

In some cases you can get all the necessary functions needed for your mobile workers from your CRM system. This is especially true if you bought your CRM from the same vendor from which you bought your ERP and/or SCM systems. This can also be done through tight integration of your CRM system with the best-of-breed modules from different vendors.

SUMMARY

By following trends in the evolution of enterprise applications we can see the progression from internally focused applications to those that are focused on helping workers who are facing the customer. This new focus is made possible by the combination of portable computing devices and wireless technology. The new computing paradigm will bring on a new breed of enterprise application that automate many of the tasks employees perform while working in the offices of their customers. We might call these applications *customer-office* applications.

Customer-office applications will make use of data that is already managed by one or more existing enterprise applications. In particular, a mobile workforce will need to access some combination of the following systems: enterprise resource planning (ERP), supply chain management (SCM), customer relationship management (CRM), knowledge management (KM), and email. A good deal of integration work will be needed to get at this data and put it into the context of customer-office business processes.

We should not forget the benefits the rest of the company enjoys when the mobile workforce has real-time access to enterprise applications. Customer-facing employees have valuable information that should be shared with others in your company. If they are equipped with the tools that allow them to easily enter new information and make that information quickly available to others in the company, you will improve your knowledge base. Mobile solutions can help prevent the formation of information silos, where each salesperson keeps information to him- or herself.

Mobile Enterprise Security

We now understand the channel between the mobile worker and the enterprise. We also know how to get critical information out of enterprise applications and pass that information over the channel so that mobile professionals can make use of it. This is all very wonderful—and exactly what we need to make our mobile workforce more efficient. The scary thing is that this critical information will be transmitted over public networks to portable devices that might get lost or stolen.

As you have probably figured out, the mobile enterprise will have to address a significant number of security risks. For this reason, security is an essential topic of discussion. You will have to understand the unique set of vulnerabilities to which the mobile enterprise is exposed—and most importantly, you will have to understand the countermeasures your enterprise can put into place to minimize risk.

You should first think about what it is you are trying to protect and the kinds of threats you can expect. Given that understanding, you should look at the kinds of tools that can be used to counter those threats. It is important to take into account the constraints of the mobile environment and how those constraints affect the tools that ensure security.

SECURITY THREATS

The evolution of security techniques is something like the evolution of the arms industry. In the arms industry there is a perpetual race between those who develop swords and those who develop shields. We only need good shields when the enemy has good swords. This is true for the arms industry and it is true for computer and network security. As hacking techniques get better and vulnerability increases, countermeasures must evolve at least as fast.

Hacking techniques and the countermeasures used to prevent hacking are both enabled by processors. That is, both swords and shields improve as we see improvements in CPUs. In fact, the assumption that a given cryptographic technique is unbreakable is based on estimations of the power of the next few generations of processors. If improvements in microprocessors were to dramatically outstrip Moore's law over the next few years, all bets would be off on most of the cryptography being used today.

Similarly to the way military planners think through who the possible enemy would be and what might be their motives, we should think through who the potential intruders are and why they might want to intrude. We should also give some thought as to what it is we are trying to protect and what it is worth.

We do not generally go through life protecting ourselves from every possible danger. I personally risk my life every day by going to work. During my trip to work, it is conceivable that somebody would choose me as a random target to shoot at. However, such an event is unlikely. First of all, not many people are interested in launching such an attack, and those who do so can only get away with it a limited number of times. In the extreme case where somebody commits such a crime, once they are discovered, the legal system prevents them from doing it again ... in theory at least.

On the other hand, I do lock the doors to my house if I am the last one out. It is an easy thing to do and it is not improbable that somebody would come in and steal things—especially if they knew the doors were left unlocked.

Just as we do in everyday life, in business we should weigh the value of the asset at risk and the probability of an attack against the cost of the countermeasure. The balance will vary to some degree from one enterprise to another.

In general, when talking about computer and network security, we are talking about ensuring some combination of the things listed in Box 9–1.

Box 9–1   Five Properties Protected through Computer and Network Security

Computer and network security ensure some combination of the following:

- **Legitimate use:** that only those people or things we want using the system can be using it. We also want to make sure that even those people who are supposed to be using the system can be closed out from specific applications.
- **Confidentiality:** that we have control over who is able to read information we send out.

- **Service availability:** that nobody can bring the system down or otherwise hamper the level of service.
- **Data integrity:** that what one side sends is what the other side receives. That is, we want to make sure the data is not changed or deleted along the way.
- **Non-repudiation:** that if a user performs a transaction, it can be proven he or she has done so. That is, the user cannot repudiate having done something at a later date.

Let's now take a look at how intruders might try to compromise each of these important areas. I will focus specifically on the threats that are of concern to the mobile enterprise.

Legitimate Use

In the mobile environment you are vulnerable to illegitimate use in two big ways. Not only do you have to be concerned with unwanted access to your corporate network and the computers on that network, but you also have to prevent intruders from picking up and using the portable devices that are being carried around by your mobile professionals. In most cases these devices hold critical information.

Since your mobile professionals will be using the portable devices just about anywhere, you are more exposed to the risk of having somebody else steal your company's passwords. For example, an onlooker might see the password as an unsuspecting mobile professional is typing it in. It is also conceivable that a drunken employee calls it out as he or she is typing it in at the airport bar. Or perhaps a disgruntled employee will simply give it away. In any of these cases, once somebody else gets the password, he or she will have no problem getting into your system. As we will see later in this chapter, one way of minimizing this risk is through a two-factor authentication scheme.

You may also see the case where somebody who is a legitimate user of one part of the system tries to get into other parts of the system he or she is not supposed to access. For example, you probably do not want to have your field service people accessing the human resources (HR) applications to change somebody's salary. Likewise, you probably do not want to have sales funnels readable by everybody in the company. Authorization and access control techniques can be applied to minimize this risk.

Confidentiality

If you are transmitting company information to mobile devices you will want to make sure that much of that data cannot be viewed by anybody other than the employees for which the data was intended. Intruders could try to view sensitive company data in several ways. One way is by stealing a portable device and looking at the data on that device. Another is by simply looking over the shoulder of an employee who is viewing data on the portable device.

If your data is sent from your company to the wireless network via an Internet service provider (ISP), intruders might try to pick it up on the Internet. An intruder might work for the network operator and he or she might be able to view your data as it is routed through the wireless network. Finally, an eavesdropper might just listen in as your data is transmitted over the airwaves.

Service Availability

Intruders might try to bring your system down. These kinds of intruders might be hackers trying to show signs of intelligence, somebody who holds a grudge against your company, a foreign country trying to damage your country's economy, or they might be your competitors.

Your service can be compromised in several ways. On the portable device side, a virus could delete data, lock out legitimate users, or make the device difficult to use. If your user has an *always-on* wireless connection, malicious individuals might keep your device busy by continuously sending packets to it. Even if your device refuses what is being sent, the acts of checking the request and then refusing it require work. All of this extra work could render the device unusable.

Intruders might try to limit network connectivity. They could do so by placing a lot of calls over the same network or by swamping the network with data traffic. This might also happen in legitimate ways. For example, in the case of an extraordinary sports event, a lot of people may be placing calls at the same time. This would limit access from your mobile employees.

Your service could also be compromised on the enterprise side. Intruders could keep your servers busy by overloading them with connection requests. Even though your server refuses those connections, it takes time to do so. If too many requests come around the same time, the server could get so busy refusing those requests that it has no time to perform the tasks you need it to perform. These kinds of attacks are sometimes known as *denial-of-service* attacks.

Data Integrity

Intruders might change the data on the way from the employee to the enterprise or on the way from the enterprise to the employee. If you are sending prices from the enterprise to a salesperson, you probably do not want to allow the wrong price to get to the salesperson.

The places where the integrity of your data can be compromised are similar to the places where confidentiality can be compromised. Somebody borrowing the portable device can change data. It might also be changed as it passes through the wireless network. If it is passed from the wireless network to your corporate network through an ISP, it could be changed at the ISP as well. It could also be changed as it is transmitted over the air interface. Changing data is of course more complicated than simply viewing data. The attacker not only looks at the data, but also has to change it in a way that is consistent with the session being intercepted.

As is the case with confidentiality, the portable device brings on additional threats to data integrity. Viruses may modify or delete important company data, or an attacker might modify or delete data on a portable device while an employee steps away for a few minutes.

Non-repudiation

Not only is it important to be able to prove that somebody is who he says he is, it is also important to be able to prove that a person conducted a specific transaction. If you are a merchant, you do not want a customer to be able to deny having bought something after the fact. If the customer signed a ticket, the merchant has proof that the person was there.

Non-repudiation is probably not something you have to worry too much about from your mobile professionals. You probably do not have employees who consciously deny having performed transactions that they did indeed perform. After all, as a matter of course, you trust your employees for a whole lot more. It is unlikely that you have to worry about non-repudiation from your own employees.

On the other hand, if your mobile professionals are taking orders and having customers sign for those orders—or perform a digital equivalent of signing—non-repudiation may be something you wish to ensure in your mobile enterprise.

TOOLS AND CONCEPTS FOR COUNTERING THREATS

Box 9–2 provides a list of tools and concepts that can be applied to ensure the five properties just discussed. This is sort of an apples-and-oranges list. Some are tools and some are concepts. Some are prerequisites to others. The purpose here is to provide you with a list of things you will need to understand as you plan to mobilize your enterprise.

Box 9–2   Tools and Concepts for Security

Tools and concepts to protect the mobile enterprise:

- **Physical security**. By keeping something locked up you help ensure *legitimate use, confidentiality,* and *service availability.*
- **Cryptography**. By encoding messages in such a way that only the intended recipient or recipients can read the messages, you will ensure *confidentiality.*
- **Digital signatures**. By employing techniques that prove a user performed a transaction at a certain time, you ensure *non-repudiation.* A digital signature can also be used as an electronic *seal* on a message to ensure *data integrity.* Finally, digital signatures can be used to ensure *legitimate use.*
- **Certification**. By establishing a method for certifying people or entities, you enable some of the other security processes, such as authentication.
- **Authentication**: By employing techniques that allow a user to prove that she *is* who she claims to be, you help ensure *legitimate use.*
- **On-device data security**. By protecting the data on your portable device, you help ensure *confidentiality* and *data integrity.*
- **Virus protection**. By protecting your portable device from viruses, you help ensure *service availability* from the device side.

Let's take a closer look at the tools and concepts you will need to understand when talking to vendors.

Physical Security

As its name implies, physical security is security by denying physical access to whatever it is that is being protected. Some familiar examples of this are bank vaults, the bolted doors protecting a data center, and the security guards protecting your company site. Before we had so many computer networks, physical security was the principal method of staving off intruders. Your data sat on a computer that was in a secure building. Back-up media was also locked away. Information could be viewed only on terminals connected to the computer by cables and sitting securely on your company premises. Printouts and employees with loose lips were the biggest threat to confidentiality.

Corporate use of Internet changed all that, requiring a virtual private network (VPN) to provide a virtual perimeter. The job of the VPN is to use some combination of authentication, cryptography, and digital signatures to allow employees to work outside of the company premises and exchange data with enterprise applications as securely as if he or she *were* on the company premises. Now wireless networks and portable devices will require some further changes to the VPN. As users move about, data must take a different path through the network to get to the users. In many VPNs this causes complications in how a *tunnel* is set up from one network end-point to another.

By itself, physical security is no longer a sufficient means of securing company information. However, it still plays a role. We will still assume that most of your company's information assets sit on servers within the corporate premises. In fact, most of the countermeasures discussed below require some set of servers on the enterprise that are physically protected. That is, only the good guys are able to get close to these servers.

Your company probably has a *firewall* sitting between the outside world and those servers that are secured within the company premises. The firewall creates a virtual perimeter by controlling access from the outside in. Your company may also use a virtual private network (VPN) to allow remote workers to connect to the corporate network and operate as if he or she were sitting in the office.

Cryptography

Cryptography is the science or study of secret writing.[1] Examples of its use go as far back as Julius Caesar, who used it to pass military plans to his generals. Today, more than ever, cryptography plays a crucial role in warfare. No modern army can do without it. Radio transmission of critical information between military units must be secure.

Similarly, though not a matter of life or death, cryptography is an enabler of secure information exchange for commerce. Cryptography has been a source of confusion for many people, but viewed from a different angle, it may not be so complicated after all. Many of us became familiar with cryptography as children, exchanging secret messages with classmates. In fact, the techniques used by children illustrate many of the basic concepts. This

---

1. *Webster's Encyclopedic Unabridged Dictionary of the English Language*

being the case, let's take a simple example of a child's cryptosystem to explore some of the fundamental concepts of cryptography.

Keys

Assume two classmates, Paul and Louise, want to exchange secret messages. They hold a private meeting to agree on algorithms for encryption and decryption. In this case, we will assume the algorithm for encryption is to add a value to each letter of the message. (The original message is known as *plain text*.) To decrypt the message, the same value will be subtracted from the encrypted message. (The encrypted message is known as *cipher text*.) To simplify, Paul and Louise agree that spaces and punctuation will not be encrypted.

At the same secret meeting, Paul and Louise also agree on a *key*—the value that will be applied to the encryption and decryption algorithms. Let's assume they agree to use a key value of 6. Figure 9–1 shows how a message exchange works.

Needless to say, there are several problems with this technique. Given enough time, other children in the class can probably figure out the algorithm and the key being used. The first thing an attacker would notice is recurring words. For example, the word *you* always produces the cipher text *eua*. Upon examination of enough cipher text, the attacker could spot some of the frequently occurring words and guess their meanings. Once a few words are known, the attacker could derive the algorithm and key value.

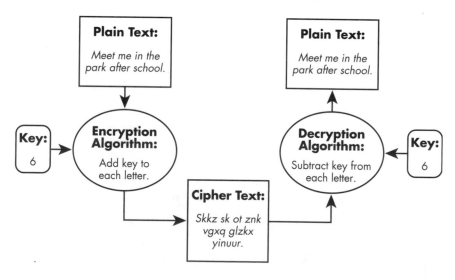

FIGURE 9–1 A child's cryptosystem.

Let's extend our example by assuming that Paul wants to exchange messages with other classmates. Furthermore, for a given exchange, he wants only the intended recipient to be able to read his message. To simplify, he will use the same algorithm with all classmates, but the secret key will be different for each exchange partner. In order to agree on a key value, he must hold a separate meeting with each partner. The process through which the two parties get together in private to agree on a key value is known as *key exchange*.

Since all classmates now know the algorithm, one with malicious intent has only to guess at different key values to decipher a message he or she is not supposed to read. In this case, there are only 26 possible key values—that is, the *key space* is only 26. It would take at most 25 guesses to arrive at the correct value. Most of Paul's classmates possess the sophistication needed to make 25 guesses in a reasonable amount of time. This means that the cryptosystem just described is very easy to crack.

The general rule is that the smaller the key space, the easier it is to apply a *brute-force* method to guess the value of the key being used in a given exchange. Think about how hard it is to guess the key when the key space is 2^{128}, which is equivalent to 3.4×10^{38}. Such a key space is achieved by using a key that is 128 bits long. It would take a tremendous amount of guesswork to crack such a cryptosystem! Certainly no school kid could do it. However, if enough computing power is applied to the problem for a long enough time, the system can indeed be cracked. Fortunately, using today's computers it would take a lot of computers working in parallel for a lot of years to guess the right key among the 3.4×10^{38} possibilities.

But let's not fool ourselves. There is no free lunch. The trade-off is that in general, the longer the key, the more computational power it takes to encrypt and decrypt messages. This fact will haunt us when we start applying cryptography to portable devices with limited computing power.

Pads

There is another way for Paul and Louise to eliminate many of the problems inherent in their simple scheme. Instead of adding the same value to each letter, they could agree on a text that would be added to each message. For example, they might agree that Lincoln's Gettysburg Address would be added to the message. Using this system, the sender would add each letter of the plain text "meet me after school" to each letter of "Four score and seven" to obtain the corresponding cipher text.

In this example, the Gettysburg Address is a special kind of key called a *pad*. The system just described is more secure than the first one. If the pad is longer than the message, there are no problems with recurring words. Note also that the key space is the number of possible pads. In fact, the only way to decipher an isolated message would be to guess from a virtually infinite number of possibilities which pad is being used.

Paul and Louise could make the system even more secure by frequently changing pads. In this way, even if somebody got a hold of a plain text message and its corresponding cipher text, they could not apply anything they learn to future or past exchanges. This is because the pad is frequently changed. Note that the agreement on which pad is to be used has to be made in private, or it has to be communicated over a secure channel.

Indeed the biggest threat to the new cryptosystem is the human factor. Neither side can reveal the pad to anybody else. Furthermore, each side must be careful not to leave any clues that would allow somebody else to guess the choice of pads.

Symmetric Keys

The cryptosystems just described use what are known as *symmetric* keys. That is, the sender and the recipient use the same algorithm and the same key (or at least the algorithms and keys of one side can be easily derived from those of the other side). Another way of putting it is that they have a *shared secret*. This means at some point in time the two sides have to exchange the key. Then each side must manage the key going forward.

There are two major problems with this. The first is that you need a secure way of exchanging the keys. The second is that if you want to exchange information with a lot of different people, and you do not want your recipients to be able to read each other's messages, you have to create and manage a lot of keys.

In cases where strangers need to exchange information over a public network, secure exchange of symmetric keys is virtually impossible. For this reason, no large-scale system for secure electronic commerce can be based on the use of symmetric keys alone.

However, for the case where you are enabling mobile services to your own employees, secure key exchange is less of a problem. In this case, the two parties—the employee and the employer—know each other. The number of potential users is also limited to a manageable number. You can in fact pass out the keys on an individual basis. After all, banks and credit card issuers do this by sending personal identification numbers (PINs) through regular mail. The banks and credit card issuers are careful to seal the PIN in an envelope in such a way as to allow the recipient to easily see when somebody has looked at it.

Data encryption standard (DES), RC5, international data encryption algorithm (IDEA), and CAST-128 are all examples of symmetric key ciphers.

Asymmetric Keys

In 1976 a revolution began when two Stanford University professors, Whitfeld Diffie and Martin Hellman, wrote a paper providing the theoretical basis for a system that works without requiring a shared secret. This system proposed different keys be used by the sender and by the recipient. One of the keys would be a *public key*; it would be available to anybody. The other key would be a *private key*; only one person would know its value. The two keys together make up a *key pair*. Since the two sides have different keys, public/private key pairs are also known as asymmetric key pairs.

To send a secret message to me, Joe Public need only obtain my public key and apply it to the encryption algorithm. Note that the public key cannot be used to decrypt the message, only the private key can do this—and only I know the value of the private key.

The reverse is also possible. A key pair can be generated such that the private key is used for encryption and the public key is used for decryption. As we see below, this is a powerful tool that enables digital signatures.

Let's illustrate the first use of asymmetric keys by extending the example of Paul and Louise. Assuming Paul wants to send a message to Louise, Louise will first have to obtain an asymmetric key pair. She will store the private key securely. Only she will know its value. She will distribute the public key to anybody wishing to send her a secret message. In this case, she will therefore send her public key to Paul. This process is shown in Figure 9–2.

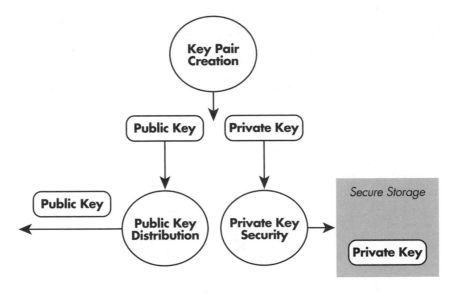

FIGURE 9–2   Creation and management of asymmetric key pairs.

Once the key pair has been created and distributed, the encryption and decryption processes occur as shown in Figure 9–3. Note that if messages are to be exchanged in both directions, that is, if Louise also wants to send a message to Paul, Paul will have to obtain his own asymmetric key pair and distribute the public key to Louise. In the end, Louise will have her own private key and Paul's public key. Likewise, Paul will have his own private key and Louise's public key.

In general, in a public key cryptosystem, each person must have one private key for all messages he or she is to receive. He or she must also obtain the public key of anybody to whom he or she is to send messages.

The system just described is an improvement on the symmetric key cryptosystems. However, there are still a few problems that have to be resolved. For example, there needs to be a scalable way of generating asymmetric key pairs. There also needs to be a way to distribute the public keys. Finally, there needs to be a way for the recipient of a public key to make sure that the public key is indeed valid. If you encrypt a message with the wrong public key, only the wrong person can decrypt the message.

Fortunately, these problems have been worked out. The infrastructure that solves these problems is known as public key infrastructure (PKI). Certification—a function of PKI—provides a mechanism by which the recipient of the public key can know that the public key is valid.

Another function that is made available through asymmetric key pairs is the authentication of an individual or an entity. If a person encrypts a value using his or her private key, the rest of the world can use the matching public

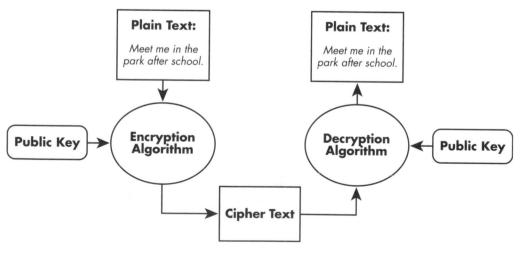

FIGURE 9–3   Encryption using asymmetric key pairs.

key to decrypt the result. Since just the unique key known only to one individual could perform the encryption, all interested parties who knew the value originally encrypted by the private keys can be sure the message was sent by that one individual. This technique is part of a challenge/response authentication system where the side performing the authentication sends a random value to the other side, which encrypts the value using a private key. Since only one individual or entity can know the private key, that person or entity must be authentic.

Examples of public-key algorithms are RSA,[2] digital signature algorithm (DSA), and DH.[3] For adequate security these algorithms require keys that are at least 1,024 bits long! However, variations on two of these algorithms limit the set of points to those that can be plotted on an elliptic curve—and in doing so, require significantly smaller key sizes for a similar level of security. These two variations are elliptic curve DSA (ECDSA) and elliptic curve DH (ECDH). Because the keys can be smaller, elliptic curve algorithms are useful for portable computing devices where memory and computing power are limited.

Secure Socket Layer (SSL) / Transport Layer Security (TLS)

A problem with asymmetric keys is that the algorithms used for encryption and decryption are computationally more intensive than those needed when symmetric keys are used. Portable devices would have trouble with this—and in fact, this is even an issue with desktop computers.

In the mid-1990s, Netscape devised a solution to this problem—and at the same time they came up with a secure communication channel that could in principal be used by a variety of applications. This was accomplished through the protocol Netscape called secure sockets layer (SSL). A distinctive feature of SSL is that it uses public key cryptography for the client to authenticate the server, and to secure a link to facilitate the secret exchange of a symmetric key. This symmetric key is called a session key because a new one is generated for each session. Once a session key is established, symmetric key encryption and decryption can be used.

SSL takes the best of both worlds. Two strangers can establish a secure link to facilitate key exchange. For the rest of the session, symmetric key cryptography can be used to cut down on the computing power needed for encryption and decryption.

---

2. Named after the developers of the algorithm: Ron Rivest, Adi Shamir, and Len Adleman.
3. Named after the developers of the algorithm: Whitfield Diffie and Martin Hellman.

Later on, the Internet engineering task force (IETF) adopted SSL and developed its successor, transport layer security (TLS). Many people use the terms SSL and TLS interchangeably. I will use the term SSL when talking about general features that apply to versions of SSL that existed before the term TLS was introduced.

SSL allows the two sides to negotiate security parameters, including the type of algorithm to be used for establishing a session key. One such algorithm is the DH algorithm (mentioned just above), which allows each side to independently derive the same session key using a combination of its own private key and the other side's public key.

Since earlier versions of cell phones did not have the memory and processing power necessary to implement a full-blown SSL, the WAP forum[4] devised a method whereby a scaled-down version of SSL could be used between a WAP phone and a WAP gateway. This scaled-down version of SSL, called Wireless TLS (WTLS), operates between the cell phone and the gateway. The gateway establishes an SSL session with the content server—the server with the content the cell phone user is trying to get at. Under this scheme, the WAP gateway decrypts WTLS messages and reencrypts them for the SSL session. In the reverse direction, messages from the SSL session are decrypted by the WAP gateway and then reencrypted for the WTLS side. The data is temporarily *in the clear* at the WAP gateway between the time it is decrypted and reencrypted. This can be a security concern if the WAP gateway is not owned by the same organization that owns the content server.

More recent generations of cell phones are more powerful, and as such the WAP forum's recent WAP 2.0 specifications allow the use of TLS from the cell phone all the way to the content server. This eliminates the issue of having the data in the clear on somebody else's gateway.

Digital Signatures

Digital signatures help ensure data integrity, authentication, and non-repudiation. This powerful technique is made possible through a combination of asymmetric key cryptography and a class of algorithms known as *hash functions*.

Hash Functions

Hash functions take as input a message of arbitrary length and output a value (*hash code*) derived from the message. Any small change in the message should produce a different hash code. This technique provides a way of detect-

---

4. *www.wapforum.org*

ing changes in a message. The sender appends the hash code to the message. When the receiving side applies the same hash function to the message, the resulting hash code should match the one attached to the message. If, on the other hand, the message was changed along the way, the recipient will get a different hash code, thereby determining that the message was changed.

Some people refer to the hash code as the *message digest*. Commonly used hash functions include Message Digest 4 (MD4), Message Digest 5 (MD5), and Secure Hash Algorithm (SHA).

Applying Digital Signatures

Note that a hash function by itself does not protect against the *man-in-the-middle* attack, where data is intentionally changed. All the attacker has to do is apply the known hash function to the changed message and append the new hash code to the changed message.

In order to provide data integrity, the hash code has to be signed by the sender. This process is shown in Figure 9–4. The hash function generates a hash code from the message. The private key of the sender is used to encrypt the hash code. The resulting cipher text is appended to the message.

On the receiving side the procedure is as shown in Figure 9–5. The recipient runs the message through the same hash function. The signed hash code is decrypted using the sender's public key. The two results are compared. If they are equal, the recipient can be sure of two things: (1) The message has not been changed along the way, and (2) it was the owner of the public key who sent the message.

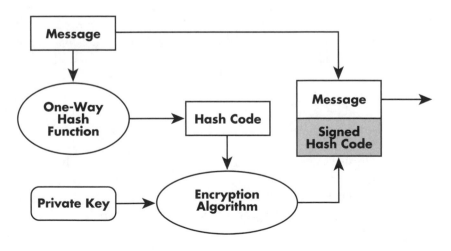

FIGURE 9–4   Signing a message.

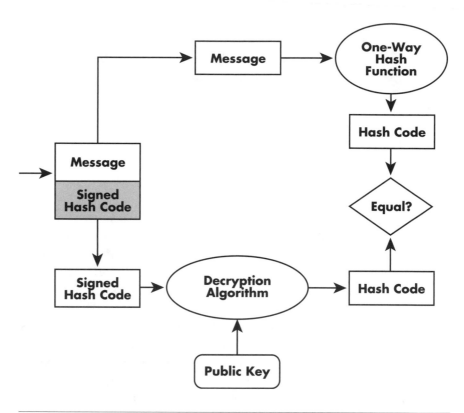

FIGURE 9–5 Checking message integrity.

Thanks to the first point, data integrity is ensured. The second point allows us to authenticate the sender, thereby helping to ensure legitimate use. It also provides a mechanism for non-repudiation; that is, the recipient can show that the sender was the only one who could have sent the message.

Digital Certificates

Frequently there is a need to certify a person or entity. Some real-life examples of certificates are passports and drivers' licenses. Certificates are generated by a trusted authority figure, for example, a government body. In the ideal case, it is impossible to forge a certificate. The notion of certification relies on two elements: a trusted third party and a document that is impossible to forge. Of course, in real life we have to make some compromises on both elements. Most of us are suspicious of the government, and nothing is impossible to forge.

In the ether world of computers and data networks, certification is also possible. Here again, we can thank asymmetric key cryptography. Similarly to the way a hash code is generated from a message, a hash code can be generated from the contents of a certificate. This code can then be signed using the private key of a trusted authority. This process ensures the integrity of the message, thereby providing the *impossible-to-forge* element of certification. The *trust* element is provided through the signature of the trusted authority.

Digital certificates provide a means of authentication. They can also be used for public key distribution. If Joe Public wants to send me a secret message, he can obtain my certificate, which includes my public key. The certificate is signed using the private key of a trusted authority; that is, Joe Public can be sure this is indeed my public key because the certificate was generated by a trusted entity and the certificate could not have been forged.

Authentication

An essential aspect of security is authentication—being able to prove somebody or something is what he, she, or it claims to be. There are many ways of doing this. Each method is based on some combination of *what you know* (password), *what you have* (an access token), or *what you are* (biometrics).

Passwords

The most common way of authenticating a person is with a password. This is a pretty basic idea that goes way back. Many of the problems passwords present in our high-tech world are the same problems that have existed as long as passwords have been used by human beings.

The more difficult the password is to guess, the more secure it is. However, it can also be said that passwords that are difficult to guess are usually difficult to remember. Some users write down passwords so they do not forget them. Of course, this represents a security risk. A malicious individual might happen onto the piece of paper on which the password is written.

It is also annoying to have to remember different passwords for different systems. Frequently people will either use the same password for all systems or they will write down the different passwords. In either case there is some security risk. The mobile enterprise should allow employees to sign on once to their portable device and then once to the enterprise. A wireless application gateway (WAG) can provide this single sign-on feature (see Chapter 7 for more on this).

When an incorrect password is given along with a valid user ID, the system should give no indication as to which input was wrong—the ID or the password. You do not want to give hackers any information they might be able to use later. If they know they got a user ID right, they are one step closer to getting in. Secure systems will also lock a user out after a small number of failed sign-on attempts. This minimizes the risk of an intruder getting in through the so-called *brute-force* method, in which all possible combinations are tried until the right one is found.

One big security risk is that a password might be intercepted. It makes no difference whether the password is encrypted, unless it is encrypted a different way each time. All the hacker has to do is pick up the string of characters and reuse it for the next session. These threats are known as *password sniffing* and *replay attacks*.

One-Time Passwords

The way around the problem of password sniffing and replay attacks is to generate a different password for each session. For example, a *challenge/response* technique might be employed. Under this scheme the client indicates that it wants to sign on. The server challenges the authenticity of the client by sending the client an unpredictable value, which the client signs. That is, the client encrypts the value using the client's private key. The client sends the result to the server, which checks out the value and accordingly either accepts or rejects the authenticity of the client. This way of generating session keys is similar to the way your Web browser gets into a secure session.

A simpler way of generating a one-time password is for the client to pass the time of day through a secret algorithm. The result is passed to the server for authentication. In this way, a different password is passed at each sign-on attempt. Note that this method only works if the client and the server have tightly synchronized clocks.

In both of these cases, a secret key must be stored in a secure, tamper-resistant place. The security and tamper resistance can be achieved through software or hardware. In either case, the software or hardware is known as an *access token*. An access token along with the secret password constitute a two-factor authentication scheme.

Two-Factor Authentication

Two-factor authentication is based on the idea that the combination of *something you have* and *something you know* can be used to prove your identity. If you lose the thing you have you will probably notice and then report the loss. Between the time the token is lost or stolen and the time administrators are able to disable access through that token, there lies a window of opportunity for misuse. However, this threat is mitigated by the requirement to use a password (something you know).

This idea is probably quite familiar to you. This is the way automated teller machines (ATMs) operate. You need an ATM card and the associated password to gain access to your account. If your card is lost or stolen you are supposed to immediately notify the bank. The bank will disable access from that card and will issue another one with a new password (or PIN, as it is called in this case).

As we shall see later in this chapter, two-factor authentication is frequently used in virtual private network (VPN) solutions. Two schemes that are frequently used with VPNs are SecurID, developed by Security Dynamics, and CRYPTOCard, developed by the company CRYPTOCard Corp.

Biometrics

Biometrics make up a class of techniques for authenticating a person based on some physical feature that is unique, electronically measurable, impossible to mimic, and stable. Since this gets right down to who a person is, biometrics are a promising way forward. Of course the idea of authenticating a person based on his or her physical traits is not new at all. We have always been able to recognize our friends, because we know what they look like or we know the sound of their voices. A more sophisticated example of how this idea has been used for quite some time now is fingerprinting, as used by law enforcement agencies. Until recently, the comparison of fingerprints has been done by careful examination of the prints by an expert with a keen eye.

Technology is now providing us with a lot of new ways of measuring individual traits. Some of the things that can now be measured electronically are fingerprints, voiceprints, and features of the eyes. By reading one or more of these traits at the point of entry, a system can keep out intruders. For example, fingerprint readers are now available on keyboards. Legitimate users are recognized by their fingerprints, and a positive check allows them access to the computer.

One day, biometrics will be an integral part of any authentication system. Today is not that day; there are still a number of problems that need to be ironed out before biometrics becomes widely accepted. First of all, these techniques are costly—the equipment to perform the measurements is expensive and the electronic representation of the trait being measured requires a lot of storage. Second, not all people have the trait that is to be measured, for example, eyes, fingers, and speech. One final difficulty is that many people find the idea offensive, some taking it as an invasion of privacy.

On-Device Data Security

The mobile enterprise will have to protect data on the portable device. In particular, there are two things to be concerned with. The first is protecting the data from illegitimate users. That is, if the device is lost, stolen, or borrowed, the wrong people might view your secret company data. To protect against this, there will have to be a file protection mechanism on the device.

The second concern is that even legitimate users should not be able to view and change all company data. You will have to either make sure only certain data is downloaded to the device, or that there is a mechanism on the device to prevent the user from viewing and/or changing certain data. In other words, there has to be an access control mechanism either as part of the download process or on the device itself.

File Protection

Portable devices should have a mechanism to ensure data privacy. This should occur with minimal user intervention. There are a variety of ways of doing this.

Files can be stored in encrypted form and decrypted as needed. In some cases, one key is used to encrypt all files on the device. In other cases, each file can be encrypted with a separate key. Key management can become a big problem here. First of all, it is not a good idea to require users to remember a lot of different passwords. A second issue is that when a key is changed, something has to be done with the files that have already been encrypted with the old key.

If only one person is to use the device, the best way to protect data is to password-protect the device itself. The screen saver could be password-protected so that the device is only usable once the password is entered. Similarly, as part of the boot-up procedures, the device could prompt for a password before allowing access to the operating system.

Remember that in cryptography, the longer the key, the harder it is for a hacker to guess its value. Also remember that the device should lock up after a small number of incorrect passwords are entered. The amount you invest in file protection, and the amount of hassles legitimate users have to put up with, should be in proportion with the value of the data on the device.

Data Access Control

In cases where synchronization is used, that is, when running in disconnected or detached mode, there will have to be some mechanism to prevent the user from viewing and/or changing data he or she is not supposed to access. The problem is that synchronization is a tricky business. It is hard to pick out the data dependencies and it is hard to know in advance what data the user will need. In fact, this might be impossible. The best case is to shoot for having the device contain data that the user is at least allowed to read, but not necessarily change. An example of this would be configuration data that only a systems administrator should be able to change, but that must be downloaded to the device in order for the application to be able to operate offline.

If there is no way of avoiding having data that should not be read by the user, some sort of access control mechanism must be designed into the applications running on the device. The case we are discussing here is one in which the device is running a *thick* client, as opposed to a *thin* client. That is, the portable device runs a significant part of the application, and does not serve as just a dumb terminal that depends on an ongoing connection. When talking to application vendors, make sure you cover the question of access control on the device.

Virus Protection

Unfortunately, there are already several viruses that specifically target hand-held devices. Bad guys do not wait to exploit a new opportunity. According to F-Secure,[5] here are some examples of the damage these viruses are already causing:

*   Performing extra activities to drain the battery of a portable device.
*   Disabling keyboard input.
*   Displaying obscene or annoying messages on the screen.
*   Deleting or hiding files.

Once you put a portable device in the hands of your employees, you have to recognize that many of them will use the device for personal reasons. To this end, many employees will access networks other than the company network—and they will download software from sites your company cannot control. They may also install software given to them by friends. Preventing this would be difficult to impossible. The result is that there is an increase in the likelihood of viral attacks.

Since viruses can come from so many different sources that cannot be controlled by your company, the best place for the virus protection to be performed is on the device itself. That is, it is insufficient to have your firewall

---

5. *www.f-secure.com*

filter viruses. Such a scheme would do nothing to eliminate viruses coming from other sources.

Virus protection works best when the software doing the protecting knows about the very latest viruses. This is usually done through a database of viruses that is updated on a regular basis by vendors of antivirus software. You will need to implement a means for the viral protection software sitting on the portable device to receive updates from this database on a weekly, and sometimes daily, basis.

Companies selling antivirus software for portable devices include F-Secure, MaGaffee, and Symantec.

SECURITY SOLUTIONS

Larger security systems employ the tools and concepts described in the preceding section. The systems that are of interest to the mobile enterprise are shown in Box 9–3.

Box 9–3   Security Solutions for the Mobile Enterprise

Security systems of interest to the mobile enterprise include:
- Public key infrastructure (PKI)
- Firewalls
- Virtual private network (VPN)
- Device protection

Public Key Infrastructure

According to the Internet Engineering Task Force (IETF), public key infrastructure (PKI) is the set of hardware, software, people, policies, and procedures needed to create, manage, store, distribute, and revoke certificates based on public-key cryptography. Perhaps the best way to explain PKI is through a simple example.

In our example, let's assume the company Acme.com wants to do business on the Internet. To encourage anonymous customers to provide credit card information, there needs to be a way for customers to authenticate Acme.com. To make this possible, Acme.com must first create a public/private key pair. Then it must have the public key certified and registered with a trusted authority. Figure 9–6 shows how this works under PKI:

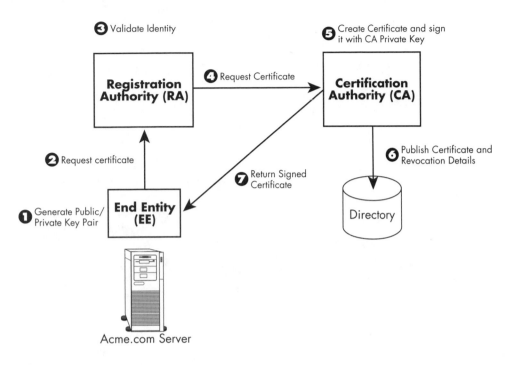

FIGURE 9–6 Certificate issuance.

1. Acme.com has a software module referred to as an end entity (EE) application. This module creates the public/private key pair using a known algorithm.

2. The EE then requests a certificate from a registration authority (RA).

3. The RA validates the identity of Acme.com through a process that may involve an in-person meeting.

4. Upon successful validation, the RA requests a certificate from a certificate authority (CA).

5. The CA creates a certificate and signs it with the private key of the CA.

6. The CA publishes the signed certificate to a directory.

7. The CA sends the signed certificate to the EE.

Now let's say that Joe Public wants to buy something from Acme.com. Mr. Public's computer will first authenticate Acme.com and then establish a secure channel. Using PKI, this would work as shown in Figure 9–7. The steps are as follows:

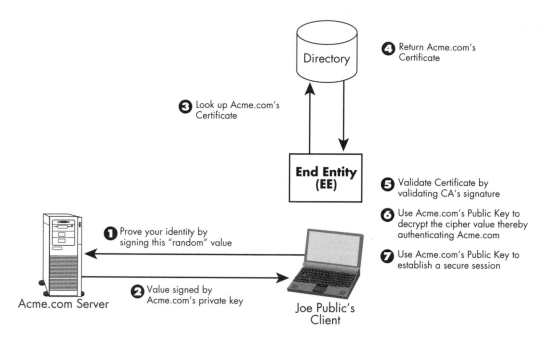

FIGURE 9–7   Server authentication through PKI.

1. Joe Public's software asks Acme.com to prove its identity.

2. Acme.com uses its private key to sign the value and sends the cipher value back to Joe Public.

3. Joe Public's client software contains an EE application, which queries a directory for Acme.com's certified public key.

4. The directory returns Acme.com's certificate, which has been signed by a trusted third party, the CA.

5. Mr. Public's software validates the certificate by decrypting the signature on the certificate with the CA's public key. Acme.com's public key is extracted from the certificate.

6. Joe Public's software uses Acme.com's public key to check Acme.com's signature.

7. Joe Public's software uses Acme.com's public key to start a secure session with Acme.com.

The preceding example was a case where a consumer was interacting with an enterprise. This is where PKI provides the most value, by allowing strangers to authenticate one another through a trusted third party and by allowing strangers to establish a secure channel.

The case where employees are communicating with the enterprise is different in that the two parties already know one another. In this latter case, a full-blown PKI is not needed. However, a scaled-down version might be useful. In any case, it is worthwhile understanding PKI, as the ideas behind it can be applied in a variety of situations.

Firewalls

To prevent fire from spreading from one building to another—or from one part of a building to another—brick walls used to be erected. These walls were of course called firewalls. In network terminology, firewalls are a single router or several routers and servers that stand between a public network and a private network and work together to isolate the private network. Firewalls prevent intrusion from unwanted elements on the outside. They can also limit traffic in the other direction. That is, they can limit access to the Internet from the internal network. For example, there might be a filter preventing the browsing of certain websites from within the company network.

Firewalls typically sit at critical points of the network infrastructure where traffic comes in (*ingress*) or goes out (*egress*). They typically perform some combination of the following functions:

- *Authentication*: To allow access to the company network from the outside, firewalls will usually attempt to authenticate the user and/or device trying to get in. Remember that this is the point of entry into your company network, so it is important that the authentication be strong.

- *Access control*: Once the firewall is sure who the user or device is, it will control access accordingly. The user might be completely locked out of the company network if he or she is unwanted. If the user is allowed into the network, there is usually some restriction on what he or she is allowed to do.

- *Audit*: By logging information on traffic patterns and subsequently scanning those logs for hints of intrusion, the firewall can raise alarms. Action can then be taken and future attacks prevented.

- *Detection of suspicious activity*: In conjunction with other routers and servers within the company network, the firewall can sometimes detect unusual behavior and subsequently lock that user and/or device out. For example, a user may repeatedly attempt to access privileged services. This can be detected and the firewall notified to lock that user out.

- *Content filtering*: Data content can be filtered at the firewall based on configurable rules. Certain words or images might be detected and some action taken.
- *Virus Filtering*: Some firewalls will specifically filter content for known viruses. In order to do this, the firewall uses a database of patterns to look for in a data stream.

Broadly speaking, there are two modes under which firewalls operate to examine traffic as it passes between the outside world and the corporate network. In these two modes the Internet Protocol (IP) packets are inspected in a different manner:

- *Stateless inspection*: where traffic is filtered per packet based on source and destination addresses and the application being requested. No consideration is given to the context of the packet; that is, the inspection does not consider whether the packet is part of a session. This kind of inspection is the easier of the two to implement and it has been used for a longer time.
- *Stateful inspection*: where the firewall keeps track of sessions and attempts to determine some of what is going on in the session. The state and history of each session must be maintained within the firewall for the duration of the session. This kind of inspection is much more sophisticated and resource intensive. However, it is a more powerful way of enforcing the company security policy.

One necessary assumption is that the firewall itself is secure. This is one case where physical security is important. No matter how powerful the firewall is, if an intruder has physical access to its component routers and servers, you are in big trouble.

Companies that make firewalls include Checkpoint Software, Nortel, and Cisco. All of these companies have taken mobility into account.

Virtual Private Networks

Virtual private networks (VPNs) allow employees to connect to the company network over the public Internet and function as if they were sitting in the office connected to the LAN. This is usually accomplished through a technique called *tunneling*, which provides secure passage of data from one end to the other.

Tunneling requires special software on both sides of the exchange. This software might sit on the client device itself, and then on the enterprise side, it typically sits on a router. The two sides of the tunnel are called *tunnel interfaces*.

In order to set up a tunnel, the two sides must first authenticate one another and negotiate parameters. As data enters the tunnel it is encrypted in its entirety; that is, even the protocol headers are encrypted. At the opposite side, the whole package is decrypted and then passed to its destination as if the two end points were sitting on the same physical network. The original protocol headers (called "inner" headers) contain source and destination addresses that define routing on the virtual network.

In addition to encryption, techniques are also applied to ensure data integrity; that is, to ensure that data is not changed as it passes through the public network.

Figure 9–8 shows how packets in the tunnel use an "outer" IP header that specifies the IP addresses of the two tunnel interfaces. From the point of view of the public network the two interfaces are just sending each other regular data. But the contents actually consist of encrypted IP packets, including an "inner" IP header specifying the IP addresses of the client and the server. Depending on the direction of the exchange, one of the IP addresses is the source address and the other is the destination.

The routers that perform the role of tunnel interface unwrap the inner IP header and pass it on to a local network. This whole process is transparent to the applications on the client and server.

We have discussed how a router may be used at either side of the tunnel. Another way of implementing a VPN is to have the tunneling software run on the client itself. In this case, and in the case where a router terminates the tunnel, the applications on the client do not have to know about the tunneling software. The VPN is transparent to applications.

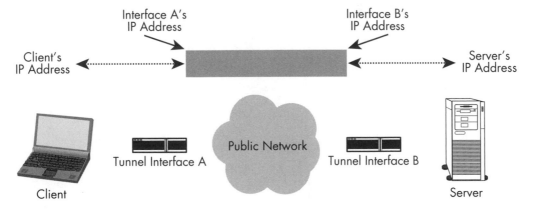

FIGURE 9–8 VPN tunneling.

Device Protection

In order to protect data, your portable devices can include an integrated smart card reader. A smart card is a card with a small CPU that can run security algorithms and hold digital certificates. Each employee is assigned a smart card with an associated password. The card and the password together make up a two-factor authentication scheme.

The smart card can contain algorithms both for file encryption on the device and for communications sessions through the VPN. When the card is inserted into the reader, the user is allowed access to the computer. The most secure systems will deny access to all computer functions without the presence of a smart card and a user who knows the correct password.

One thing to be careful of with smart card systems is that users tend to leave their cards in the computer. This defeats the purpose of such a system. To minimize this occurrence, users should be trained in proper use of the smart card.

Device protection schemes should include virus protection software. Remember, there must be a mechanism for updating the virus database so the most recent viruses can be detected.

PECULIARITIES OF THE MOBILE ENVIRONMENT

There are several aspects of the mobile environment that need to be taken into consideration when designing security countermeasures. In particular, one must be concerned with the things listed in Box 9–4.

Box 9–4   Peculiarities of the Mobile Environment

Security systems must give particular attention to these aspects of the mobile environment:

- Always-on connections
- Low bandwidth
- The broadcast nature of wireless
- Low powered devices
- A new breed of user

Let's now take a closer look at the special problems presented by the mobile environment.

Always-On Connections

Many of the data services that will be useful to the mobile enterprise are of the so-called *always-on* nature. This means data can be sent at anytime on an as-needed basis. A connection does not have to be established each time.

When I say that a connection does not have to be set up, what this really means is that a circuit does not have to be established. In fact, some sort of a virtual connection *does* have to be set up. A virtual connection simply means that the two sides of the exchange have agreed to parameters, and they track the state of the exchange. For example, each side has to keep track of which messages made it to the other side, and which ones need to be resent.

Of particular importance to the subject at hand, the two sides have to agree on security parameters. Some authentication must occur, and key exchange must take place. Since the connections are always on, session keys have to be *refreshed* from time to time. That is, the two sides have to change the key value periodically throughout the duration of the connection, so as not to give hackers enough time to discover any one key.

Low Bandwidth

Wireless networks are inherently slower than fixed-line networks. Less bandwidth is available to any single user when the transmission medium is shared by a lot of other users, as is the case with wireless. This means that security protocols cannot add as much overhead in terms of message size. It also carries implications as to how the messages are broken up into fragments and reassembled on the other side.

Broadcast Nature of Wireless

Wireless is by nature a broadcast medium. Signals are sent in all directions, and therefore, anybody in range could potentially pick up *your* signals. This will rarely happen unintentionally. Only somebody who makes a special effort to tune in to your channel can pick up your data. In order to do something with the data, they would have to understand the protocol in which it is packaged and they may have some decryption to perform.

The level of security that you get automatically from the wireless network depends on the protocol being used. Advanced Mobile Phone System (AMPS) networks, for example, provide no encryption service over the air interface. GSM networks have some encryption services, but they are not very strong. CDMA is by nature difficult to listen in on because each side of the conversation has to know the hopping sequence.

Perhaps the best attitude to take is to assume that you get no automatic encryption over the airwaves. After all, once the data is on the operator network, it may be passed over the public Internet to arrive at your enterprise.

The best thing to do is to set up end-to-end encryption, that is, from the portable device to the enterprise. By doing this, you will not have to be concerned with eavesdropping either over the airwaves or on the Internet. You will have a secure tunnel from the device to your company.

Low Powered Devices

Portable devices are by definition smaller than desktop computers. This means they have less powerful CPUs, less memory, limited keyboards, and limited screen space.

Up until now most applications were designed for the desktop. Many software developers got greedy with their use of CPU and memory. This holds true for security algorithms and the software modules that perform those algorithms. They were designed for more powerful computers.

Now that we are trying to bring some of these algorithms to the portable device, special care has to be taken. Earlier in this chapter, I discussed wireless TLS (WTLS), which was developed to provide security on cell phones. This is an example of specialized security procedures.

A New Breed of User

Mobility brings technology to a new set of people, many of whom have done their best to avoid anything technical. They were too busy talking to customers. These people had no time to deal with buggy software, cryptic error messages, and operating systems that crash several times a day. Can you blame them?

Now we are asking customer-facing employees to carry a small computer with them to "help" them do their work. If security procedures are too complicated, they will probably either stop using the device or they will find a way of working around the procedures.

SECURING THE MOBILE ENTERPRISE

It is worth noting that over the past six or seven years, most enterprises have undergone a major shift in the way they protect corporate data. Before, companies could rely on *perimeter* security. That is, by securing company premises, most data was protected. Then with the major paradigm shift brought on by the Internet, company computers were suddenly open to remote access from anybody with a computer and an Internet connection.

Perhaps one way of measuring the magnitude of a paradigm shift is by noting the number of new words that have to be invented to talk about it. The words needed to describe some of the new ideas simply do not exist before the change. With all the revolutions it brings, technology must be the number-one contributor of new words to the English language. For example, in the particular case where companies began to open up their networks, we got the words *intranet* and *extranet,* and the term *virtual private network* (VPN).

Suddenly a whole different set of countermeasures had to be put into place to protect against electronic intrusion. Firewalls had to be erected to isolate the company from the public network, thus delineating the intranet. Secure tunnels had to be established with selected partners, thus defining an extranet. And finally, VPNs had to be set up to allow remote employees to work as if they were at the corporate site.

The countermeasures that have been deployed as a result of the Internet revolution are applicable to the mobile enterprise as well. There are a few variations that are required to address the peculiarities of the mobile environment.

A Fully Secured Mobile Enterprise

Let's take a look at the components of the mobile enterprise and see all of the different points where security has to be considered. In other words, we should consider which components have to authenticate one another, which components need to perform cryptographic functions, where data integrity is required, and so on. I will err on the side of caution and let you consider where some of the functions can be combined or left out.

A fully secured mobile enterprise will implement all of the features shown in Figure 9–9. The tools discussed throughout this chapter can be applied at the various points shown in the diagram to perform the necessary countermeasures. How secure your mobile enterprise is will depend on the quality of the tools you apply at each of these points:

1. *Authentication of the user by the device.* The user will need to authenticate him- or herself to the portable device. The most secure system will not allow the operating system on the portable device to run without the presence of an authentic user. Alternatively, access can be denied to certain applications and/or data.

2. *Authenication, encryption, and data integrity from device to enterprise.* The device should be authenticated by the enterprise—and the enterprise

by the device. This might be done through an exchange of digital certificates. Data passed between the enterprise and the portable device is encrypted, and data integrity techniques are applied.

3. *Authentication of user to the enterprise.* The user will also have to be authenticated by the enterprise. This process is entirely different from the authentication of the user by the device. This process involves logging into the company VPN.

4. *Authentication of user to WAG.* The user will have to be authenticated by the wireless application gateway (WAG). This process is the single sign-on process. It might be the case that once the enterprise has authenticated the user, the identity of the user can be passed to the WAG, which would no longer require a separate sign-on directly from the user.

5. *Authentication of user to enterprise applications.* The WAG will sign on to the back-end applications on behalf of the user.

6. *Physical security.* Servers and routers are physically secured within the corporate premises.

7. *Virus protection, encrypted files, and access control on device.* The portable device is running virus protection software. The device is also capable of encrypting files. The portable devices can control access to applications and/or data based on authentication of the user and what access that user is allowed.

8. *Careful behavior of users.* Security procedures are put in place. These procedures do not place a significant burden on the user. Users are trained in these procedures. Adherence to these procedures is audited.

Note that while authentication needs to occur between several different entities, in some cases this can be done automatically. It could also be done through a simple trust model. For example, you could decide that if the enterprise knows who the user is, the enterprise can trust the user to only use authentic devices. In other words, if the enterprise trusts the user, and the user can recognize a device, the enterprise can rest assured that the device is valid once the user is authenticated.

Many applications do not require security at all points shown in Figure 9–9. However, you should use this diagram as a checklist. Are you securing all points? If not, is there a good reason why you are not?

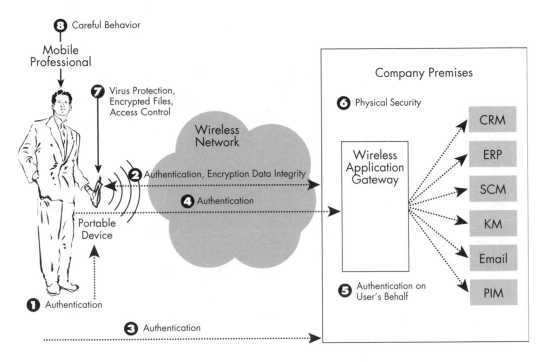

FIGURE 9–9 A fully secured mobile enterprise.

Updating the Corporate Security Policy

Your company may already have a security policy written by management to reflect overarching security requirements of your company to protect its electronic assets. In Chapter 1 it was suggested that at a minimum, your company's IT department should start planning for the adoption of wireless technology. As part of that planning process, security policies should be updated.

Here is some food for thought in developing a security policy for the mobile enterprise:

- The value of what is being protected should determine how much you are going to spend to protect it. If the information you are sending over wireless links is information you are willing to make public, you will not need to encrypt that data.

- It is important to think through who might be a perpetrator and what might be their motives. Think about the level of sophistication of the potential intruders. Are they capable of intercepting data transmission over airwaves?

- Careful consideration should be given to user procedures, how they are to be audited, and how they are to be enforced. Some of the new procedures involve the use of smart cards, taking care not to leave devices lying around, and being cautious when viewing data in public places. The company should make clear statements to employees about adherence to security procedures and what the company will do when procedures are not followed.

Do not underestimate the human factor in security. Procedures must be easy to use, and the users' perception of how secure the system is should be commiserate with how secure the system really is.

SUMMARY

Security is an essential feature of the mobile enterprise. The basic concepts of security are not too hard to understand if you examine a simple model, such as children exchanging secret messages in a classroom.

The hard part is that rapidly advancing technology is fueling a race between those wielding swords and those wielding shields, that is, between attackers and defenders. The result is that products and techniques are constantly evolving. Another difficulty is that computer-usage paradigms are evolving. Security was pretty simple when the only people who used a computer were those who were standing next to it. Now, with users who are not only remote, but who are also moving around and broadcasting information over the airwaves, the rules of the game have changed.

It is important to consider what it is you are trying to protect and from whom. Do not spend a lot of time and money countering improbable threats. Also make sure that the security countermeasures you implement do not make your users jump through hoops just to use the system. In other words, do not get carried away with security.

On the other hand, do not make your company vulnerable. You should make sure to address all points shown in Figure 9–9. If you choose not to implement a countermeasure at a given point, there should be a good reason why. For example, you may not have sensitive data at that point, or there may not be a significant threat at that point.

We have just covered a whole lot of material. Hopefully this will provide you with a good enough understanding to evaluate products and services being offered to secure your mobile enterprise.

Ready, Set...

CHAPTER 10

Reengineering
Business Processes

Needless to say, businesses have already reaped enormous benefits from applying computing and networking technology. Much of this benefit has to do with information management—capturing it, storing it, and making it readily available. Business processes have improved because quality information can now be easily retrieved by employees connected to the company LAN or to the company intranet.

Unfortunately, though, there is a class of business processes for which the lack of information is still one of the biggest bottlenecks. These are customer-facing activities. As we have discussed throughout this book, a little bit of mobile magic should clear this bottleneck up and get things working more efficiently. The trick is to identify when this is appropriate and when it is not. Indeed, understanding where to apply mobile technology might just be crucial to your business.

Let's first discuss the advantages of process-oriented business, and then business process reengineering in general. Then let's consider a methodology for reengineering business processes by applying mobile technology. To illustrate, we can apply this methodology to specific cases—pharmaceutical sales representatives and high-tech field engineers.

Hopefully you will use this methodology—or something similar—to evaluate your own business processes and assess the case for adopting mobile technologies.

PROCESS-ORIENTED BUSINESS

A lot has been written about process-oriented business over the last two decades. Much of this movement was inspired by technology and how it could be applied to achieve higher efficiencies and new revenue opportunities. In particular, a lot of progress was made as a result of applying software to automate back-office tasks such as order management, purchasing, and invoicing.

A side effect of applying technology to business was that people became forced to work in a more uniform manner. Nowadays two people in different locations of a company use much of the same software to perform the same tasks. When several steps of a task are supported by technology, people tend to perform the whole task in a uniform manner. Business becomes process oriented.

There is a great deal of value in this uniformity. In particular, consistency and economy of scale are achieved. At the same time, there is a need to remain flexible to allow workers to discover better ways of doing things, and to respond to unforeseen customer demands. This flexibility can lead to improved processes as best practices are recognized and then adopted as standard.

Consistency

By having unified processes, customers are served the same way by different employees. They come to know what to expect from your company. The key is to ensure the customer receives the same high level of service from each employee regardless of who makes the sales call, services equipment, answers the phone, or responds to their email request.

Having consistent processes also means that employees can be moved around between different parts of the company. Employees can replace one another as needed and step right into a new job function. If the process is well documented, and training programs are built around the process, new employees can come up to speed more quickly.

Economy of Scale

Process-oriented businesses achieve a certain economy of scale. Technology to support the processes can be bought wholesale. Training and documentation can be developed once and propagated. Support systems can be duplicated.

The ceiling on company growth is raised by an order of magnitude. If everybody in the company is doing things differently, as the company grows, so does the chaos. If, on the other hand, employees performing different job roles know what each other is doing, they can know what to expect from one another. In large organizations without well-defined business processes, employees can spend most of their work time just trying to figure out how the company works.

The Importance of Flexibility

On the other hand, the danger in process-oriented business stems from it's rigidity. What if the way we choose to perform the tasks is no good? Do you want everybody in the company to be making the same mistakes? No, we want the opposite. We want some variation in our business processes—we want to allow some experimentation. In this way, best practices will emerge, and others can learn from examples. There needs to be some scope for competition among the different groups performing similar tasks. And of course, there needs to be ways of measuring which groups are performing better than others.

Since not all customers have the same needs, there should be enough flexibility in processes to allow the company to respond to customer needs that may not have been predicted. You should not believe that a central design team is able to think of all of the right answers. Leave room for variation and creativity in the field.

At the same time it is useful to capture the variations in writing. If employees document how they veer off the standard process, you can review these variations at regular intervals, and decide which ones are really best practices that should be incorporated into the corporate standards.

OBJECTIVES IN REENGINEERING BUSINESS PROCESSES

Whether or not your business is already process oriented, you are now considering changing the way things work. If you currently do not have well-defined processes, the outcome of the work you are doing now will probably be to define and implement some. If you are already using well-defined processes, the outcome of the work you are doing here will probably result in changes to what exists. This could involve incremental change or it could involve a fundamental shift and organizational changes. Either way, you will be reengineering business processes.

In most cases the kinds of things that you are trying to achieve through business process reengineering can be broken down into some combination of the following kinds of objectives:

- *Cost reduction*: activities and resources might be removed from processes because they do not add value from a customer or company perspective.

- *Cycle time reduction*: sales, service, expense, and billing cycles might be reduced.

- *Optimal of use of time*: at points in a business process where there is a wait state, we can look for other useful tasks the worker can perform.

- *Increased customer satisfaction*: the quality of the service to the customer might be maximized.

- *Increased employee satisfaction*: we can look for ways to keep employees happy by reducing tedium, unnecessary trips to the office, and extra paperwork.

- *Increased revenue*: we can try to introduce revenue-generating activities that would not otherwise be possible. For example, we can look for cross-sell and up-sell opportunities.

All of these objectives are pertinent when mobile technology is introduced in the business process.

A SIMPLE METHODOLOGY

In order to determine whether or not your business processes can be improved through mobility, you can follow a simple methodology. The general flow of this methodology is shown in Figure 10–1.

Having read this chapter, you are interested in reevaluating one or more of your business processes. The first step is to model the way things are done now. This is called the *as-is* process. The next step is to model a new process where mobile technology is applied. This is optimistically called the *improved* process. Both the as-is process and the improved process should be presented extensively to others in the company to check your work—and to get help in analyzing whether or not change is worthwhile.

Having compared the improved process with the as-is process, you must ask yourself if it is worth proceeding. We will not even consider the cost of a solution at this point. Setting the matter of cost aside, is it worth the effort to change how you do things? If it is, then go on to read Chapter 11 where we will look at how to fit a solution to the problem and how to evaluate the total cost.

If you determine that it is not worth proceeding, plan to reevaluate at some later point in time. Going through this process is a healthy exercise anyway.

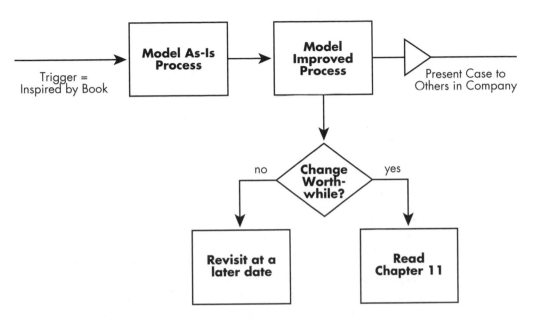

FIGURE 10–1 Business process reengineering.

Notation

Let's consider the things that need to be modeled. In this discussion I will introduce a little notation, which is borrowed from standard flowchart representation. You might use this, or you might come up with your own notation. Whichever way you choose, it is important that everybody involved understand what the symbols represent, what kinds of things get put in the model, and what kinds of things are intentionally left out.

Triggers

Triggers are external events that start out the process or that require a reaction in the middle of the process. Triggers can be represented as shown in Figure 10–2. In this example, the trigger is a request from a customer.

FIGURE 10–2 Trigger.

```
┌─────────────┐
│   Suggest   │
│  a related  │
│  product to │
│   customer  │
└─────────────┘
```

FIGURE 10–3 Key activities.

Mobile technology can help when a trigger involves notifying a field worker. In this case, the notification can be sent over a wireless network to the field worker's portable computing device.

Key Activities

A key activity is an important task that is performed as part of the business process. Key activities are represented in Figure 10–3. In this example, the activity is to attempt a cross-sell by suggesting a related product to the customer.

Mobile technology can help by enabling workers to carry out activities more quickly or to eliminate some activities altogether.

Conditions

Conditions are represented in Figure 10–4. The conditional statement should be worded in a way that results in a "yes" or "no" outcome. In this example, the condition is whether or not the customer is interested in the suggested alternative.

FIGURE 10–4 Conditions.

Mobile technology can sometimes help with conditions, especially when the condition involves somebody's making a decision. Through mobile technology, the information that feeds into the decision is more readily available.

Wait States

We have to understand where in the current business process workers are waiting for something to happen. This is likely to be *dead time*—a period

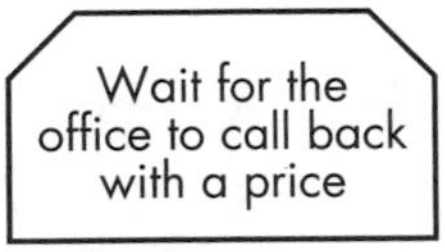

Wait for the
office to call back
with a price

FIGURE 10–5   Wait states.

during which nothing productive occurs. Wait states are depicted in Figure 10–5.

In this example, the salesperson is waiting for somebody in the office to call back with price information—a perfect example of a wait state that could be eliminated by mobile technology. With a mobile solution, the salesperson could find the price himself.

In addition to completely eliminating wait states, mobile technology can help by enabling field workers to perform useful tasks during a wait. Using a portable device, they might read email, perform planning activities, fill out an expense report, and so on.

Information Exchange

Since our objective is to loosen up bottlenecks caused by poor information flow, we need to model how information is exchanged throughout the business process. It is important to note what information is exchanged, from whom, to whom, and the channel by which that information is currently exchanged. It is also worthwhile indicating how valuable that information is to the recipient, and how much subsequent steps in the process depend on it.

Information exchange is represented in Figure 10–6. In this example, the exchange involves using a phone to provide an office administrator information about an order just taken.

Mobile technology helps in information exchanges that involve mailing something through the postal service or making an extra trip to deliver a form. Through mobile technology, information can be sent electronically.

Call Office
Admin to provide
Order Info

FIGURE 10–6   Information exchange.

Variations

It is not wise to assume a business process is performed uniformly throughout the company and under all conditions. Failure to understand significant variations might cause us to design a new business process that does not work under all conditions. Trying to impose the new process where it does not really work will result in a lot of frustration. If this occurs, your new process is likely to be ignored, with the whole reengineering effort being a waste of time and effort.

Significant variations in the business process should be noted along with the model.

Assumptions

Note any assumptions you make along the way. By noting them you let others in on your thinking—and if any of your assumptions are invalid you want somebody else to be able to point that out to you as soon as possible. Ideally you will be performing the business process reengineering as a group. In this way, it is more likely that invalid assumptions are spotted more quickly.

Cost

When there is a cost associated with an activity or information flow, it should be noted. Cost may be incurred as a result of time spent, materials used, services purchased, or lost revenue opportunities.

In addition to the costs associated with events, you can evaluate the cost of mistakes or things going wrong. You might estimate the probability of such an occurrence and multiply that by the cost incurred when the event does happen. In this way you can arrive at an overall cost.

Modeling As-Is Processes

The first thing to do is understand the current business processes. If you cannot get agreement on how things work now, you are not likely to make the right changes.

The as-is processes should be plotted using formal notation to avoid ambiguity. A few paragraphs of text should accompany the model to provide further explanation. Costs should be associated with the steps in the process flow. Costs might be noted in terms of time, materials, or lost opportunity.

Most process mapping is an iterative effort that starts with a high-level process (for example, sales), and breaks it down into subprocesses (for example, preparation, customer visit, and follow-up). You should strike a balance between capturing the essence of the process without getting bogged down in minute details that are not pertinent.

Management's View

Service managers, call center managers, sales managers, and line-of-business managers all have a view of some of the business processes performed by customer-facing employees. They might have even written down a process flow. This view is the way things are *supposed* to happen.

One of the problems with this is that the process flow might have been designed without input from the people actually doing the work. When people really get out and do the work, they discover tricks here and there that make them more efficient. They learn which corners can be cut to achieve an objective.

Even if field workers were involved in the design of the process flow, things might have changed since. The result is management might not understand what really happens in the field—and documented process flows might not depict the real process.

Still it is important to get management's view on the business process. While they might not have an understanding of which corners are being cut, they have a better overall view of how the process fits in with other parts of the company. They have also thought through the process with the intent of optimizing productivity.

Field Worker's View

To understand what really happens, field workers should be interviewed. A focus group might be formed to discuss processes and share best practices. Maybe some of the field workers do not know the best tricks their colleagues have picked up. They can learn as a result of the group discussions, and in this way the discussion itself might result in some efficiency gains.

Another good way to find out what happens in the field is to have an independent observer ride around with field workers for a few days, taking notes on activities performed, the amount of time spent, and any resources utilized. The person accompanying a field worker should not be the field worker's manager. It should be somebody whose presence is not likely to alter behavior. After all, you do not want the worker to put on an act.

As you are writing down what happens, note any assumptions you, management, or field workers are making. Also note variations in the process. At different times, the process might work differently or different workers may perform tasks differently. Note all significant variations, when they occur, where they occur, and why they occur.

Once you think you understand a business process, test your understanding through simulations or walkthroughs with field workers and managers.

Customer's View

Insofar as possible you should try to get customer feedback on your business process. How do they perceive your services? How are you doing on customer satisfaction and why? Is your company easy to do business with?

You might get this information through customer focus groups. Invite a cross-section of your customers—or would-be customers—to a discussion. You might also use a survey to get some information.

In the absence of direct input from customers, you might hire industry consultants to serve as proxies for the customer. They can help you look through your business processes from a customer's point of view.

Redesigning Processes

Having fully evaluated the as-is business process, you are now ready to redesign using mobile technology. Start out by considering what kinds of things mobility can change. This will help you spot areas for improvement.

What Mobility Can Change

Mobile technology can minimize the kinds of problems listed in Box 10–1. In your business, can you apply mobile technology at the points where these problems are occurring?

Box 10–1 Candidates for Improvement through Mobile Technology

Areas of a business process you can look to improve with mobile technology:

- **Bottlenecks caused by lack of information**: places in the process where somebody is waiting for information, or where somebody has to make extra trips to obtain information.
- **Data reentry**: places in the process where data is written down on paper and later typed in to the system.
- **Wait time**: places where the field worker is waiting for something to happen and has nothing useful to do during the wait.
- **Lack of coordination**: places where individuals need to coordinate activities, but are unable to do so.

Mobility can also introduce value-generating activities that were not possible before. For example, with mobile technology you can suggest more complex configurations. Since you are able to access back-end systems containing information on related products, you can cross-sell and up-sell.

Modeling the Changes

Model the improved process using the same notation you used to model the as-is process. Where activities are eliminated, or where the cost of an activity is reduced, record the savings. At the bottom of the process model, add the savings and any new revenue-generating activities. This is the incremental value of the improved process.

Review your work with colleagues. Simulate the process, if possible, through software tools. Otherwise, simply step through the process. Have you accounted for all important activities and information flows? Are your assumptions valid? Have you covered all significant variations in the business process?

Review your work with end-users. Does the new business process assume the user will be using technology in ways that are not possible? You might be assuming the worker has a free hand to carry a device at a point where this would be impossible. You might be assuming a high degree of technical literacy from people who generally do not like technology. You might be requiring complex input operations from people who would not be frequent-enough users to remember the operations.

Consider what happens when the technology the new process relies on fails. Would a failure shut down your entire business? Is there a backup plan in your new process?

Evaluating the Case for Mobility

We have not yet talked about the cost of a solution. In fact, I will only give parameters on estimating the cost, as it would not be of much use trying to tell you what solutions cost. Prices change so often and the particular solution you want may not be covered in my estimation. In Chapter 11 I will talk about total cost of ownership (TCO) and provide guidelines for estimating the total cost. To work through the questions of whether or not it is worth changing business processes through mobile solutions, you will have to work in the estimated cost.

Alternatives to Achieve Same Result

Having worked through the as-is model, how it can be changed, and what value that brings, the first question you should ask yourself is, "Can I achieve the same value by doing something else?" For example, if I buy my employees a fast car, cycle times might be improved by as much or more than if I employ mobile technology.

Business as Usual

Remember that your best alternative might be business as usual—at least for the time being. If the sky is not falling down, there may not be a compelling reason for you to change your processes now.

It is healthy to run through this exercise now and again to reevaluate with respect to the state of the technology and with respect to the business practices of your competition and the expectations of your customers and employees. But also remember that in many cases, a nice side effect of adopting new technologies is that it keeps work fun for employees who happen to be technophiles. Also it is important for employees to feel they are keeping up their skill set with respect to the requirements of the job market.

EXAMPLE 1: PHARMACEUTICAL SALES REP

Let's work through a couple of examples. The first will involve the work life of a pharmaceutical sales representative.

Pharmaceutical companies make a large part of their profits by selling prescription drugs. Since the principal sales channel for prescription drugs is the physician, these companies strive to keep physicians well informed about their latest products, and gain their preference. They do this by sending sales representatives to visit physicians' offices to talk about the drugs and leave behind brochures—a process known as *detailing* in the pharmaceutical industry.

Since detailing is the principal means with which companies gain preference, the physician's office is one of the key battlefields for competitive advantage in the pharmaceutical industry. Indeed, according to Forrester 2001, 70% of the marketing budgets of pharmaceutical companies is being spent on the sales force.

The need for face-to-face interaction with physicians is so strong that pharmaceutical sales forces have more than doubled in recent years as companies compete for detailing time in front of physicians. Large pharmaceutical companies have traditionally had multiple sales forces selling different products to physicians. But recently, the need to create as much noise as possible during the early launch phase of a drug means that companies also deploy mirror sales forces, promoting overlapping products to the same physicians. It is not unusual to have between two and five medical representatives on the same territory with overlapping product portfolios.

Supporting Staff:
1) **Manager:** reviews business plan, cycle plan, and weekly plans; monitors performance and coordinates field teams
2) **Admin:** supports field teams, coordinates reports and field administration
3) **Marketing Department:** analyzes information on doctors, customer relationship management (CRM), analyzes market, etc.; develops marketing campaigns
4) **Sample Management:** maintains records for regulatory compliance, takes sample orders, and sends out samples accordingly

FIGURE 10–7   Work life of pharmaceutical sales rep.

Another aspect of the visit at the physician's office is leaving behind drug samples. The pharmaceutical sales representative will frequently leave a handful behind. As a regulatory measure, the physician may have to sign a form upon receipt of the samples. This is to track samples, and thereby minimize abuse.

Let's now evaluate the case for using mobile technology to help the pharmaceutical sales force. The work life of a pharmaceutical sales rep is shown in Figure 10–7.

The manager helps develop the various plans: the business plan for the year, the cycle plan for the quarter, and the weekly plan. The administrative assistant enters data into enterprise applications. The marketing department analyzes new information returned by the sales rep and makes sure information from other channels (for example, the Internet) is available to the sales rep. The sample management department maintains records for regulatory compliance and fills sample orders.

Pre-Call Planning

At the beginning of the week the pharmaceutical sales rep needs to develop a weekly plan and send it to his manager. The manager needs this plan to track activities and to help coordinate the activities of the different sales reps in the company. For example, the company wants to ensure all target doctors are covered in a marketing campaign. Different reps might visit the same physician to talk about similar lines of drugs. It is better for the company not to send more than one sales rep to a given physician on a given day.

At the beginning of the workday, the pharmaceutical sales rep prepares for visits to physicians by performing several activities. He collects drug samples to leave behind during visits. These drugs are kept at his house so he does not have to make extra trips to the office.

He may also develop a daily plan for his own use. This might help him choose an optimal route. This daily plan will also help him think what kinds of information he needs to bring along and what kinds of things he will need to talk about.

The sales rep does some research on physicians from his home computer. He tries to find out about recent interactions between his company and the physician. He may remind himself of some of the personal hobbies of physicians to help personalize the visit.

As-Is Pre-Call Planning Process

The pre-call planning process is modeled in Figure 10–8. At the end of the week, or over the weekend, the pharmaceutical sales rep creates a plan for the coming week. This indicates which physicians he intends to see, what he intends to talk to them about, and which samples to leave behind. This work is done on a home desktop computer or a notebook computer.

Once he is finished developing the plan, he sends it to his manager through email or by fax. The manager does not sit around all weekend waiting for plans to review. But she does dial in from time to time to check. Once she gets a plan, she reviews it. If there are any issues with it, she sends it back to the sales rep. Otherwise, she saves it for the record.

If a plan is sent back for changes, it probably will not be changed right away. By this time, it is unlikely that the sales rep is still online, so he will probably not see the email until later.

Improved Pre-Call Planning Process

Pre-call planning can be improved through mobile technology. An improved process is shown in Figure 10–9.

It is still necessary to load the car with samples at the beginning of the workday—there is no way around that. However, big savings can be achieved due to the fact that a lot of the planning activities can take place while the rep is waiting for doctors. In the as-is process, the time spent waiting for doctors is dead time. In the new business process, we will use this time to perform planning activities. This translates to less work at home—and time for more doctor visits.

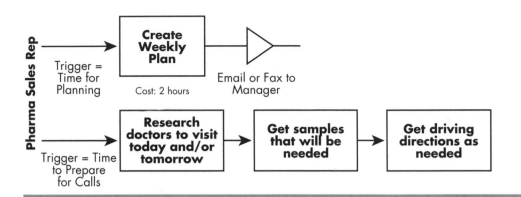

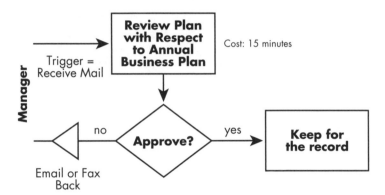

Things that can go wrong:

1) Pharma sales rep may not get the disapproved plan back in time. He may not check his email often enough.
2) If pharma rep has to change plan while on the road, he cannot research the doctor before the visit.

Variations:

1) In many cases, the rep does not even create a weekly plan. Pharma reps do not see value in this—and it has to be done from home—so they try to avoid it.

Overall Costs:

1) Employee is not happy spending up to 2 hours planning from home on the weekend.

FIGURE 10–8   As-is pre-call planning process.

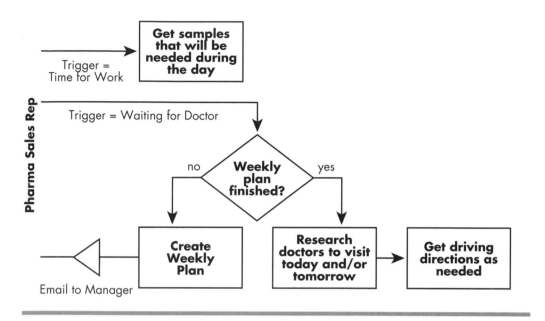

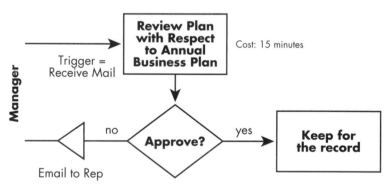

Savings:

1) Pharma sales rep can do all planning and research during wait states of the physician-facing process.

Other Benefits:

1) Pharma rep can easily change plan while on the road. Then he can update schedule and research unplanned visits.

FIGURE 10–9   Improved pre-call planning process.

The other benefit to the new process is that the pharmaceutical sales rep can make schedule changes while on the road. Furthermore, after changing the schedule, he can do all pre-call research from the mobile device.

Since planning can be done during wait time, the sales rep will have a more positive attitude toward generating plans and sending them into his manager. The manager is more apt to respond quickly during a workday than on the weekend, so the weekly plan has a better chance at being reviewed and approved quickly. This is of benefit to the manager, and it helps others in the company to coordinate the activities of sales reps.

Physician-Facing Activities

The pharmaceutical sales rep spends a lot of time driving from one doctor's office to another. The other big time waster is sitting in the doctor's office waiting to see him or her.

As-Is Physician-Facing Process

The sales rep will go from one doctor to the next according to his daily plan. Ideally he will have chosen optimal routes to maximize the number of visits he can make per day. The physician-facing activities are modeled in Figure 10–10.

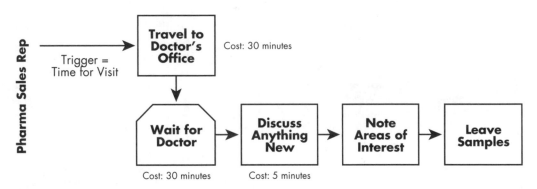

Things that can go wrong:
1) Waiting too long for one doctor causes rep to be late for visit with the next doctor.

Variations:
1) Sales rep does not always leave samples.

Overall Costs:
1) A lot of dead time while waiting for doctors.

FIGURE 10–10 As-is physician-facing process.

When it is time to visit a doctor, the sales rep drives to the doctor's office. He then has to wait for the doctor. This wait can be anywhere from a few minutes to over an hour. When the sales rep finally sits down to talk to the doctor, the doctor usually allows less than 5 minutes for the visit. During this time, the sales rep will go over anything new about the drugs sold by his company. He will find out the areas where the doctor needs more information and note this so that he can follow up by sending her more information.

During the visit, the sales rep will leave samples behind. For prescription drugs, the sales rep has to get the doctor's signature as confirmation that she accepted the sample. This signature is required for legal reasons.

There is no easy way for one sales rep to know if another sales rep from his company has visited that same doctor during the same day. The different reps work in different groups promoting similar drugs and their activities are usually not well coordinated. While there is no tangible cost to this lack of coordination, it is probably not so impressive to the doctor—and it might result in her developing an unfavorable attitude toward the pharmaceutical company.

Improved Physician-Facing Process

The model for the improved physician-facing process is shown in Figure 10–11. As discussed in the section on pre-call planning, mobile technology allows the sales rep to perform planning activities while waiting for the physician. The other benefit of the new process is that during the visit the sales rep can enter areas of interest directly on the mobile device—there is no need

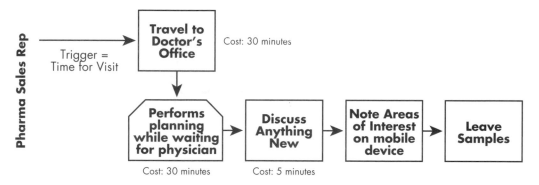

Savings:
1) Sales rep performs useful tasks while waiting for the physician.

Other benefits:
1) Sales rep can note interests directly onto mobile device.

FIGURE 10–11 Improved physician-facing process.

to jot down notes and enter them later, by which time the most important information is forgotten.

While the sales rep is waiting for the doctor he might also review training documentation or he might view targeted news feeds to keep up on what is happening in the pharmaceutical industry.

Post-Call Activities

At some point after visiting a physician, the sales rep has to update enterprise applications with new information on the physician. He must also order any follow-up documentation on areas of interest to the doctor. If he got the doctor's signature for samples left behind, he has to send the signatures into the office to be filed. He may order new samples to restock.

As-Is Post-Call Process

The current way of working after a call is shown in Figure 10–12. The sales rep usually waits until the end of the day to perform these activities. Though he does have a lot of free time during the day while driving from office to office, or while sitting in a waiting room, he cannot perform these tasks while driving, and his laptop is too big to use in a doctor's waiting room.

Using a home computer, he makes the updates to the enterprise applications and orders follow-up documentation. He may send signatures to the office and he may order new samples.

The marketing department makes use of the updates to the enterprise applications. From time to time they will generate reports to draw some conclusions about physician preferences and other things that may influence marketing campaigns.

The sample management department fulfills any orders for new samples. The samples are shipped directly to the sales rep's house. If any signatures are received they are filed away.

Since the sales rep cannot enter new information into the enterprise applications until he gets home at night, the rest of the company has to wait to act on the new information. If the doctor uses the Internet to access pharmaceutical information, she might be frustrated by having to wait to see updates resulting from the visit.

The sales rep has to enter data from home every night. This is not a pleasant task and because of this, sales reps do not generally do it well. In fact, if they can get away with not doing it, they may not even do it at all.

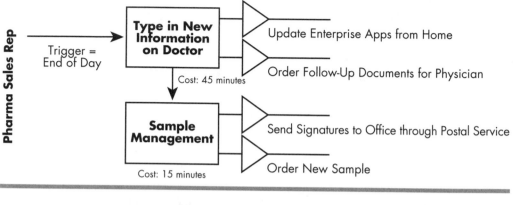

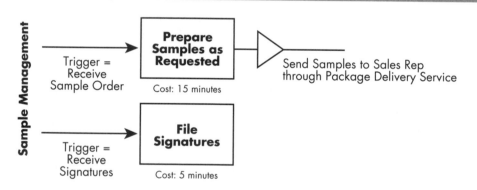

Things that can go wrong:

1) The delay in updating enterprise applications means that new information on a doctor is not available to other channels—for example, other reps on the Internet.

2) Difficulty in entering updates means it gets done less frequently.

Variations:

1) Signatures are not needed for certain drugs.

2) Sales rep may pick up samples instead of having them sent to him.

Overall Costs:

1) Employee is not happy spending 60 minutes entering data from home at night.

FIGURE 10–12 As-is post-call process.

Improved Post-Call Process

As shown in Figure 10–13, we can model a new post-call process using mobile technology. During the visit the sales rep can already enter new information on the doctor's interest. Immediately after the visit, or during the wait for the next doctor, the sales rep can enter other new information.

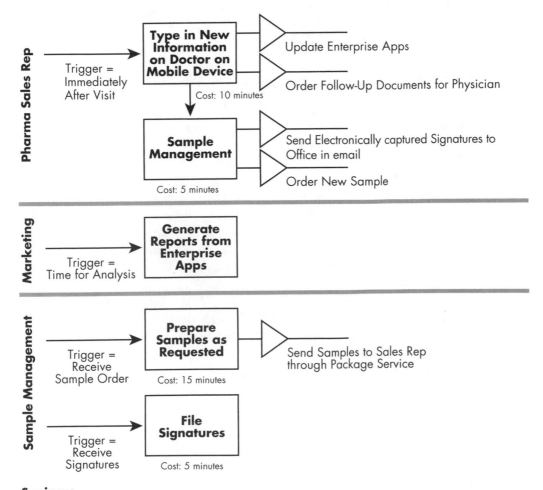

Savings:

1) Sales rep can enter information during and immediately after visit. This does not have to be done at the end of the day from home. More calls can therefore be made or the sales rep can have a better lifestyle.

Other benefits:

1) Rest of company benefits from quick information.

FIGURE 10–13 Improved post-call process.

He can then upload all new information, allowing the rest of the company to immediately benefit. This information can be instantaneously applied to other channels, such as the Internet site the doctor might access shortly after the visit.

He can order new documents according to the expressed interests of the doctor. He might also plan some follow-up activities to cater to those interests.

If new samples are needed, the sales rep can order them at any time through the mobile device.

Advantages Gained through Mobile Technology

In the pharmaceutical industry, the use of mobile technology has the potential to add value in a number of areas. The current flow of information to and from the sales force is far from ideal, even though pharmaceutical companies have been early adopters of sales force automation through the use of laptops. Sales representatives are often preoccupied finding the next potential call or rushing to the next appointment. Waiting for a laptop to boot up before and after each call is impractical and often the information is entered days after the customer event has occurred, leading to the questionable value of such data. The capture of reliable data after each call requires a significant change in behavior, as current technology is not integrated into the daily activities of the sales force.

A further problem that tends to get overlooked is that the current pharmaceutical sales process is disjointed and inefficient. Sales representatives need to carry out all their pre-call activities at home or in the office, execute their customer-facing activities in the field, and then return to their office or home where they complete administrative and follow-up tasks, such as ordering literature or recording customer information. Because companies are accustomed to the sales process taking place in three separate and disjointed environments for each call, the cost of these inefficiencies is often overlooked. Value is often lost when information is not recorded immediately and sales representatives may just enter irrelevant data to complete a customer contact on their information systems. Post-call follow-up activities may not get recorded or acted upon because of the time lag between activities. Mobility fundamentally changes everything by enabling representatives to access all the sales tools they need to complete the sales activities in the field—as close to the customer event as possible.

On portable computing devices functionality includes access to the company portal, email, diary management, personalized news, and information from the Internet. Typical sales force tools are also available, allowing representatives to access customer records, call history, best access times, and planning objectives. Representatives can also analyze sales data for accounts or territories—or by product or product group—and set objectives accordingly. Providing these tools to sales representatives at the point of contact will lead to efficiency and productivity gains in these areas and allow them to use time more effectively in waiting rooms and between calls. Personalized training can also be provided via handheld devices, reducing the amount of time spent off territory. For example, after the launch of a new drug, companies can reduce the amount of time representatives need to come into the office for training by making product and disease training modules available on handheld devices, so the sales force can utilize their dead time more efficiently and focus on areas of individual weakness.

EXAMPLE 2: HIGH-TECH FIELD ENGINEER

Let's now take a second example of business process reengineering. This example involves the work life of a high-tech field engineer, who goes to the customer site to fix equipment as needed.

High-tech field engineers are under constant pressure to complete tasks quicker—and at the same time support an ever-growing list of products. These workers need quick access to various kinds of information, including parts information, self-test information, configuration data, and failure codes.

Let's take a look at the work life of a high-tech field engineer and of all those people in the organization supporting her. As shown in Figure 10–14, these workers perform at least three separate and distinct business processes

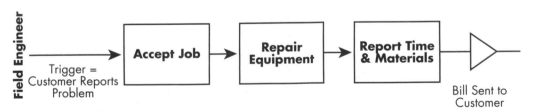

Supporting Staff:
1) **Call Center:** receives customer problem report and starts dispatch process.
2) **Field Coordinator:** approves T&M forms.
3) **Service Admin:** enters time & materials information into computer.
4) **Finance:** uses time & materials information to generate invoice and send to customer.

FIGURE 10–14 Overall work life of field engineer.

that can be improved through mobile technology. These processes are strung together in a sequence initiated by a customer problem report and terminated with a bill being sent to the customer.

Dispatch

The quicker a company can fix broken equipment, the happier its customers are. Two of the biggest causes of delay in getting equipment fixed are the time it takes to get parts and the time it takes to get a field engineer to the customer site.

As-Is Dispatch Process

The current dispatch process works as shown in Figure 10–15. At the beginning of the week, the field engineer will plan her week either from a home computer or at the office. She will then send her schedule to the dispatch center via email. The dispatch center uses the schedules of all engineers to determine where each engineer is likely to be at any time during the week. Unfortunately, things come up during the week, and by mid-week, the schedules are pretty much obsolete.

When a problem arises, the customer calls the help desk where the problem is identified and information is captured, including customer details and the serial number of the equipment in question. The help desk generates a job ticket and sends the job to the dispatch center.

Viewing the nature of the problem, the dispatch center generates a list of engineers who have the skills to fix the problem. This list is ordered by proximity and availability—according to the schedule sent in by each engineer at the beginning of the week. The dispatch center pages the first engineer in the list and gives that engineer 30 minutes to reply.

If the engineer rejects the job, or if 30 minutes go by with no response, the dispatch center may decide that 30 minutes makes enough difference in availability that another list of engineers must be generated. Alternatively, they might just proceed to the next engineer on the original list. This process goes on until an engineer accepts the job.

The field engineer receives a dispatch page and responds to accept the job. She does this by either calling the dispatch center or returning a page, if she has a two-way pager. Then the field engineer calls the customer to discuss the problem. Even if she is not sure she will need parts, she will go ahead and order some, just in case. She then schedules a visit to the customer site based on the delivery date of the parts. She notes the date on a piece of paper, which she will consult at the beginning of the next week when she does planning.

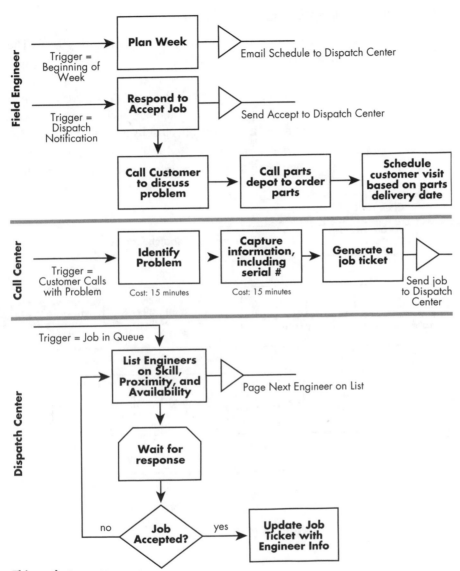

Things that can go wrong:
1) Engineer schedules become obsolete after a few days. Dispatch Center can no longer figure out where engineers are.

Variations:
1) For some equipment the engineer goes to the site without bringing parts.

Overall Costs:
1) Engineer orders more parts than necessary just in case.
2) The dispatcher may not be able to find an available engineer.

FIGURE 10–15   As-is dispatch process.

Improved Dispatch Process

The dispatch process can be reengineered, as shown in Figure 10–16. The field engineer immediately views information on the job as part of the dispatch notification.

She can order parts without having to call the parts depot. Now she can order them through the mobile application, which can access the parts database. The parts management application returns a delivery date immediately.

A separate dispatch center is no longer needed. Dispatch can be an automatic process initiated and monitored by people in the call center. More

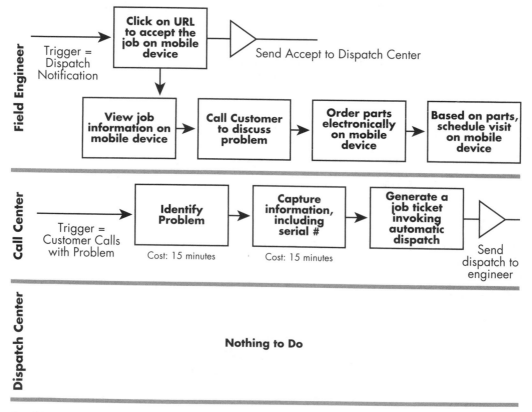

Savings:

1) Dispatch center is no longer needed for this particular process.

Other benefits:

1) Field engineer gets more information with the dispatch.

FIGURE 10–16   Improved dispatch process.

information can be sent along with the dispatch notification, thereby allowing the field engineer to make more informed decisions about accepting a job.

Repair Equipment

To repair equipment the field engineer needs easy access to technical documents and other information, including reports on how similar problems have been fixed in the past by other engineers in the company.

As-Is Repair Process

Under the current process (see Figure 10–17), the field engineer first collects documentation and problem history. Then she travels to the site and examines the equipment.

At the site, if she has all the necessary information with her, she works on the problem. Otherwise, she calls the help desk to ask coworkers to get more information from knowledge management applications.

If she fixes the problem on the first visit, she writes down information on what she did and she notes the parts she did not need. At some later point, she mails the problem update to the service admin who enters the information into computer systems.

When the help desk gets a call from a field engineer they consult the knowledge management system as needed. This system contains documentation on equipment and information on fixing the equipment.

When the service administrator receives a problem update report from the field engineer, he enters it into the computer system.

This current process has several problems that might result in the field engineer having to schedule a second visit. If not all information is available and nobody on the help desk is available to help out, the field engineer either waits around or schedules a second visit. If the problem is not as initially reported, or if the wrong information was recorded, the field engineer might show up unprepared to fix the problem. Here also the field engineer has to schedule a second visit.

Another problem with the as-is repair process is that collecting relevant documentation prior to the call requires an extra trip into the office.

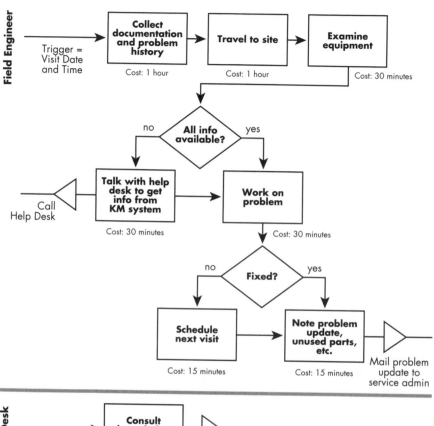

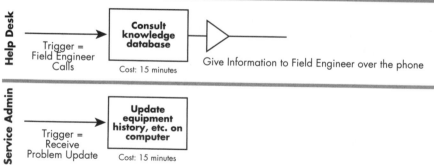

Things that can go wrong:

1) FE does not have all information needed, and help desk is too busy to help out.

2) The wrong information was provided prior to the call, so the FE shows up unprepared.

Variations:

1) Instead of sending product update to project coordinator, FE might drive into office.

Overall Costs:

1) Extra drive to the office to pick up documentation on the equipment.

FIGURE 10–17   As-is equipment repair process.

Improved Repair Process

The repair process can be redesigned as shown in Figure 10–18. The field engineer no longer has to make a special trip to the office to pick up the nec-

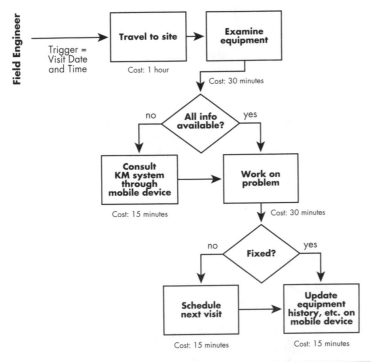

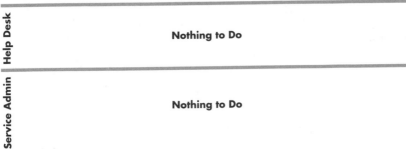

Savings:
1) Help desk no longer has to assist engineer in looking up information.
2) Service admin no longer has to reenter problem update information.
3) Field Engineer no longer has to make special trip to pick up documentation.

Other Benefits:
1) With easier access to information, the engineer fixes the problem faster and is more likely to fix it on the first visit.

FIGURE 10–18   Improved equipment repair process.

essary documentation. Instead, she can browse documents from the portable computing device.

For the same reason, the field engineer no longer relies on help desk support to retrieve more information. All information can be viewed on the portable device.

Once the job is completed, the field engineer updates the problem status directly on the mobile device. This eliminates the extra data entry step previously performed by the service administrator.

With easier access to information the field engineer is able to repair the equipment more quickly—and she is more likely to complete the repair on the first visit. We can expect these improvements to result in a reduced repair cycle, thus increasing customer satisfaction as well as the productivity of the field engineer.

Time and Materials

After completing a repair, the field engineer must record the amount of time spent on the problem, and the materials used. This information is needed to generate an invoice so the company can get paid.

As-Is Time and Materials

The as-is business process for entering time and materials information is modeled in Figure 10–19. When a job is completed the field engineer completes the time and materials (T&M) form for the job. Then she must get the customer's signature at the bottom of the form.

She makes a call to the service administrator to indicate that she has a T&M form to send in. The service administrator enters this information into the computer system and gets a reference number back. The field engineer jots the reference number on the form and mails the form to the field coordinator. Alternatively, she brings the form into the office. Some engineers will collect forms for several days and bring them all in at once.

The field coordinator receives the form in internal mail. The form could have come through the postal service, or it could have been brought into the office and placed in the internal mail system. The field coordinator reviews the form marking it as either approved or disapproved with a reason. Then he sends it to the service administrator.

The service administrator receives the form in internal mail. If the form was marked as disapproved, he calls the field engineer and collects missing information. He fills in the changes and sends the form back to the field coordinator for inspection.

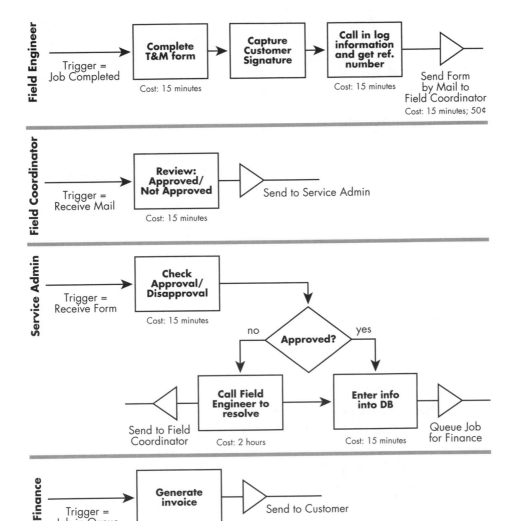

Things that can go wrong:

1) FE does not have correct form—may not even invoice.
2) Invalid forms take a long time to resolve.
3) Form lost in mail.

Variations:

1) Instead of sending form to project coordinator, FE might drive into office.

Overall Costs:

1) At least 1 extra day is built into the invoicing because information has to be mailed in. This adds to the delay in getting paid.

FIGURE 10–19   As-is business process for time and materials.

If, on the other hand, the form was approved, the service administrator enters the information from the form into the computer system. As long as the field engineer's handwriting is legible, the service administrator is able to enter the information in about 15 minutes. After entering the data, he selects the option to send the job to finance.

The finance department gets the job from its queue and generates an invoice. The invoice is then mailed to the customer. Note that there is a delay of at least one day built into this process. That is the time it takes to get the T&M form to the service administrator. This delay results in a delay in getting paid.

The paperwork causes at least two problems. First of all, the engineer has to have all the right documents with her. Second, an extra step is required to get the information into the computer system.

Improved Time and Materials

Now consider how the time and materials billing process can be improved by applying mobile technology. The new process is modeled in Figure 10–20.

Because the field engineer is able to enter all information on a mobile device, and even get the customer's signature on the device, the service administrator does not have to get involved. The whole step of data reentry is eliminated. As the field engineer is entering job data, the mobile application validates the input to some extent. This minimizes the number of T&M forms that get rejected by the field coordinator.

The field engineer no longer has to call in to report that she is about to send in a T&M form. Instead, she just goes ahead and sends in the form electronically. Because the form is sent immediately, the billing cycle is reduced by at least one day—the best case in the previous process was that the postal service gets the form to the field coordinator overnight.

Since the mobile application performs validity checks on the data entered by the field engineer, the field coordinator rejects fewer T&M forms. When he does reject a form it is immediately sent back to the field engineer. Since the time between the entry of the T&M data by the field engineer and the rejection of the form by the field coordinator has been compressed, there is a good chance the field engineer will not be too far from the customer site when she receives the rejected form. If she has to go back for more information, it does not take too long.

This improved business process saves time, involves fewer people, and allows the company to get paid at least one day sooner.

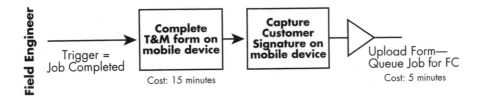

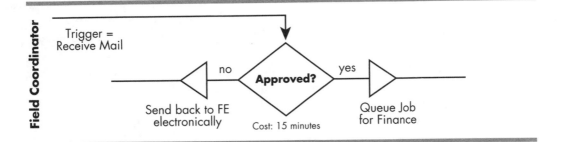

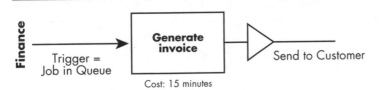

Savings per job:
1) 25 minutes from FE
2) 30 minutes from Service Admin
3) Service Admin no longer gets involved
4) Form validated immediately—mistakes caught right away

Other benefits:
1) Reduce accounts receivable by at least one day—bill can be generated almost immediately

FIGURE 10–20   T&M improved through mobility.

Advantages Gained through Mobile Technology

Equipped with mobile technology, the field engineer is more autonomous. She no longer relies on support from people in the office to help her track down information. Mobile technology allows her to access more information quicker. The result is that she is able to fix problems quicker. This increases customer satisfaction; and it also increases the number of jobs the engineer can work on.

A nice side effect of this extra level of automation is that we can now obtain accurate metrics on the performance of a field engineer. For example, we can know when the engineer gets to the customer site and when she leaves. We can also log repair and service history to a finer level of detail throughout a call. This helps track call status, and it allows your company to better inform the customer.

When engineers are able to access enterprise applications from the field, they are better able to respond to changes and reprioritize accordingly. A higher degree of coordination can be achieved.

SUMMARY

Our intuition might tell us that somewhere beyond the "gee-whiz" effect of mobile technology, there is some real value. We get this feeling inside that somehow this stuff might actually help us do business more effectively. But intuition alone is not enough to build a strong case when others in your company need to be convinced. And even if others think that somehow mobility makes sense, exactly where and how it makes sense is not always so easy to determine.

By formalizing your analysis of business processes and how they might be improved though mobile technology, you stand a better chance of making the right choices. If you know what to model, and how to spot the things that mobility can improve, you can more quickly arrive at the right answers.

Indeed, the right answer might be that mobility is not much help to you. The important thing is that you have a way of determining that.

Fitting the Solution to the Problem

The old adage goes "when all you have is a hammer, every problem looks like a nail." This says a lot about our approach to problem solving in general. Carpenters see all problems as nails, doctors as diseases, boxers as punching bags, and so on. From here on out we will divorce ourselves from this way of thinking. When it comes to solving problems with high-tech solutions, the last thing we need is more confusion. The right thing to do is first understand the problem, and then work your way toward a solution.

Let's start out by defining some guidelines you can use to think through your requirements. This will help you generate a shopping list. Given this list, we will look for where to shop. To this end, we will look at how the industry is structured and what competitive forces are acting on the different kinds of players. Finally, we will establish guidelines to help estimate the total cost of ownership (TCO) of a mobile solution.

DEVELOPING A SHOPPING LIST

If you have thought through your business processes in Chapter 10, and are prepared to move forward, the next step is to shop around. Let's start out by developing a good list of what it is we are looking for. We need to examine requirements in these areas:

- *Device*. What kind of device is most appropriate for you? Do you need ruggedized devices?

- *Online versus offline access.* Do you need a wireless connection at all times, or is it more appropriate to preload data onto the device and work off that data?
- *Network connectivity.* What are your bandwidth requirements?
- *Thin client versus thick client.* Can your device act more or less as a "dumb" terminal, or do you need a relatively large application running on the device?
- *System load.* How much data traffic does your system have to handle?
- *Uptime.* Does the system have to be up and running at all times?
- *Security.* How much security is appropriate for your needs?

As much as possible, we will think through the requirements independently of one another.

Device Requirements

The first thing to consider is which device is appropriate for your users. There are several dimensions to this problem. Perhaps the three most important are screen, keyboard, and ruggedization.

The more reading your users have to do, the larger the screen you should choose. The more data entry your users have to perform, the larger the keyboard should be. Where not much data entry is required, you might not even need a keyboard. A stylus or a voice interface may suffice in this case.

The more likely it is that the device gets dropped or that somebody spills liquid on it, and the more extreme the weather conditions under which it is to be used, the higher your need for a ruggedized device.

Do not forget to weigh in the cost of a ruggedized device. They can be expensive. If you think the device is only going to be dropped three times a year, you might want to evaluate the cost of just buying three new nonrugged devices a year. That might be the most cost-effective solution.

It is possible that different users will have different device needs. In this case, you will require a system that can simultaneously handle multiple device types, and that has some features for managing those devices.

Think about device replacements. If a device is lost, how quickly do you need a replacement?

Online versus Offline Access

You should consider whether you need *online* access to data or if *offline* access will suffice. Remember that online access means that a connection is required in order to get at the data you need. Offline access means work is done on the device without a connection. In between the two there are various caching schemes you can consider, including:

- The data is fetched every few hours and stored on the device.
- Whenever there is unused bandwidth, the device checks for updates from the enterprise.
- Software on the enterprise side pushes updates to the devices whenever there is unused bandwidth.

Consider the business process models and note where information is needed. For each point at which information is needed, think about how much you need the most recent version of the data versus how often the data changes. The graph shown in Figure 11–1 is a rough sketch of different cases and how they translate to requirements for online, offline, or cached models.

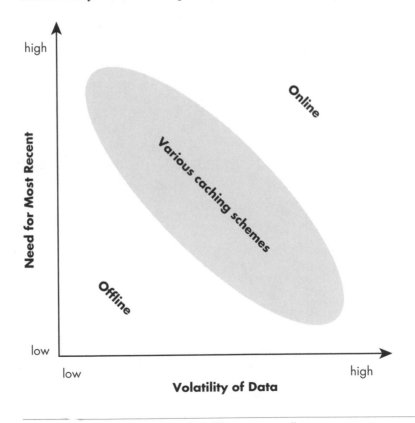

FIGURE 11–1 Requirements for offline versus online.

Consider your requirements for online versus offline access independently of the network coverage available to you.

Network Requirements

Given the information exchanges from your business process reengineering exercise, you are ready to determine which network services you need. There are several dimensions to this problem. You have to consider bandwidth, latency, cost, and service availability.

One way of selecting a data service is by considering the sizes of the individual data exchanges. As shown in Figure 11–2, if your individual transfers are small, your main selection criteria for the network coverage might be cost. If, on the other hand, your individual transfers are large, you might make your choice based on bandwidth.

To get an idea of the network coverage available, you can start out by looking at network coverage maps. Appendix A lists the Web sites of several network operators; most of them includes coverage maps.

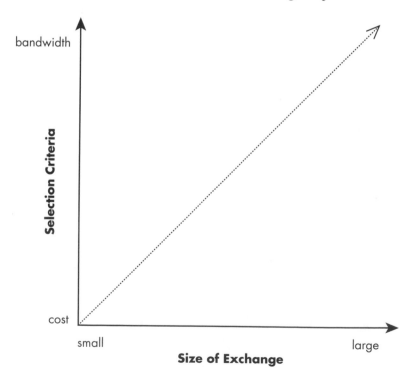

FIGURE 11–2 Selection criteria for data services.

Finally, you can conduct surveys of the sites you know your workers are going to be. To do this, bring a sample device if possible—or at least bring a device that uses the data services you are interested in. If your workers need access indoors, make sure you test network coverage indoors.

Thin Client versus Thick Client

Having looked at your requirements, and having obtained information on network coverage, now compare the two. For each point where you need information, consider the network coverage versus your requirements. The graph shown in Figure 11–3 might help you.

If you need online access, but the network coverage is low, you may get yourself into trouble by adopting mobility at this point. In this case, you should rethink your business processes to see if you can live with offline access. If you cannot, maybe it's better to go on with business as usual. Remember that not changing at all is also a perfectly valid alternative.

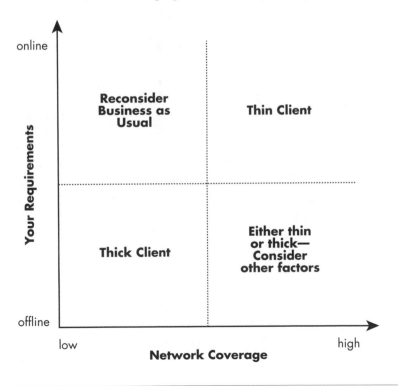

FIGURE 11–3   Thin client or thick client.

If offline access is acceptable, and if network coverage is good, you can use either a thin client or a thick client. Consider other factors, such as the cost of network access versus the cost of a thick client. Remember though that if at any one of the points where you need information you do not have good network coverage, you will need a thick client.

System Load

Your requirements for system capacity might run along several dimensions. Box 11–1 lists some of the dimensions you should consider.

Box 11-1 Dimensions to Consider for System Load

In thinking about your requirements for system performance and capacity, you should think along the following dimensions:

- **Throughput**: the amount of time it takes to respond to a request.
- **Requests per second**: the number of requests the system can handle in a second.
- **Simultaneous sessions**: the number of sessions that can be open simultaneously.
- **Synchronization throughput**: the amount of time it takes to perform synchronization for your average data volume.
- **Simultaneous synchronization**: the number of users who can be synchronizing simultaneously.
- **Number of users**: probably the most misleading. The number of users can be limited by the size of the user database. It can also be limited by system load, but to understand that you have to know something about peak utilization and the characteristics of your applications.

For each of these dimensions you should look at the peak time behavior; that is, how you require the system to behave at the time when the load is at its heaviest.

Uptime

Think about how much uptime you require. Another way of putting it is to think about how much downtime you can tolerate (see Figure 11–4). Think in terms of planned downtime and unplanned downtime. The former occurs when you perform backups or maintenance; the latter is when the system crashes.

It is likely that you can tolerate periods of planned downtime at night and during the weekend. This makes things easier. You do not have to buy an extra

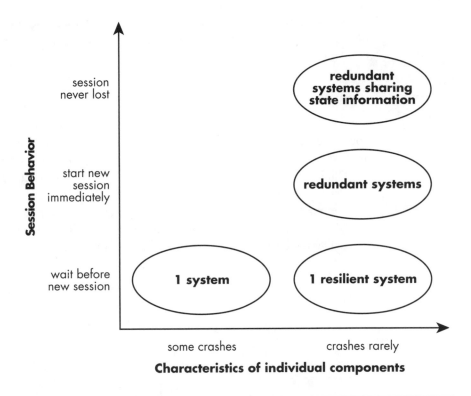

FIGURE 11–4   Session behavior on failure.

standby system—and you do not have to go through special procedures to switch to the standby system before performing the backup or maintenance.

Think about how you require the system to react in cases of failure. Is it okay for the user to just wait a little and then start all over? Or should the user be able to start all over immediately? The most stringent requirement would be that the session is never lost on system failure.

How you want sessions to behave on failure conditions will drive your requirements for redundant hardware. If you can tolerate crashes from time to time, and have the user wait a few minutes before trying back, then all you need is one system. If you want fewer crashes, that one system should be pretty resilient. If you want the user to be able to try back immediately, you need redundant systems, but session state does not have to be shared between servers. If you want sessions to carry on in the event of a failure, you need redundant systems and a way for those systems to share information on the state of ongoing sessions. By sharing this state information, one system can take over the session of a system that crashes.

At a minimum you will want to make sure that your solution guarantees transaction integrity; that is, when a session is broken in the middle of a transaction, the transaction is rolled back.

Security

Remember that, as shown in Figure 11–5, as soon as you implement some kind of security, there are associated costs and some extra hassle for users and system administrators. Avoid overkill on your security requirements.

Think through each of the aspects of your system and what kind of security you require. Box 11–2 lists some of the things you can consider.

You might try listing your security requirements in terms of *must-have* versus *nice-to-have*. That will allow you some flexibility when it comes time to consider the costs of implementing what you require.

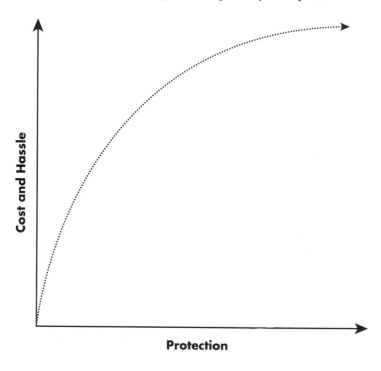

FIGURE 11–5   Relationship between security and costs and hassle.

Box 11–2 Considerations for security requirements

Things to consider for security requirements:

- **User behavior**. Think about their attitude toward security, how well they will follow rules, and how much hassle they will tolerate for security.
- **Device**. Think about virus protection, file encryption, access control (so that if there is data on the device the user is not supposed to access, there is some way of preventing his or her access), and operating system lockout for nonauthenticated users.
- **Network**. Think about encryption and data integrity.
- **Intranet access**. Think about authentication and access control. Do you want to authenticate the user, the device, or both?
- **Application access**. Think about single sign-on. The user can be authenticated once and then gain access to the different back-end application based on his or her profile.

GOING SHOPPING

Armed with your shopping list, you are now ready to talk to vendors. But first you have to figure out which ones to talk to. You will find that today there are a lot of companies selling products and services designed to mobilize the enterprise—so many that you could easily spend all your work time talking to the different vendors and still not meet the requirements on your shopping list.

If, on the other hand, you start out with a good understanding of how the industry is structured, you will have a better idea of who to call. By understanding the competitive pressures acting on the different companies, you will have a better feel for the direction they are likely to take.

The Structure of the Industry

The overall structure of the industry is shown in Figure 11–6. At the top is the enterprise whose only concern is improving business. Below are all the different kinds of companies and the kinds of things they are telling would-be customers.

To mobilize your enterprise you will need something from each of these classes of company. You probably will not deal with each of them directly, and unless you like to do a lot of in-house integration work, you probably do not *want* to have to deal with more than one or two of them. The better way to go is to rely on one company to put the whole thing together. Pick a company with competencies in several areas and/or with strong complementary part-

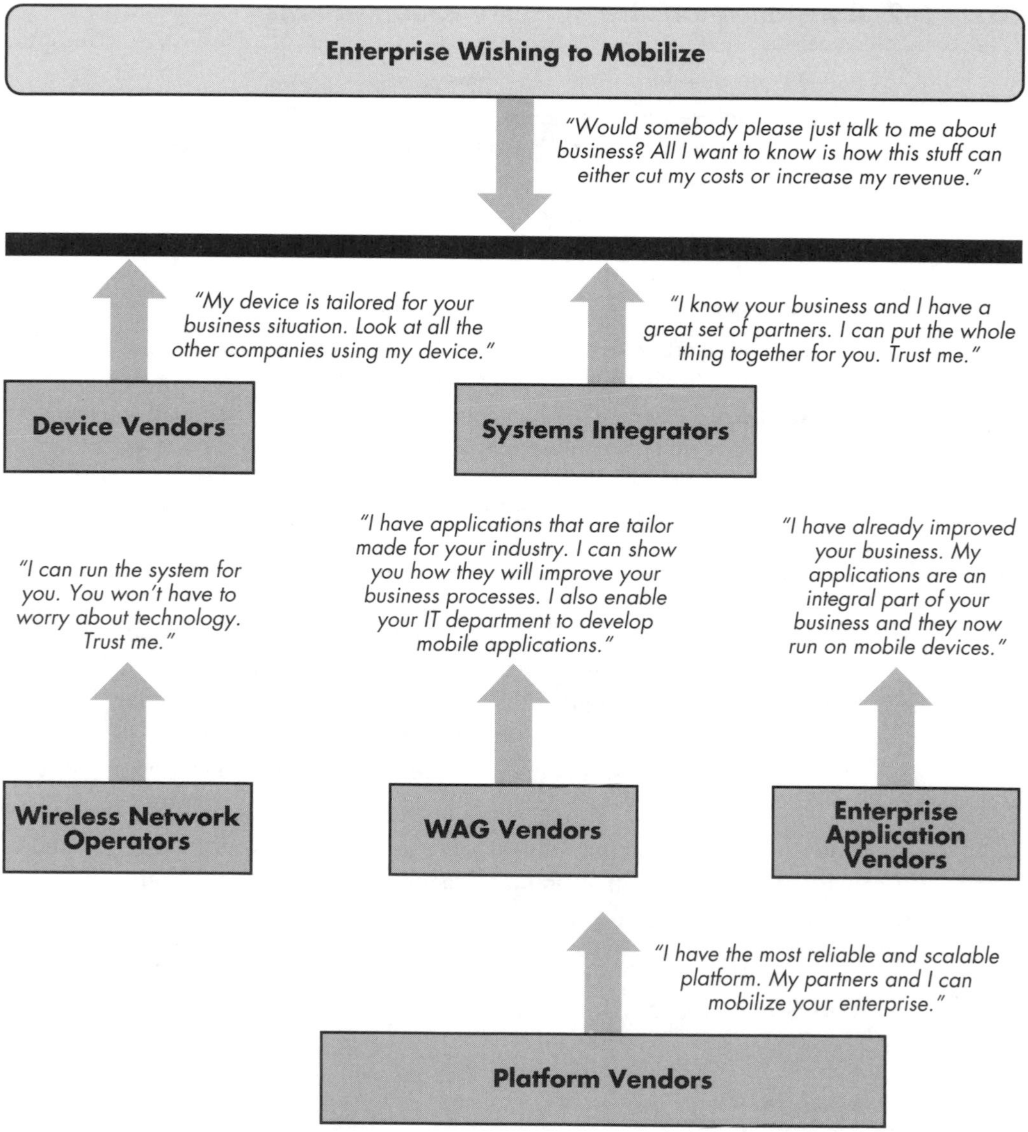

FIGURE 11–6   The structure of the industry.

nerships. For ongoing support issues, you have that company to beat up on. Let them deal with all the others.

In some cases, one company is positioned in several categories. For example, both HP and IBM act as device vendors, systems integrators, WAG vendors, and platform vendors. Another example is that Siebel, SAP, Oracle, and PeopleSoft are all well positioned as enterprise application vendors. Each has also developed its own mobile platform tailored to access its applications. Furthermore, these companies all have systems integration capabilities.

Figure 11–6 shows how each of these classes of company is trying to position themselves. Let's now examine each class more closely to see what they can do well, with whom they are likely to partner, and the evolutionary path most natural for them.

Device Vendors

Portable computing devices are the most prominent feature of the mobile enterprise. This is the part of the mobile enterprise that people see and touch. The companies selling portable devices include those shown in Table 11–1.

TABLE 11–1 Device Vendors

Company	Notes
Ericsson	Ericsson markets cell phones and smart phones primarily to consumers. They are now trying to gain a better position in the enterprise market.
Handspring	Handspring has innovative devices, including a successful smart phone.
HP	HP sells PDAs, Tablets, and Notebooks to the enterprise. Because they also fit in the systems integrator, WAG vendor, and platform vendor categories, they are able to package devices as part of a larger sale.
IBM	IBM sells PDAs and Notebooks to the enterprise. Like HP, they also fit in the systems integrator, WAG vendor, and platform vendor categories, and are able to package devices as part of a larger sale. With Lotus Notes, IBM also fits in the enterprise application vendor category.
Intermec	Intermec sells ruggedized devices.
Itronix	Itronix sells ruggedized devices.
Motorola	Motorola markets cell phones. They are particularly strong in the paging market. Their PDAs run a proprietary OS, so there is not such a rich set of third-party applications running on these devices.
Nokia	Like Ericsson, Nokia does a good job of marketing cell phones and smart phones to consumers—and they are now trying to gain a stronger position in the enterprise market.
PALM	PALM sells well in the consumer market, but they are struggling with the enterprise market.
RIM	RIM messengers are very good at wireless email. They are a relatively small company and rely on partnerships to increase their reach.
Symbol	Symbol sells ruggedized devices.
Two Technologies	Two Technologies sells ruggedized devices.

There are two broad markets for portable computing devices: consumer and enterprise. Some of the device vendors do very well in the consumer market, but not so well in the enterprise market, where they have to establish account relationships and set up support infrastructure. Devices are positioned differently in the consumer and enterprise market in terms of the fashion statement they make. For example, while purple cell phones might sell very well among teenage consumers, they would be a hard sell to business users. Another difference is in the price points—consumers are not willing to pay as much as the enterprise customer.

Device vendors may try to partner with wireless network operators. The operator might subsidize the purchase of a device in order to lock a user into a subscription plan. This has worked for cell phones and RIM messengers. There have also been some efforts to apply this model to PDA sales. The danger in this approach to the device vendor is that if there is nothing to differentiate the device, the operator can play one device off another and apply price pressure.

Device vendors also try to win the preferences of systems integrators, WAG vendors, and enterprise application vendors. In this way, they create a pull-through effect. When any of these kinds of companies wins a deal, they are most likely to pull along the device with which they are most familiar. The customer may differ and demand a different device. The customer should be aware that the decision to use a different device may result in some extra hidden costs. While the systems integrator, WAG vendor, or enterprise application vendor might say that they are device-independent, they could have some trouble working out a relationship with a different device vendor and learning to use the different device.

A strengths/weaknesses/opportunities/threats (SWOT) analysis of the situation of device vendors as a class is shown in Figure 11–7.

STRENGTHS	WEAKNESSES
• Brand-name recognition translates from the consumer market to the enterprise market. • The device is the most prominent aspect of the mobile enterprise, thus increasing brand strength even further.	• Many vendors are well positioned for consumer sales, but they are not as well prepared to provide the extra support required by enterprise customers. • Device vendors cannot by themselves mobilize an enterprise.
OPPORTUNITIES	THREATS
• Vendors must gain the preference of application developers and systems integrators to create pull-through sales. • Seduce users. Users tend to become attached to a device, resulting in more brand loyalty.	• The lack of clear differentiation in a crowded market means there will be downward price pressure. • The technology is changing quickly and there are always new entrants.

FIGURE 11–7 SWOT analysis of device vendors.

A device vendor alone could never mobilize your enterprise. A different kind of company would have to lead this effort. The best thing the device vendor can hope for is to have the preference of the customer and/or the company leading the sale.

Systems Integrators

Of all the classes of companies involved in mobilizing enterprises, systems integrators (SIs) are the best suited to talking to customers about strategy and return on investment—and to putting the whole solution together. The downside is that they tend to be expensive.

The systems integrators working in this area include those listed in Table 11–2.

TABLE 11–2 Systems Integrators

Company	Notes
Accenture	Accenture, along with network operator partners, offers two types of services to enterprises. One is for larger enterprises to run wirelessly enabled business systems in their own data centers. The other offers a hosted wireless service for small and midsize enterprises.
CGE&Y	Cap Gemini Earnst & Young's "Mobile Insight" service is designed to get clients started on wireless through education on wireless technology and through help in devising a strategy. CGE&Y has worked with clients to add wirelessly enabled enterprise applications.
Deloitte Consulting	Deloitte Consulting offers several services in wireless, including the "mTransformation" and readiness-assessment services, which helps clients identify areas for potential wireless investment. Where mobility is required, DC will frequently bring in the WAG of its subsidiary, Telispark.
EDS	Electronic Data Services offers a suite of mobile and wireless services ranging from consulting to integration services. The consulting services include strategic as well as tactical advice and security assessments.
HPC	HP Consulting leverages its broad experience with both telcos and in the area of enterprise applications to provide a set of services to help enterprise clients go mobile. These services include an "Art of the Possible" workshop to help clients determine the business case for mobility.
IGS	IBM Global Services is the world's largest systems integrator. For customers interested in wireless, IGS provides services such as implementation planning, site survey, predelivery preparation, installation and rollout, network and cellular access, training, and support.
KPMG Consulting	KPMG Consulting's "readySetGo!" framework is designed to help clients evaluate ROI potential, to select wireless carriers and devices, and to determine how to wirelessly enable applications.
PwC Consulting	PricewaterhouseCoopers Consulting "mBusiness" strategy focuses on helping clients develop new business models through mobility, lowering costs, and demonstrating return on investment (ROI).

STRENGTHS	WEAKNESSES
• SIs have knowledge in the industries of their clients, and are quite capable of talking to their clients about business problems. • Because they are defining strategy for their clients, they are well positioned to get implementation projects.	• SIs are not able to do anything inexpensively. • SIs usually have no products of their own.
OPPORTUNITIES	THREATS
• SIs must partner with WAG vendors and enterprise application vendors to provide services around product sales. • Win large, high-profile deals to gain credibility in an emerging market.	• Smaller systems integrators who are deeply entrenched in special niches threaten the big systems integrators.

FIGURE 11–8   SWOT analysis of systems integrators.

All of the systems integrators have experience in consulting around the big enterprise applications, such as ERP and CRM. Most also have experience working with wireless operators. All have industry-specific groups.

Given such organizational structures, there is no clear place to put a mobility practice. Most systems integrators have opted for having a cross-organizational mobility practice, while also having mobility expertise in the CRM groups and in the industry groups.

Figure 11–8 shows a SWOT analysis of systems integrators as a class. Systems integrators are very well positioned in that they are usually involved in defining their clients' wireless strategies.

Wireless Network Operators

There is no question that wireless networks are an essential part of the mobile enterprise, but they will have trouble positioning themselves the way they would like, that is, hosting enterprise applications and WAGs. Their biggest fear is ending up just providing data transmission services.

A list of wireless network operators is shown in Table 11–3.

TABLE 11-3 Wireless network operators.

Company	Notes
Arch	Arch Wireless Enterprise Solutions (AWES) includes access to email, Internet, and CRM.
AT&T Wireless	AT&T Wireless runs a network that uses several technologies—AMPS, TDMA, and GSM.
Cingular	Cingular's "Wireless Internet" and "Interactive Messaging" services allow limited Internet access and messaging through cell phones.
EarthLink	EarthLink's "Wireless Email and Internet" services allow access to email and Internet.
GoAmerica	GoAmerica's "Enterprise Desktop" services include wireless access to email, CRM, and sales force automation (SFA).
Metrocall	Metrocall offers data services to enterprises.
Motient	Motient offers a variety of enterprise solutions based on their data network.
Nextel	Nextel's "Wireless Business Solutions" allow wireless use of strategic business applications.
Sprint PCS	Sprint PCS's "Clear Wireless Workplace" includes access to email, Internet, and enterprise applications from cell phones, PDAs, and notebook computers.
SkyTel	SkyTel offers data services to enterprises.
Verizon	Verizon's "Mobile Office" service offers secure access to email for business users.
VoiceStream	VoiceStream's "Wireless Inbox" services offers secure access to email for business users.

As it stands today, there is not a big difference in service from one operator to another. Customers tend to switch networks frequently—and they do so based on price. This has two big effects on operators:

1. The average revenue per user (ARPU) is declining over time.
2. They have to spend a lot of money to attract new customers—and those new customers usually have to be taken from a competitor.

These competitive pressures are causing network operators to look for new revenue streams and for new ways of locking customers in. Some operators are attempting to accomplish these two things by hosting wireless services for enterprise customers. This might involve hosting the WAG and/or some mobile applications.

The value proposition to customers is that they do not have to run the IT infrastructure themselves. Such services might be subscription based, so the customer does not have to pay as much up front. However, there are several problems with this proposition, which make it unlikely to prevail. These problems are:

- *Security.* If the operator is providing a value-added service, that is, if they are doing anything other than providing a data transmission service, your enterprise data will probably have to be *in the clear* (unencrypted) at some point in the operator network.

- *Performance.* Data has to be fetched from your enterprise applications and transformed on the operator network. This is not likely to occur as fast as when the transformation occurs at the enterprise.

- *Operator lock-in.* If a given wireless network operator becomes an integral part of your method of accessing enterprise data, you will have a hard time changing operators. Once you are locked in, the operator has a great deal of control, which puts upward pressure on prices. While this is exactly what the operator wants, it is very undesirable for customers. Such a win–lose arrangement is not a good foundation for ongoing business.

The data services offered by the different operators depends to a large extent on the network technology used (see Chapter 6). Operators are also able to determine the location of a user through different techniques described in Chapter 6. The choice of techniques used will result in different levels of service.

While wireless network operators would love to get into the hosting business, this will probably not work in the long run. In the long run, the role of the wireless network operator will be to sell data services and location-based services (Figure 11–9).

Operators do not have good channels into the enterprise market. They also know very little about enterprise applications and the integration of these applications. For these reasons they could not lead the effort to mobilize your enterprise. Instead they will rely on partners.

STRENGTHS	WEAKNESSES
• Network operators are alone in the ability to determine the location of a user (remember that GPS does not work indoors). • High startup costs make it hard for new competitors to enter their particular market.	• Network operators have very little understanding of enterprise applications. • Network operators cannot by themselves mobilize an enterprise.
OPPORTUNITIES	**THREATS**
• Operators partner with device vendors and systems integrators. • Develop location-based services that do not involve sensitive enterprise data.	• Network operators are constantly faced with the threat of becoming just utility companies delivering a commodity-like service.

FIGURE 11–9   SWOT analysis on wireless operators.

Operators naturally partner with device vendors. The operator subsidizes the sale of the device in return for the sale of a subscription. In some cases, the operator puts its brand on the device. For example, Sprint PCS brands a smart phone made by Samsung.

Operators also like to gain the preference of systems integrators who are making recommendations to customers. The systems integrator might get a bulk discount on data services in return for selling these services to large enterprises.

Wireless Application Gateway Vendors

The initial strategy of most WAG vendors has been to provide a platform, which allows IT departments and third-party developers to create wireless applications to meet their specific needs. Most have since realized that they have to provide a suite of vertically oriented applications as well. These are applications that respond to a specific industry need, for which a clear case can be made for business value. For example, some vendors have specific applications targeting pharmaceutical sales.

The list of WAG vendors is long. Table 11–4 shows some of the most prominent ones.

TABLE 11–4 WAG Vendors

Company	Notes
724 Solutions	724 Solutions' Wireless Internet Platform (WIP) is a robust platform positioned for high-volume transactions.
Aether Systems	Aether Systems' Fusion framework integrates various pieces of software to provide a wireless platform that allows access to enterprise applications.
Air2Web	Air2Web's Mobile Internet Platform uses a patented approach to content rendering called Cascaded Rendering.
AvantGo	AvantGo's Mobile Business Server (MBS) performs content aggregation, compression, intelligent caching, and content transformation to provide access to multiple device types.
Brience	Brience's Mobile Processing Server provides access from multiple devices to multiple back-end applications.
Everypath	Everypath's Mobile Application Gateway provides access from multiple device types to back-end applications such as those from Oracle, Siebel, and SAP.
Extended Systems	Extended Systems' OneBridge platform allows customers to mobilize back-end applications.
HP	HP's Total-E-Mobile is built on HP Application Server, combining a robust platform with a set of tools to interface with back-end applications and render content on multiple device types.
IBM	IBM's WebSphere Transcoding Publisher (WTP) adapts application output to a format appropriate for smaller devices.

TABLE 11–4   WAG Vendors (Continued)

Company	Notes
iConverse	iConverse's Mobility Platform allows customers to create and deploy mobile applications by linking into existing enterprise applications.
Oracle	Oracle's 9iAS allows customers to access back-end applications and databases from mobile devices.
Sybase	Sybase iAnywhere Solutions, a subsidiary of Sybase, include platforms for access to enterprise applications from mobile devices.
Telispark	A subsidiary of Deloitte Consulting. Experts in wireless technologies and enterprise application integration.

The WAG market is very crowded. Competitive pressures are likely to reduce the crowd significantly over the next year. A SWOT analysis of WAG vendors as a class is shown in Figure 11–10.

A threat to WAG vendors as a group is that with enterprise application vendors mobilizing their applications, the need for a WAG is reduced. However, the thing that is likely to keep the need for WAGs alive is the fact that most mobile professionals need access to several different enterprise systems. It makes more sense to have one platform sit in front of several applications rather than adding mobile features to each of the individual applications.

STRENGTHS	WEAKNESSES
• Because the WAG is the piece that ties the whole solution together, WAG vendors have the best understanding of the overall solution. • The WAG is the centerpiece of the mobile enterprise, defining the feature set and operational aspects.	• Most are small companies, a fact which tends to scare customers. • For those WAGs marketed by large companies, since today's market is small, the management in these companies sees the WAG business as too small a portion of their revenue to focus on.
OPPORTUNITIES	**THREATS**
• WAG vendors can seize the day by developing vertically oriented customer office applications. • Those WAGs that are scalable and reliable will beat the others to the punch once demand picks up. • Smaller WAG vendors should partner with large companies for large channels and to add legitimacy. This will reduce their chances of being squeezed out once bigger companies get into this business.	• Enterprise application vendors with mobile features minimize the need for a WAG. • When the market takes off, more large companies will get into this business and try to squeeze out the smaller WAG vendors.

FIGURE 11–10   SWOT analysis of WAG vendors.

Enterprise Application Vendors

Enterprise application vendors have already been through a cycle of applying technology to improve the business processes of their clients. In doing this they have realized the importance of understanding specific industries and fitting the technology to the business problem. Table 11–5 shows a list of prominent enterprise application vendors.

TABLE 11–5 Enterprise Application Vendors

Company	Notes
IBM	IBM sells Lotus Notes.
Microsoft	Microsoft sells Exchange E-Mail.
Oracle	Oracle uses its 9iAS wireless edition to mobilize some of its CRM applications.
PeopleSoft	PeopleSoft mobilizes CRM and some of its parts management modules.
SAP	SAP mobilizes sales modules of its CRM suite.
Siebel Systems	Siebel Systems mobilizes sales modules of its CRM suite.

Enterprise applications assume the user is working on a computer with a large screen and a full-sized keyboard. They also assume access is over a high-bandwidth, fixed-line connection. These assumptions play into the way data is presented, the size of the applications, the amount of data exchanges that occur between the application and the client computer, and in the general flow of the application logic.

Customer-office applications depend on back-office and front-office applications for data, but they require a different flow. This new breed of application has to fit into the business processes of customer-facing employees. Forward-looking vendors recognize this and are working to evolve their products accordingly.

Figure 11–11 provides a SWOT analysis of enterprise application vendors.

Over time, wireless may just be another channel for accessing applications. In a mobile environment, the devices on which the applications are being accessed will be small by definition. This means that the application has to work well on a small screen. The application logic also has to fit naturally into the workday of a mobile professional.

STRENGTHS	WEAKNESSES
• Their applications hold all the business information that we are trying to get to the mobile professional. • They are accustomed to speaking to clients about business process reengineering.	• They generally do not have good skills in wireless technology.
OPPORTUNITIES	THREATS
• Develop the customer-office applications that are needed by the mobile professional. • Develop offline versions of their applications that operate through synchronization.	• WAG vendors might gain the upper hand in developing customer-office applications. This will become the most important class of applications.

FIGURE 11–11 SWOT analysis for enterprise application vendors.

Platform Vendors

Platform vendors are almost by definition large companies. Who else could have the capacity to design, manufacture, sell, and support computer hardware? Because these companies are large, they tend to have skills in several other areas as well. Table 11–6 shows a list of platform vendors.

TABLE 11–6 Platform Vendors

Company	Notes
HP	HP sells computer platforms along with middleware.
IBM	IBM sells computer platforms along with middleware.
Sun	Sun sells computer platforms along with middleware.

In their capacity as platform vendors, the selling opportunities for these companies are to systems integrators, WAG vendors, and enterprise application vendors. The best thing they can do in this capacity is to gain the preference of these other companies to create a sell-through effect. A SWOT analysis of platform vendors is shown in Figure 11–12.

As already mentioned, HP and IBM are also in the business of selling solutions. To sell solutions, they tend to form a range of partnerships and integrate various components.

STRENGTHS	WEAKNESSES
• There is a high cost of entering this business. Newcomers are few and far between. • The size and reach of their sales force makes them a great channel for their partners.	• Platforms do not offer the core functionality of the mobile enterprise. They are enablers of other pieces.
OPPORTUNITIES	**THREATS**
• Vendors must gain the preference of application developers and systems integrators to create pull-through sales. • Scalable and reliable platforms will rule as demand picks up. • Storage area networks (SANs) will be in high demand.	• Platform vendors have to be careful not to have their products become mere commodities.

FIGURE 11–12 SWOT analysis of platform vendors.

The Size of the Vendor

Since this industry is so new, it is heavily populated with startup companies. This presents a risk to the customer. You do not want to buy a complex solution from a company that does not have the infrastructure to provide support—and you definitely do not want to buy a product and have the vendor go bankrupt 6 months later.

The WAG vendors are most likely to be start-up companies. These platforms are based on new technology—and larger companies cannot react quickly enough to put a product in this space. The larger companies also tend to focus on larger markets. There is not yet enough volume in WAG sales to put a dent in a large company's bottom line.

This will change over the next few years. As mobile technology reaches a higher rate of adoption, the industry will consolidate and larger companies will begin to sell WAGs. Microsoft and Oracle are already moving in this direction.

WAG vendors tend to partner with larger companies to extend their reach. The proposition to the customer is that the large vendor can provide ongoing support for the overall solution.

There are also some small device vendors, but they are generally at least an order of magnitude bigger than the WAG vendors. As long as the device is running a standard operating system, the cost of changing is not so high. All you have to do is find another device running the same operating system, and your applications should be able to run on the new device with, at most, only a small number of modifications. Portable computers are evolving so rapidly that you will probably look to the market for a new device every eighteen months or so anyway.

The issues you will face with device vendors are around ongoing support. You need quick access to replacement devices. If you are operating in several geographical areas, you need to do business with a company that can get you those replacements where you need them.

Finally, if your business processes are highly specific, you might have to rely on a small systems integrator staffed with experts in your industry. The larger systems integrators will not see a big enough market in your industry to train people to the degree you require. The best way to mitigate risk in this case is to insist on a lot of documentation and on the use of standards wherever possible. If your systems integrator goes out of business, you want a new one to come up to speed quickly.

TOTAL COST OF OWNERSHIP (TCO)

Before mobilizing your enterprise, take an honest assessment of all the costs. As shown in Box 11–3, costs will come in many forms and at many different points in time.

Box 11–3 Costs to Remember

Remember to take the following costs into account in assessing TCO:

- **Business consulting**. You may have a consulting firm analyze your business processes for you and make recommendations.
- **Software and hardware**. There will be an upfront cost to purchasing system components.
- **Customization and configuration**. You will never encounter the situation where you can buy a mobile enterprise solution shrink-wrapped and ready to go. There will always be some customization and configuration work somebody has to do.
- **Training costs**. You will have to train your IT department to run the new platform. You will also have to train users.
- **Replacement costs**. Do not forget to stock up on replacement devices. Once your mobile workforce comes to depend on this technology, you will need to make replacements quickly.
- **Ongoing support**. Your solution provider will probably offer a support contract.
- **Service charges**. For wireless data services, there will probably be some fixed monthly charge.

- **Consumption charges**. There may also be usage charges for the wireless data services.
- **Enhancements**. Remember that this is all very new. Your solution provider will offer enhancements from time to time.

In estimating the total cost of ownership, take all of these things into account.

SUMMARY

Be careful not to apply technology just for technology's sake—and definitely do not let your vendors get away with this. Your business is already complicated enough as it is. There is no room for technology that makes things worse.

Think through your requirements carefully. Try to consider each one in isolation, and try to separate the requirement from the technology you think you will apply. This is never completely possible, but it is what you should strive for. The technology you apply to your business should be simple to deploy, easy to use, and tailor-made for your business flows.

We have discussed the structure of the industry and how the different kinds of companies are positioning themselves. There are certain natural partnerships between the different classes of company. No one kind of company is able to mobilize your enterprise alone. They will rely on partners.

You, as the buyer, should understand which kind of company to call. You should know why they are in this business and get an idea of where they are trying to go. Hopefully, this chapter has helped you understand the structure of the industry today and how it is likely to evolve.

CHAPTER 12

Deploying a Mobile Enterprise Solution

Now you are at the point where you want to deploy a mobile enterprise solution. Having worked through your business processes and spotted areas where mobility can make significant improvements, and having considered your requirements and shopped around, there are still several questions that need to be resolved. These range from questions about how to run a pilot to questions concerning health and safety.

Early on in the process you will need to decide on how you can measure the benefits of your mobile solution. There are a good deal of metrics from which to choose. Make decisions on how you measure success before starting.

When it comes time to deploy, you will need to plan in such a way as to minimize your company's risk exposure. It is wise to start out on a small scale and monitor the results. Once you establish success, you are ready to roll out.

Be sure to familiarize yourself with some of the concerns that have been raised about the health risks of using cell phones. It is important to review these issues, and understand the various studies that have been conducted. You certainly do not want to put your employees, and those around them, at risk.

MEASURING THE BENEFITS OF MOBILE TECHNOLOGY

There are a number of benefits you expect to derive through mobile solutions. Some are tangible—others are not. As much as possible, you should try to measure change so you can accurately assess the value of mobility to your enterprise. But also remember to take into account intangible benefits, such as better communications between employees, less wasted time during travel, and a better work environment.

Pick a small number of metrics. Then establish a baseline on a control group or during a control time period preceding the use of your new mobile solution. Keep in mind that you will need to filter out other factors that could contribute to observed changes. For example, sales are subject to seasonable economic factors—you probably already experience a certain amount of fluctuation in the number of orders taken just before Christmas.

Be meticulous about metrics. They will help you demonstrate the business value of a mobile solution.

Metrics for Sales

Salespeople benefit from mobile solutions by being able to answer customer questions more quickly, take orders on the spot, prepare for customer visits more efficiently, close higher value sales, complete administrative tasks more efficiently, and coordinate sales efforts with colleagues. Most of these new capabilities should translate to measurable benefits.

Number of Calls

If your mobile solution is making your sales force work more quickly and more efficiently, you can expect an increase in the number of sales calls that can be made per salesperson. This is something you probably measure on a regular basis already.

Number of Orders

Mobile solutions can help your salespeople keep momentum going during a sales call. They also make it easier for salespeople to take orders. The average number of orders should be measured to help demonstrate the effect of your mobile solution.

Average Size of Order

If a salesperson has access to more information to sell higher-value items, you might expect an increase in the average order size. For example, with a mobile solution a salesperson might be able to explore complex product configurations with the customer. As part of this process, the salesperson can work out the price of such unusual configurations and the profit he or she would make on a sale.

Number of Up-Sells and Cross-Sells

If your mobile solution includes functionality that enables the salesperson to cross-sell and up-sell, you should consider measuring the number of times a cross-sell or an up-sell occurs. It may take some time to get this process going, as you need some history in order to make the correlations between products.

Close Rate

Since a mobile solution can help a salesperson move toward a close, you should measure the rate at which salespeople are able to close deals. You can expect a bigger change in this metric for low-value products than for high-value products.

Revenue per Salesperson

In the end you want to take in more revenue per salesperson. This is definitely something you should measure in the long run. In the short run it might be difficult to see a difference. For example, you might not be able to take such a measurement over the duration of a pilot. However, you should look for improvement in revenue over the long term—over several months or a few years.

Metrics for Service Workers

Service workers benefit from mobile solutions by being able to fix equipment faster, get dispatched more efficiently, order parts faster, coordinate more effectively with colleagues, access problem history and technical documents, generate bills faster and more easily, and make fewer trips to the office. These new capabilities should translate to a number of measurable benefits.

First-Time Fix Rate

When an engineer cannot fix equipment on the first visit, he or she must then schedule a follow-up visit. This is wasteful—and it causes further delay in getting the equipment up and running.

This usually occurs because either not enough information was communicated to the engineer at the time of dispatch, or the information that was communicated was wrong. In either case the engineer might show up with the wrong documentation and spare parts.

Another reason engineers cannot fix equipment on the first visit is that they need help from colleagues or they need more information. If they cannot phone somebody to get that information, they have to schedule a second visit.

A mobile solution helps in both of these cases by allowing the engineer to retrieve information as needed. He or she can connect to the company intranet and query knowledge management (KM) systems.

The first-time fix rate is something many companies measure already. We expect to see a higher first-time fix rate when mobile technology is put to use.

Time to Repair

The quicker equipment gets fixed, the more benefit your customer derives from the equipment. If the equipment you sold a customer is down for a long time, your customer is not likely to be very happy.

Because there is a potential to reduce dispatch time, and to enable engineers to retrieve information to help them fix equipment, we can expect a mobile solution to reduce the average time it takes to repair equipment.

Dispatch Time

Mobile solutions can reduce the dispatch time in several ways. First of all, either through location-determination technology or by having engineers update their schedules as changes occur, mobile technology makes it easier to keep track of where the engineers are at any given time. With this knowledge, a dispatch system is able to select an engineer for a job based on proximity and availability, in addition to skill set.

Second, mobile solutions make the dispatch process more efficient. Information can be sent with a dispatch notification, enabling the engineer to make a more informed decision as to whether or not he or she is the right person for the job. The dispatch notification might even include a low-resolution map or driving instructions.

Finally, the engineer does not have to stop in the office to pick up documentation or to review problem history. Because he or she can download and read documents from a portable computing device, less time is wasted in getting to the problem site.

Calls Serviced per Engineer

If mobile technology can help engineers work faster and more efficiently, we can expect an increase in the number of calls that can be serviced by each engineer. This is relatively simple to measure.

Invoices per Engineer

If your mobile solution makes it easier for field engineers to fill out the forms necessary to generate an invoice, you might find that more invoices get generated. That which is easy to do is more likely to get done.

Revenue per Engineer

One of the overall results you are looking to achieve is to generate more revenue per field engineer. It may take some time before revenue gains are achieved. For this reason, it might not be a useful metric for your pilot. However, this is certainly something you should measure over the long run.

General Metrics

The rest of the company benefits by being able to learn more about customers, serve customers better, operate more efficiently, and stay in touch with mobile workers. These capabilities sometimes translate to measurable benefits.

Update Rate

One key benefit of the mobile technology is that customer-facing employees can make updates to customer relationship management (CRM)—or other enterprise applications—as they learn something new. Because these employees can make updates easily, they are more likely to do so. Because they can do so immediately, they are not likely to forget just what it is they want to say.

With up-to-date information in your CRM system, you can get closer to your customers. Where possible, you should measure how more often updates are made after a mobile solution is deployed.

Reduction in Paperwork

Our intuition tells us that mobile solutions will reduce the amount of paperwork required to perform business functions. The benefit here is not necessarily the reduced cost of buying paper—remember that if you are using a wireless data network you will incur a transmission cost, which will offset your savings in paper. The benefit of reducing the amount of paperwork is that you have less work to do to read the information from the paper and type it into a computer system. You can also expect fewer errors if the data is entered only once—and by the person with the information to be entered.

You can measure the reduction in paperwork by counting how much new paper has to be ordered during a given period.

Miles per Job

For any worker who has to travel to and from the office to retrieve documents and data, or to fill out forms, you can expect a reduction in the number of miles traveled. This equates to a reduction in wasted time and in travel costs. A good thing to measure in this case is the average number of miles traveled per job.

Customer Satisfaction Survey

Customer satisfaction is a leading indicator of customer retention. If you are loosing customers, you have to spend a lot of time and money getting them back or getting new customers. Customer acquisition is expensive.

If you try to measure customer satisfaction through customer retention, by the time you find out you have a problem it is too late. The best way of measuring customer satisfaction is by asking the customer. Take the time to carefully plan and conduct customer surveys targeted to measuring any difference brought on by the mobile solution.

Another thing you might measure is the number of customer complaints. If your mobile solution has some effect on customer satisfaction, you might notice a reduction in the number of customer complaints.

Employee Satisfaction Survey

Employee satisfaction is a leading indicator of employee retention. We all know that it takes a lot of money to hire new employees and to bring them up to speed. The best thing to do is not lose employees.

Furthermore, you should be concerned with what employees think about using the mobile solution. If they do not like the solution, you probably will not derive much business benefit from it.

Some of the ways you can measure employee satisfaction are through employee surveys, focus group meetings, and user group meetings.

DEPLOYMENT PHASES

Once you have chosen vendors, you are ready to try out your mobile solution. To minimize the risks associated with new technology, you should start with a pilot. As shown in Figure 12–1, the steps to deployment should start with a carefully planned pilot, followed by a phased implementation. In between the pilot and the initial implementation should be a careful analysis of the pilot results.

One problem companies face when running a pilot is that not everybody has the same objectives. Even worse is that frequently people do not make the difference between a proof-of-concept and a pilot.

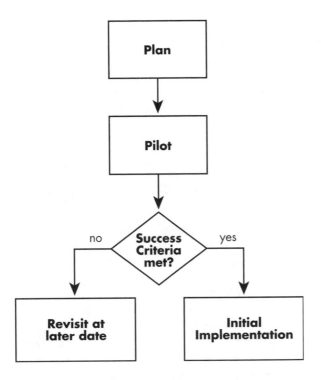

FIGURE 12–1 Steps to deployment.

Proof of Concept versus Pilot

A proof-of-concept makes sense when it is necessary to try out some new idea. Usually this is accomplished by putting together different technology in a one-off configuration just to see if the concept works.

For example, an IT team within HP hypothesized that salespeople would want to listen to their email on a cassette tape while driving to customer sites in the morning. To test this idea, they put together a system whereby a text-to-speech converter read the salesperson's email overnight and recorded it onto a cassette tape. In the morning, the salesperson took the tape and put it in his or her car to listen to on the drive to the first customer site.

This proof-of-concept worked well in that it showed the hypothesis was wrong. The last thing salespeople want to do is listen to email while driving to a customer site. Most would prefer to spend the time thinking about the imminent customer visit.

A proof-of-concept makes sense to test a new paradigm. It is usually based on a set of components put together just for the test in order to get user feedback. If feedback is positive, a real solution might be put together. Mobile enterprise solutions are way past the proof-of-concept phase.

A pilot, on the other hand, makes sense once you have decided on a concept and a set of features. The purpose of the pilot is to test the entire value chain, including support and training. It is entirely appropriate to run a pilot of your mobile solution. This is to test all aspects of the service.

Pilot Objectives

People in your organization may have different definitions about what a pilot is. This can lead to problems in running the pilot and in evaluating its success. This might also lead to a situation where the pilot simply becomes the initial deployment with no evaluation whatsoever.

A pilot should be a small-scale version of the real deployment minus mission-critical aspects. It is run to test support infrastructure and scalability. Some of the other things you might want to validate:

*   *A hypothesis for return on investment (ROI)*: Although your business case looks good on paper, it is a good idea to test it on a small scale. In this case, during your pilot, you will need to measure values that you can reasonably expect to change throughout the pilot. For example, you might measure miles traveled per customer visit or number of updates to the CRM system. But you cannot reasonably expect to be able to measure a change in revenue.

*   *Integration with enterprise applications*: A pilot can help you determine how well your mobile solution integrates with existing enterprise applications. Does the data remain consistent as updates are posted in either direction—from the user to the enterprise, as well as from the enterprise to the user?

These objectives may work for you—or you may have a few others of your own. What is important is that all stakeholders agree on the objectives that make sense for *your* company's pilot.

Remember also that a pilot, which allows you to determine the system does not work, is in fact a successful pilot. You save a lot of time and money by making that assessment early and on a small scale. A failed pilot is one in which you do not make an accurate determination of what to expect from a full deployment.

Planning a Pilot

A good deal of time should go into planning the pilot. All aspects of the service should be included in your plans. As shown in Box 12–1, some of the biggest pitfalls in piloting are results of poor planning.

Box 12–1 Mistakes in Running a Pilot

Some of the worst mistakes made around piloting new systems are:

- **Not planning all aspects of the value chain**: Remember that the pilot is a test of the entire service. This includes training, documentation, user setup, and support.
- **Not planning how they will be evaluated**: If you do not have clear objectives and measures to distinguish success from failure, you might as well not run a pilot. Your measures should include all aspects of the value chain.
- **Not planning how they will end**: A pilot should have success and failure criteria. In addition, there should be a clear start date and end date. If success or failure is apparent before the end date, you should stop then. If pilot runs up to the end date, be sure to carefully evaluate the outcome.
- **Poor timing**: Do not start a pilot the week before everybody goes on vacation, the last week of the quarter, or the week before a major sporting event.

It is important to share your plans with other stakeholders to make sure they understand your intentions. It is even better if you can get them to participate in developing the plans.

Organizational Alignment

In cases where your plans require services from other departments in your company, make sure you get some kind of written agreement to avoid misunderstandings. One department you will certainly need to have on board is the support group. In order to get the pilot off the ground, you will need to be sure users can call somebody to get help.

You will probably have to allow time for people working the help desk to get trained to provide the necessary support. Documentation should be made available for the help desk. Procedures should be put in place to incorporate user feedback into future changes to the system.

Choosing Users

You should carefully select the users of the pilot system. They should be enthusiastic about the pilot. One way to make sure they take it seriously is to require users—or their organizations—to pay a nominal fee for participating in the pilot. Even if they just pay a small amount, this gives them some skin in the game.

Establishing Success Criteria

From the outset you should recognize three possible ends to the pilot. One is that the end date is reached. Another is that complete disaster is recognized early. And the third—and best case—is that great success is recognized early. Start out with a plan that takes these three eventualities into account.

Metrics around the success of the pilot should include those for determining return on investment (ROI), as well as those around the success of the service. The service includes software, hardware, training, documentation, support, and billing.

Running the Pilot

After careful planning, and after all stakeholders are in agreement on objectives and success criteria, you are ready to start your pilot.

Gaining User Acceptance Early

To start out on the right foot you might consider giving the portable computing devices to users a little early to allow them to play around with it and get to like it. You might even entice employees through the "fun factor" by putting games on the devices.

At a minimum you should make sure you have smooth processes for setting up and getting users started. There is no bigger turn off than starting out with a buggy system—especially when the system is supposed to be a way of making work easier.

Communicating with Pilot Participants

Throughout the pilot you should have a way of collecting user feedback. This might include reviewing calls to the help desk, collecting feedback through user groups, conducting surveys, or making direct inquiries to individuals. In many cases, a pilot is started and nobody can tell how many people are actually using the system. When testing a service that makes use of new technology, it is especially important to make sure the service is in fact being used.

If it is not, why not? The answer to this question could indicate that the system is a complete failure and there is no need to continue. More often, though, the problem turns out to be that users have not received enough guidance. You will want to catch this problem early.

Checkpoint Meetings

All stakeholders in the pilot should participate in regular checkpoint meetings to gage progress. These checkpoints should include discussions on how much the system is being used, user feedback, and progress with respect to success criteria. Participants should review the objectives to make sure they still make sense.

Evaluating the Pilot

In many cases, pilots accidentally become initial implementations; that is, they creep in with a lot of wrong expectations. You should avoid this. By making the distinction between pilot and early deployment, you allow your self room to experiment during the pilot.

Make a clean cut between the pilot and the initial implementation with a thorough analysis between the two. If your pilot demonstrates that the mobile service will not work for your company, do not proceed. Document your results, and revisit mobility at a later date. Sooner or later you probably will want to take it on, but now may not be the right time. While *you* are an early adopter, your users may not be.

It is wise to leave open the possibility of changing vendors as you move from pilot to initial deployment. The pilot as a whole may be successful, but you might have noticed some problems with one or more vendors.

Initial Implementation

Once you have decided to go ahead with deployment it is best to use a phased approach. For example, plan to roll out to a hundred people first, another hundred people after that, and so on. Your choice of where to roll out will depend on both geography and organizations.

Choosing Geographies

Geography will be an important factor in deployment for two reasons. First of all, wireless network service and coverage may vary from region to region. Second, your IT infrastructure, training, and support is probably regional in nature.

Strategy might be global but implementation is local. Implementation might not even make sense in certain geographies.

Choosing Organizations

It is usually best to deploy new technology work group by work group, and business by business. Users in the same work group or business area tend to communicate. User communities are an important factor in the deployment of new technology. Also you should not underestimate the value of unintended IT activities. For example, a few users might happen to be technically oriented and they might tend to help their colleagues with the new system.

FISCAL PLANNING ASPECTS

As is the case for any part of life, money makes things happen. Somebody in your company has to pay for the new mobility service.

Somewhere between planning a pilot and initial implementation you will have to figure out how to bill users or organizations for the service. To do this you will have to estimate the lifetime of the service and the total number of users during that lifetime. The cost will have to be spread out accordingly.

Some IT managers prefer to charge early users a little more. There is some rationale behind this, since early users get benefits earlier. Also during the early phases the costing structure is less sure, so you might have to charge more to spread the risk. While the early adopters might pay more, they should not have to pay the full cost of your mobile solution.

A well-advertised success from the pilot could go a long way in getting organizations to contribute funds and/or make commitments to pay for the service. This is yet another reason why it is important to be able to demonstrate success from the pilot.

Another question you will have to answer is what gets billed? Do you bill based on usage? Or do you charge for the service on a monthly basis?

HEALTH AND SAFETY CONCERNS

Before deploying a mobile solution, consider some of the safety issues. There are some that are real, for example, using a portable computing device while driving. There are also some things that are *perceived* as being unsafe, without any supporting evidence. You need to address both kinds of issues. In the former case, you should establish rules to keep workers out of harm's way. In the latter case, you need to make information available to workers who perceive danger.

Somebody in your company should follow developments in both of these areas to keep abreast of any new findings. Not only is this clearly the right thing to do—it is also a good way of keeping your company out of lawsuits.

Working while Driving

In many countries it is illegal to use a cell phone while driving. In the United States, there is still much debate on this topic. Some argue that talking on a cell phone is no more dangerous than talking to a passenger while you are driving. Others contend that while holding a phone to your ear as you are driving might present some risk, using a hands-free phone does not.

Researchers have produced evidence, which refutes both of these viewpoints. Consider the four different kinds of distractions human factors experts tell us a driver can experience:

- *Visual*: Looking at a cell phone display constitutes a visual distraction, because it causes you to look away.

- *Auditory*: A ringing phone is an example of an audio distraction.

- *Mechanical*: Typing on a keypad is a mechanical distraction. It requires use of your hands.

- *Cognitive*: Engaging in a focused conversation with somebody is an example of cognitive distraction, since it turns your mental attention away from driving.

Few people will argue that drivers who are visually or mechanically distracted by a cell phone are putting themselves and others in danger. If you have to look at a screen or keyboard while driving, you are taking your eye off the road. If you have to type on the keypad, you are taking your hand off the steering wheel, reducing your ability to turn quickly to avoid an accident.

As for cognitive distraction, a recent study conducted by researchers at the University of Utah, and published in the November 2001 issue of *Psychological Science,* found that the probability a driver will fail to react is significantly increased when the driver is engaged in conversation on a cell phone. Research published in the February 1997 issue of *The New England Journal of Medicine* suggests that drivers using a cell phone have four times as many accidents as drivers who are not using cell phones. The article points out that this risk is similar to the accident risk for drivers who are legally drunk!

Both these articles also provide evidence suggesting there are no safety advantages to hands-free as compared to handheld phones.

The difference between talking on a phone and talking with a passenger is that the passenger, being in the same situation as the driver, is able to alter the conversation according to what is happening on the road. In fact, the passenger can even spot signs of danger and warn the driver.

While cell phone use and driving are a dangerous combination, it is even more dangerous to use more powerful computing devices while driving. Larger screens and more complex applications divert the driver's attention even more.

No business process should include activities that distract workers while driving. In fact, it would be a good idea to require employees to sign an agreement *not* to use cell phones or other portable computing devices while driving. Even if you are not convinced of the danger, such a policy could protect your company from lawsuits.

Effects of Radio Frequency (RF) Signals on Health

Many studies have been conducted to determine the effects of RF signals on health. In particular, many people have been concerned that radio signals emitted by cell phones could cause cancer. So far no serious study has supported this belief. But do not take my word on this. Take a look at some of the Web sites shown in Table 12–1 to find out more.

TABLE 12–1   Sources of Information on Health Effects of RF Signals

Organization	Web site	Notes
International Electromagnetic Field (EMF) Project	*www.who.int/peh-emf*	This group was established by the World Health Organization (WHO) in 1996 to study the effects of electromagnetic fields on humans.
Federal Communications Commission	*www.fcc.gov/cellphones*	This is the FCC's RF safety page.
Nokia	*www.nokia.com*	Search Nokia's site using the keyword "Health."
Ericsson	*www.ericsson.com*	Search Ericsson's site using the keyword "Health."
Motorola	*www.motorola.com*	Search Motorola's site using the two keywords "Health" and "RF."

To be on the safe side, the FCC has put together guidelines around a value, called the specific absorption rate (SAR), which corresponds to the relative amount of RF energy absorbed in the head of a user of a wireless handset. The FCC limits cell phones to a SAR level of 1.6 watts per kilogram.

To get more information on these guidelines, and to find out the SAR value for specific phones and devices, you can visit the Web site *www.fcc.gov/cellphones.* You might also look for this value on the Web site of your phone or device manufacturer.

SUMMARY

At this point it is best to start out by running a pilot. Make sure that others in your organization understand your definition of a pilot and that it has a start and an end date. You should define other criteria for terminating, such as early indications of total failure or incredible success.

Before starting the pilot make sure you have defined metrics to evaluate whether or not you should move on to full rollout. Use either a control group or a control time period to benchmark on these metrics. When evaluating results be sure to remove other factors, such as seasonality in sales volumes. For example, you do not want to assume that your mobile solution accounted for the great increase in sales you experienced just before Christmas!

Be careful not to have the pilot turn into initial implementation unintentionally. Your first deployment should be more scalable and robust. The value of making the clean break between pilot and initial deployment is that it gives you the freedom to be more experimental during the pilot. On the other hand, real deployment should not involve such unknowns.

An important consideration is your financial model to spread out the cost of deployment. How do you charge your users internally? You should avoid having the early users bear all of the cost. To spread out the costs you will have to make some estimates as to the lifetime of your deployment and the total number of users during that lifetime.

Afterword

Companies all over the world are taking their first steps toward a fully mobilized workplace. Wholesale distributors are implementing wireless order entry—for up-to-the-minute order accuracy and same-day delivery—turning inventory into cash, and delighting their customers. Technical service personnel, dispatched instantly in the field, can carry tools and parts instead of books and manuals—completing more repairs quickly and with fewer callbacks. Insurance claims processors carry their database in their pocket, and document claims instantly—for quantum leaps in efficiency and customer satisfaction.

It is not surprising that big technology companies like Bellsouth, Boeing, and HP have been quick to equip workers with mobile solutions. But smaller companies in diverse industries around the world are doing the same.

In Israel, Trading Pharma, a subsidiary of Schering Plough, understands this. They outfitted their pharmaceutical sales reps with a mobile solution to let them manage their schedules, write call reports, view doctors' history, order samples, and take doctors' signatures electronically. Mobile technology has transformed the way they do territory management.

South East Water Ltd (a member of the SAUR Group), an English water utilities company, knows about customer satisfaction. By equipping field service workers with wirelessly enabled notebook computers, they drove down service cycles, miles driven per job, resources per completed activity, and customer service complaints. At the same time, data quality rose for both operational and regulatory purposes.

In New Zealand these ideas have not escaped NZMP, a division of Fonterra Dairy. A critical function in their business is monitoring the location and quality of dairy products through all stages of production. Because they equipped workers with wirelessly enabled PDAs with attached barcode readers, they now have less spoilage and faster workflow.

Handleman Company, a distributor and category manager of audio CDs in the United States understands how to maintain its lead over the competition. They are equipping their field sales people with wirelessly enabled computing devices, empowering them to review music sales by store and monitor in-transit orders. Through instant two-way communications salespeople are able to resolve inventory discrepancies, shift support resources, and send merchandising alerts to support local concerts, promotions, or other events. Handleman knows that smooth in-store execution maximizes retail sales.

As you were reading these examples—wherever you are in the world—you probably had two or three ideas how wireless technology could help your business. I urge you to act on those ideas. The technology is already capable of supporting real business solutions, and is growing more powerful every month.

Start now.

Online Resources

An enormous amount of information is available on the Internet to help you learn more about the mobile enterprise. These Web sites range from those targeting a technical audience to those targeting a business audience.

DEFINITIONS/ENCYCLOPEDIAS/TUTORIALS

Several Web sites provide definitions of technical terms, encyclopedia entries on technology, and tutorials. You might start out by looking at these sites.

www.iec.org/online/tutorials/	A source of tutorials on a variety of telecom-related technical topics.
www.techguide.com/	A library of papers written on a lot of different business/technical topics.
www.tiab2b.com/glossary/	A guide to the telecom industry.
www.webopedia.lycos.com/	An online dictionary and search engine for computer and Internet technology.
www.whatis.com/	An online encyclopedia on technical topics.

INDUSTRY NEWS/OPINION

There are a large number of sites offering up-to-date news and information and opinions on different topics relevant to the mobile enterprise. In many cases these are Web sites of magazines to which you might also subscribe.

www.3gnewsroom.com/	Contains news and information on 3G technology.
www.cio.com/	A magazine and a Web site targeting IT managers.
www.destinationcrm.com/	A magazine and a Web site. It is a great resource for information on CRM.
www.destinationffa.com/	A magazine and a Web site. It has a lot of information on the mobile enterprise.
www.destinationkm.com	A magazine and a Web site. This is a good source for knowledge management (KM).
www.eaijournal.com/	A magazine and a Web site focused on enterprise application integration (EAI).
www.emobinet.com/	Contains information for wireless Internet users, enthusiasts, developers, and businesses.
www.mbusinessdaily.com/	A magazine and a Web site. It is dedicated to mobile business.
www.mformobile.com/	Focused on mobility.
www.mobilecomputing.com/	Focused on portable computing devices.
www.rcrnews.com/	Containing news on wireless.
www.realmarket.com/	Provides news on CRM.
www.telecomweb.com/wirelessdata/	Contains news and information on wireless data.
www.unstrung.com/	Online publication focused on the global wireless market.
www.wapsight.com/	Online resources delivers news with a focus on wireless data on cell phones and PDAs.
www.wired.com/news/wireless/	A section of "Wired News" that is dedicated to wireless.
www.wirelessinternetmagazine.com/	A magazine and an Internet site devoted to wireless Internet news.
www.wirelessreport.net/	Has a lot of information on the wireless enterprise and it has monthly articles by various industry leaders.
www.wirelessweek.com/	A weekly magazine and a Web site covering wireless news.
www.wow-com.com/news/	Web site of the Cellular Telecommunications and Internet Association (CTIA). Here you will find news and information on industry conferences.

INDUSTRY FORUMS

You might check out the Web sites of some of the relevant industry forums. These sites list meeting details and contain information on how to join.

www.3gamericas.org/	Attempts to unify wireless operators around popular wireless technologies, including TDMA, GSM, GPRS, EDGE, and UMTS.
www.3gpp.org/	The 3rd Generation Partnership Project is a collaboration of different standards bodies to produce global specifications for 3rd-generation mobile systems.

www.bluetooth.com/	The Bluetooth consortium is a forum of companies, including major cell phone manufacturers, working together to specify Bluetooth.
www.cwta.ca/	The Canadian Wireless Telecommunications Association includes wireless network operators, paging companies, mobile radio, mobile satellite carriers, and fixed wireless service providers in Canada.
www.fcc.gov/e911/	This is the FCC's Web site on Enhanced 911 rules. Here you will find out about drivers behind some of the location technology.
www.iec.ch/	The International Electrotechnical Commission prepares and publishes international standards for ruggedization of portable computers. The Ingress Protection (IP) standards from the IEC address ingress protection—protection of devices from dust, rain, etc. Look for IP Standard 60529 at this Web site.
www.mda-mobiledata.org/	The Mobile Data Association is a global association for vendors and users of mobile data.
www.mobitex.org/	The Mobitex Operators Association consists of wireless data network operators, software developers, hardware manufacturers, and customers.
www.nema.org/	The National Electrical Manufacturers Association develops American standards on device ruggedization. In particular, you can look for "Enclosures for Electrical Equipment," Publication 250 at this site.
www.openmobilealliance.org/	The Open Mobile Alliance is an industry alliance focused on mobile data. This group grew out of the WAP forum.
www.pcia.com/	The Personal Communications Industry Association promotes the wireless industry. This Web site includes news and information.
www.w3c.org/	The World Wide Web Consortium (W3C) develops interoperable technologies for the Web.

INDUSTRY ANALYSTS AND RESEARCH FIRMS

There is a good deal of market research on the mobile enterprise. Here is a list of companies performing research in this area, and from whom you might obtain reports. Look for reports on mobility and on enterprise applications.

www.bwcs.com/	BWCS
www.canalys.com/	Canalys.com
www.datamonitor.com/	Datamonitor
www.forrester.com/	Forrester Research
www.gartner.com/	Gartner
www.idc.com/	IDC
www.instat.com/	In-Stat/MDR
www.metagroup.com/	Meta Group
www.ovum.com/	Ovum
www.pmpresearch.com/	PMP Research

www.shosteck.com/	The Shosteck Group
www.strategyanalytics.com/	Strategy Analytics
www.summitstrat.com/	Summit Strategies
www.yankeegroup.com/	The Yankee Group

HEALTH AND SAFETY

To find out more about health and safety issues concerning cell phone use while driving, or the effects of radio frequency signals on humans, have a look at some of these Web sites.

www.ericsson.com/	Search Ericsson's Web site using the keyword "Health."
www.fcc.gov/cellphones/	The FCC Web site on radio frequency safety contains information on regulations around RF output.
www.motorola.com/	Search Motorola's Web site using the keywords "Health" and "RF" together.
www.nhtsa.dot.gov/	The National Highway Traffic Safety Administration contains information on the effects of cell phones on driving. Search on "cell phone."
www.nokia.com/	Search Nokia's Web site on "Health."
www.who.int/peh-emf/	The International electromagnetic Fields (EMF) project was established by the World Health Organization (WHO) to study the effects of electromagnetic radiation on humans.

RESOURCES FOR IT PROFESSIONALS

Here are some sites containing useful information of a technical nature.

www.3gamericas.org/English/Technology_Center/	The technical section of 3G Americas contains technical information on wireless in the United States.
www.allnetdevices.com/	allNetDevices™ contains news and features for developers and vendors of devices.
www.fcc.gov/wtb/	The FCC Wireless Telecommunications Bureau includes information on rulings and licensing in the United States. Go here for a lot of facts on wireless in the United States.
www.forum.nokia.com/main/	Nokia's Web site includes tools and software development kits for developers creating mobile applications on Nokia platforms.
www.javamobiles.com/	JavaMobiles is a guide to mobile phones and PDAs running Java.
www.pdabuzz.com/	PDA Buzz contains information on PDAs.

www.thinkmobile.com/	ThinkMobile contains a lot of technical news and information on wireless.
www.wireless.internet.com/	The wireless section of internet.com contains technical information on many different aspects of the mobile enterprise.

DEVICE VENDORS

There are a number of device vendors to look at. In some cases, especially with cell phone vendors, the Web site will contain a lot of information on wireless networking.

www.casio.com/	Look for their mobile computing products, which includes PDAs and Pen Tablet/Notebook computers.
www.dell.com/	Look for notebook computers.
www.dolch.com/	Look for ruggedized portable computers.
www.ericsson.com/	Look for cell phones and smart phones. You will also find a lot of useful material on wireless networking.
www.fujitsu.com/	Look for notebooks and tablets.
www.gateway.com/	Look for notebook computers.
www.getac.com/	Look for ruggedized portable computers.
www.handspring.com/	Look for the PDAs and smart phones.
www.hitachi.com/	Look for notebook and tablet computers.
www.hp.com/	Look for notebooks, tablets, and PDAs.
www.ibm.com/	Look for notebook computers.
www.intermec.com/	Look for ruggedized portable computers.
www.itronix.com/	Look for ruggedized portable computers.
www.kyocera.com/	Look for cell phones and smart phones.
www.motorola.com/	Look for cell phones and pagers. You will also find information on processors and wireless networks at this site.
www.nokia.com/	Look for cell phones and smart phones. You will also find information on wireless networks at this site.
www.palm.com/	Look for PDAs and information on the PALM OS™.
www.psion.com/	Look for mobile computing and rugged devices.
www.qualcomm.com/	Look for information on cell phones and on CDMA networks.
www.rim.com/	Look for information on two-way pagers, PDAs, and wireless messaging. RIM also markets a smart phone.
www.samsung.com/	Look for information on cell phones and smart phones.
www.sonicblue.com/	Look for information on tablet computers.

www.sony.com/	Look for handheld computers or PDAs.
www.symbian.com/	Look for information in the EPOC operating system for PDAs and smart phones.
www.symbol.com/	Look for ruggedized handhelds.
www.toshiba.com	Look for PDAs and notebook computers.

ENTERPRISE APPLICATION VENDORS

Here is a list of the Web sites of the major enterprise application vendors. Pay special attention to references to mobile versions of their applications.

www.baan.com/	Look for ERP and CRM.
www.dendrite.com/	Look for CRM.
www.epiphany.com/	Look for CRM.
www.i2technologies.com/	Look for SCM.
www.ibm.com/	Look for Lotus Notes Email.
www.jdedwards.com/	Look for ERP, SCM, and CRM.
www.manugistics.com/	Look for SCM.
www.microsoft.com/	Look for Exchange Email.
www.oracle.com/	Look for ERP, SCM, and CRM.
www.peoplesoft.com/	Look for ERP, SCM, and CRM.
www.sap.com/	Look for ERP, SCM, and CRM.
www.siebel.com/	Look for CRM.

WAG VENDORS

Here is a list of the Web sites of some of the WAG vendors. Have a look at these sites to see the different strategies for providing mobile platforms and applications.

www.724solutions.com/	The 724 Solutions Platform is designed to mobilize applications.
www.aethersystems.com/	The Aether Fusion framework brings together components to mobilize business applications.
www.air2web.com/	The Mobile Internet Platform offers a development environment for rapid wireless deployment.
www.avantgo.com/	The M-Business Server can be used to mobilize applications.
www.brience.com/	Look at their Mobile Processing Server.
www.cellexchange.com/	They have various tools for mobilizing an enterprise.

www.covigo.com/	The Covigo Platform™ is a suite of solutions to mobilize applications.
www.everypath.com/	Their Enterprise Mobile Application Gateway extends enterprise applications to mobile devices.
www.extendedsystems.com/	They have a variety of products for device management and for making applications available to mobile devices.
www.ianywhere.com/	This is a subsidiary of Sybase.
www.iconverse.com/	They have a suite of products for enterprise mobility.
www.oraclemobile.com/	Oracle offers hosted solutions and a wireless platform to mobilize enterprise applications.
www.telispark.com/	Telispark offers a variety of mobile applications designed for specific industries.

SYSTEMS INTEGRATORS

It is not always easy to find information on the mobility practices on the SI Web pages. Try searching on "wireless" or "mobile" at these sites. You will sometimes also find mobility practices within the CRM practices of these companies, as they see mobilizing CRM as the most promising market.

www.accenture.com/	Look for the "Mobile Service Bureau."
www.cgey.com/	Look at their CRM, ERP, and network infrastructure solutions.
www.dc.com/	Deloitte Consulting has a variety of mobile and wireless services, including those around its subsidiary, Telispark, which is a WAG vendor.
www.eds.com/	Look for "Mobile Services."
www.hp.com/	Look for mobility solutions.
www.ibm.com/	Look under industry solutions for wireless e-business.
www.kpmg.com/	Look for mobile and wireless.
www.pwcconsulting.com/	Search on mobile, wireless, and M-Business.

WIRELESS NETWORK OPERATORS

Here is a list of operators in North America. Most of these operators will have information on their networks, including a coverage map.

www.arch.com/	Learn about the ReFLEX two-way paging protocol and look at the Arch Wireless Enterprise Solution.
www.attwireless.com/	Look at AT&T Wireless's progress in rolling out GSM and GPRS. Also look at their enterprise services.
www.cingular.com/	Look at the business solutions. You can also find out about wireless data services.
www.earthlink.com/	Look at Earthlink's wireless email and Internet services.

www.goamerica.com/	Look at their mobile office solutions and enterprise solutions.
www.metrocall.com/	Learn about their wireless email and PIM services.
www.motient.com/	Look at their wireless data services. Learn about ARDIS and about indoor data services.
www.nextel.com/	Look at Nextel's Wireless Business Solutions and their Wireless Web services.
www.skytel.com/	Look at their paging and messaging services.
www.sprintpcs.com/	Learn about Sprint PCS's wireless Web services and their business services.
www.verizon.com/	Look at their enterprise solutions, which include virtual office services for mobile workers.
www.voicestream.com/	Look at their business rate plans and their wireless email services.

Platform Vendors

The Web sites of platform vendors contain information on computing platforms, including hardware, middleware, and network management software.

www.hp.com/	Look at UNIX, Linux, and NT Servers. Look also at the nonstop Himalaya fault tolerant computing platform.
www.ibm.com/	Look at servers and at the WebSphere platform.
www.sun.com/	Look at Unix servers and at the "Sun ONE" platform.

Vendors of Security Products

The Web sites of the vendors of various security products are not only good to visit when shopping around—they are also useful places to learn more about computer and network security.

www.checkpoint.com/	Learn about VPN and firewalls.
www.cisco.com/	Find out about VPN solutions.
www.f-secure.com/	Look for virus protection software.
www.mcafee.com/	Look for virus protection software.
www.nortel.com/	Find out about VPN and firewall solutions.
www.rsasecurity.com/	Find out about cryptography.
www.symantec.com/	Look for virus protection software.
www.verisign.com/	Look for information on securing the enterprise.

OTHER VENDORS

Here are some other vendors who do not quite fit into the other categories I have defined.

www.handago.com/	Handago sells applications for mobile devices.
www.synchrologic.com/	Synchrologic market synchronization and device management solutions.
www.xcelleNet.com/	Xcellenet offers synchronization and device management solutions.

Recommended Reading

TECHNOLOGY ADOPTION

Cairncross, Frances. *The Death of Distance*. Cambridge, MA: Harvard Business School Press, 1997.

Cutcliffe, Stephen H., and Terry S. Reynolds. *Technology and American History (A Historical Anthology from Technology and Culture)*. Chicago: University of Chicago, 1997.

Dell, Michael, and Catherine Fredman. *Direct from DELL*. New York: Harper Business, 1999.

Ettighoffer, Denis. *L'Enterprise Virtuelle (Ou Les Nouveaux Modes de Travail)*. Editions Odile Jacob, 1992.

Gates, Bill. *The Road Ahead*. New York: The Penguin Group, 1995.

Moore, Geoffrey A. *Crossing the Chasm (Marketing and Selling High-Tech Products to Mainstream Customers)*. New York: Harper-Business, 1999.

Moore, Geoffrey. *Inside the Tornado*. New York: HarperCollins, 1995.

PERSONAL COMPUTING DEVICES

Carlson, Jeff. *PALM Organizers*. Berkeley, CA: Peachpit Press, 2002.

Hanttula, Dan. *Pocket PC Handbook*. Hungry Minds, 2001

Underdahl, Brian. *Pocket PCs for Dummies*. Indianapolis, IN: IDG Books, 2001

WIRELESS NETWORK TECHNOLOGY

Bedell, Paul. *Wireless Crash Course*. New York: McGraw-Hill, 2001.

Burkhardt, Jochen, Horst Henn, Stefan Hepper, Klaus Rintdorff, and Thomas Schäck. *Pervasive Computing*. New York: Addison-Wesley, 2002.

Burnham, John P. *The Essential Guide to the Business of U.S. Mobile Wireless Communications*. Englewood Cliffs, NJ: Prentice Hall, 2002.

Faigen, George, Boris Fridman, and Arielle Emmett. *Wireless Data for the Enterprise (Making Sense of Wireless Business)*. New York: McGraw-Hill, 2002.

Held, Gil. *Data Over Wireless Networks (Bluetooth, WAP, and Wireless LANs)*. New York: McGraw-Hill, 2001.

Kikta, Roman, Al Fisher, and Michael Courtney. *Wireless Internet Crash Course*. New York: McGraw-Hill, 2002.

Redl, Siegmund M., Matthias K. Weber, and Malcolm W. Oliphant. *An Introduction to GSM*. Boston: Artech House, 1995.

Redl, Siegmund M., Matthias K. Weber, and Malcolm W. Oliphant, *GSM and Personal Communications Handbook*. Boston: Artech House, 1998.

Rhoton, John. *The Wireless Internet Explained*. Boston: Digital Press, 2002.

Webb, William. *The Future of Wireless Communications*. Boston: Artech House, 2001.

ENTERPRISE APPLICATIONS

Anderson, Kristin and Carol Keer. *Customer Relationship Management*. New York: McGraw-Hill, 2002.

Chorafas, Dimitris N. *Integrating ERP, CRM, Supply Chain Management and Smart Materials*. Boca Raton, Fl: Auerback, 2001.

O'Leary, Daniel E. *Enterprise Resource Planning Systems (Systems, Life Cycle, Electronic Commerce, and Risk)*. Cambridge: Cambridge University Press, 2000.

Shields, Murrell G. *E-Business and ERP (Rapid Implementation and Project Planning)*. New York: Wiley, 2001.

Siebel, Thomas M. *Taking Care of eBusiness*. New York: Doubleday, 2001.

Tiwana, Amrit. *The Essential Guide to Knowledge Management*. Englewood Cliffs, NJ: Prentice Hall, 2001.

SECURITY

Adams, Carlisle and Steve Lloyd. *Understanding Public-Key Infrastructure (Concepts, Standards, and Deployment Considerations)*. New York: Macmillan Technical Publishing, 1999.

Clark, David Leon. *IT Manager's Guide to Virtual Private Networks*. New York: McGraw-Hill, 1999.

Kaeo, Merike. *Designing Network Security*. Indianapolis, IN: Macmillan, 1999.

Oppliger, Rolf. *Security Technologies for the World Wide Web*. Boston: Artech House, 2000.

WIRELESS APPLICATION GATEWAYS

Cattell, Rick and Jim Inscore. *J2EE™ Technology in Practice, Building Business Applications with the Java™ 2 Platform, Enterprise Edition*. Sun Microsystems, 2001.

Platt, David S. *Introducing Microsoft.NET*. Redmond, WA: Microsoft Press, 2001.

BUSINESS PROCESS REENGINEERING

Galloway, Dianne. *Mapping Work Processes*. Milwaukee, WI: ASQ Quality Press, 1994.

Hammer, Michael. *Beyond Reengineering: How the Processed-Centered Organization is Changing Our Work and Our Lives*. New York: Harper-Collins, 1997.

Hammer, Michael, and Steven A. Stanton. *The Reengineering Revolution*. New York: HarperBusiness, 1995.

Jacka, Mike J., and Paulete J. Keller. *Business Process Mapping (Improving Customer Satisfaction)*. New York: Wiley, 2002.

INTERNET

Amor, Daniel. *The E-business (R)EVOLUTION (Living and Working in an Interconnected World*. Englewood Cliffs, NJ: Prentice Hall, 2000.

INDUSTRIES

Porter, Michael E. *Competitive Strategy (Techniques for Analyzing Industries and Competitors)*. New York: The Free Press, 1980.

Shaker, Steven M. and Mark P. Gembicki. *The Warroom Guide to Competitive Intelligence*. New York: McGraw-Hill, 1999.

HEALTH AND SAFETY

Redelmeier, Donald A., and Robert J. Tibshirani. *Association Between Cellular-Telephone Calls and Motor Vehicle Collisions. New England Journal of Medicine*, February 13, 1997.

Strayer, David L. and William A. Johnston. *Driven to Distraction: Dual-Tasks Studies of Simulated Driving and Conversing on a Cellular Telephone. Psychological Science*, November 2001.

An Investigation of the Saftey Implications of Wireless Communications in Vehicles. National Highway Traffic Safety Administration (NHTSA), November 1997.

PERIODICALS

.Net Magazine
    www.thedotnetmag.com

Field Force Automation
    www.destinationffa.com/

Laptop (Mobile Solutions for Business & Life)
    www.techworthy.com/

M-Business
    www.mbizcentral.com/

Mobile Computing
    www.mobilecomputing.com/

Pen Computing
    www.pencomputing.com/

PC World
    www.pcworld.com

PocketPC
    www.PocketPCmag.com/

Wireless Business & Technology
    Sys-Con Media

Glossary

1G

First-generation wireless network, based on analog signaling. The dominant 1G networking technology in the United States is AMPS.

1xRTT

A fast packet-switched data service offered on cdma2000 networks. Theoretically, this service can offers data rates of 144 kbps in a mobile environment. In practice, however, average data rates are from 28 to 80 kbps. The 1x refers to the 1.25 MHz of bandwidth needed for this service; RTT is short for Radio Transmission Technology. This service is also sometimes referred to as cdma2000 1x.

2.5G

Two-and-a-half-generation wireless network: Wireless networks that are somewhere between 2G and 3G. These networks have packet-switched data service that are not as fast as 3G. GSM, CDMA (IS-95), and TDMA (IS-136) networks become 2.5G when modifications are made to add GPRS or EDGE (for GSM), 1xRTT (for CDMA), or EDGE (for TDMA) capabilities.

2G

Second-generation wireless network. These networks are based on digital signaling, but do not offer a fast packet-switched data service. CDMA (IS-95), TDMA (IS-136), and GSM are all examples of 2G networks.

3G

Third-generation wireless networks outlined in a set of proposals called International Mobile Telecommunications-2000 (IMT2000). Important features of 3G include high data rates, multimedia, location technology, wireline voice quality, and security. The good news is data rates of up to 2 megabits per second will be offered; the bad new is 3G will not be widely deployed until a few years from now.

3xRTT

The second phase of the cdma2000 standard (1xRTT is the first). 3xRTT will provide data rates of up to 2 Mbps. The 3x refers to the three 1.25 MHz channels needed to accomplish these data rates; RTT is short for Radio Transmission Technology. This service is also sometimes referred to as cdma2000 3x.

802.11

The first of a series of specifications developed by the IEEE for wireless LAN. 802.11 operates in the 2.4 GHz band and uses either frequency hopping spread spectrum (FHSS) or direct sequence spread spectrum (DSSS) to support data rates of 1 or 2 Mbps.

802.11a

A revision of 802.11 that operates in the 5 GHz band and supports data rates up to 54 Mbps. 802.11a uses orthogonal frequency division multiplexing (OFDM) rather than FHSS or DSSS.

802.11b

A revision of 802.11 that operates in the 2.4 GHz band and uses direct sequence spread spectrum (DSSS) to support data rates up to 11 Mbps. 802.11b is also referred to as Wi-Fi.

Access Control

The security countermeasures that prevent unauthorized access to system resources.

Access Point (AP)

An essential hardware component of 802.11b networks that serves as the interface between the wired LAN, and the wireless LAN. The access point is an antenna that communications with stations using radio frequency (RF) signaling.

Active Scanning

A procedure through which an 802.11b station connects to a network by probing for nearby access points (APs).

Active Server Page (ASP)

A page addressed by a uniform resource locator (URL) with the suffix ".asp". ASPs contain a mixture of dynamic scripting content and static content, allowing a dynamically generated page to be created in response to an HTTP request. Similar to Java server pages (JSPs) and common gateway interface (CGI) scripts.

Advanced Mobile Phone System (AMPS)

The first analog cellular phone system deployed in the United States. AMPS is also used in over 35 other countries. This technology is sometimes also called Analog Mobile Phone System.

Advanced Radio Data Information Service (ARDIS)

A packet-switched wireless network based on the DataTac technology developed by Motorola and IBM. The original ARDIS network provided IBM service employees remote access to mainframes. Today the network is owned by Motient and is used for messaging, field service, and transportation applications. The ARDIS network delivers data rates of up to 19.2 kbps and provides deep penetration into buildings.

A-GPS

See *Assisted Global Positioning System.*

AI

See *Artificial Intelligence.*

Air Interface

The interface between the base station (on the wireless network) and the mobile handset using radio signaling and communication protocols.

Alert

A message pushed to a user to notify him or her of an event, for example, the arrival of an email message, a document update, or a price change. Synonym for notification.

Alert Engine

Software that manages alerts. Alert engines include a mechanism for users to configure what they want to be alerted on and how the alerts are sent to them. For example, an alert might be sent by email during certain times of the day, and by fax at other times.

ALI

See *Automatic Location Identification.*

Always-on

Connectionless network service. Because connection setup and termination are not required, data can be exchanged as needed, therefore, the service is "always on."

AM

See *Amplitude Modulation.*

Amplitude Modulation (AM)

Modulation technique in which the amplitude of a carrier wave is varied to communicate data values. See also *Frequency Modulation* and *Phase Modulation.*

AMPS

See *Advanced Mobile Phone System.*

Analog

Signaling in which data is directly and linearly encoded onto a carrier by modulating the carrier's frequency.

AP

See *Access Point.*

API

See *Application Programming Interface.*

Application Programming Interface (API)

Software and procedures allowing an application to interface with another application or system.

Application Server

A program that provides an interface to back-end applications or databases. Typically this kind of an interface is needed for complex, transaction-based applications; the application server is usually built on a scalable, high-availability platform.

ARDIS

See *Advanced Radio Data Information Service.*

ARPU

See *Average Revenue Per User.*

Artificial Intelligence (AI)

The branch of computer science that attempts to mimic human intelligence using computers and software.

ASP

See *Active Server Page.*

Assisted Global Positioning System (A-GPS)

Location-determination technology that works by complimenting the global positioning system (GPS) with processing in the network or on the handset. GPS by itself is expensive, does not work indoors, and requires several seconds to determine a position. The extra processing in the network or handset overcomes these problems by extrapolating from previous GPS readings to estimate location.

Association

A process defined in 802.11 by which a station and an access point (AP) exchange information about capabilities.

Asymmetric Cryptography

Cryptography involving pairs of keys, with one key in a pair being a public key and the other, a private key. The public key can be distributed freely, whereas the private key is known to only one person or entity. The public/private key pair is such that the two keys cannot be easily derived from one another, and one is used to decrypt messages encrypted by the other.

ATP

See *Available-to-Promise.*

Automatic Location Identification (ALI)

Algorithms and technologies used to determine the location of a wireless handset with a higher degree of accuracy than simply locating the cell serving the handset.

Authentication

Security process that verifies the claimed identity of a person or entity.

Authorization

Security process that allows a person or entity access to system resources.

Availability

The state of a system in which it provides services at the level required by its users. Availability is one of the properties a security system might ensure.

Available-to-Promise (ATP)

A feature of supply chain management (SCM) systems that returns information on the capacity of the supply chain to fulfill an order.

Average Revenue Per User (ARPU)

A financial metric associated with the wireless network operator business. This is computed by taking the total amount of subscriber revenue divided by the number of subscribers. Since users tend to switch network providers based on price, this value has been steadily decreasing, and is expected to continue doing so.

Back-Office Application

Enterprise application that addresses business activities of an operational nature, such as invoicing, order management, finance, accounting, human resources, and loan processing.

Band

A specific range of radio frequencies.

Bandwidth

(1) The width of a range of frequencies; that is, the highest frequency minus the lowest frequency, or (2) data rate: the amount of data that can be communicated in a given interval. The amount is usually expressed in bits, and the interval in seconds, giving bits per second (bps).

Base Station

The central transceiver and associated equipment serving a cell.

Basic Service Set (BSS)

In an 802.11b infrastructure configuration, this consists of an access point (AP) and one or more stations. Each BSS is controlled by an AP.

Basic Trading Area (BTA)

One of 493 geographic areas defined by Rand McNally & Company based on grouping counties whose residents do most of their shopping in the same area. The FCC grants personal communications system (PCS) licenses based on BTAs and Major Trading Areas (MTAs). See also *Major Trading Areas*.

BER

See *Bit-Error Rate*.

BI

See *Business Intelligence*.

Biometrics

The use of biological properties to authenticate individuals. Traits used for biometrics must be unique, stable, easy to measure electronically, and difficult to imitate. Commonly used traits include fingerprints, retinas, and voice.

Bit-Error Rate (BER)

The ratio of erroneous bits to the total number of bits sent.

Bit

Binary digit: a base 2 digit, therefore having a value of either 0 or 1.

Bits Per Second (bps)

Unit for expressing data rate (or bandwidth). The number of bits that can be transmitted per second.

Bluetooth

A standard for short-range omnidirectional wireless communications operating in the 2.4 GHz band. Using Bluetooth, devices equipped with low-cost transceiver chips are able to communicate directly with one another, thereby minimizing the need for cables. The name of this standard is taken from the 10th-century Danish King Harald Bluetooth.

Bps

See *Bits Per Second.*

BPR

See *Business Process Reengineering.*

Browser

A program allowing users to access and view documents on the World Wide Web, typically using the HTTP protocol to fetch documents, and interpreting HTML or xHTML markup languages to present them to the user.

Brute-Force Attack

Attacks that attempt to break through a cryptosystem by applying every possible key until the resulting plaintext looks meaningful.

BSS

See *Basic Service Set.*

BTA

See *Basic Trading Area.*

Business Intelligence (BI)

The set of applications and technologies for capturing, cataloging, storing, analyzing, and providing access to information.

Business Object

Data and a set of operations on that data, which together form an abstraction of some part or function of a business. A good example is a business object representing opportunities. This includes the following data: customer name, address, and the amount of potential sales. Functions on that data include insert, update, and delete.

Business Process Reengineering (BPR)

The practice of analyzing existing ways of performing business activities and then making changes to increase efficiency and reduce complexity.

Byte

Eight bits taken together to represent a value from 0 to 255.

CA

See *Certificate Authority.*

Caching

The process of storing data locally in order to speed future access. Some prediction is made as to which data is likely to be needed again—and as to the likelihood the data will change between the first and subsequent accesses.

Capable-to-Promise

A supply chain management (SCM) function used to determine if a product can be delivered to a customer by specific data.

Cardholder Present

In credit card transactions, to minimize fraud, it is important to show the owner of the card is present, and therefore in agreement, during a transaction. One way of doing this is to get the customer's signature.

Carrier

A reference signal known to both sides that can be modulated by the transmitting side to convey binary values to the receiver.

CC/PP

See *Composite Capabilities/Preferences Profile.*

CDMA

See *Code Division Multiple Access.*

cdma2000™

Upgrade to cdmaOne. The evolutionary path for cdmaOne networks to 3G, consisting of two phases: 1xRTT and 3xRTT.

cdma2000 1x

See *1xRTT.*

cdma2000 3x

See *3xRTT.*

cdmaOne™

The brand name for IS-95 Code Division Multiple Access (CDMA).

CDPD

See *Cellular Digital Packet Data.*

Cell

A geographic area from around 1 to 20 miles in diameter, in which telephone service is provided by a single antenna, or a cluster of antennas acting as one.

Cell Phone

A telephone that communicates with a wide area public wireless network to provide phone service.

Cell Site

Physical location of the main equipment serving a cell.

Cellular

(1) A network model in which the network is made up of a set of contiguous radio coverage areas, or cells. (2) Wireless telephone licenses in the 800–900 MHz band. See also *PCS*.

Cellular Digital Packet Data (CDPD)

A packet-switched data service provided on AMPS networks and implemented by transmitting data during idle time on voice circuits. This service is more efficient than CSD in that it does not require a dedicated voice circuit. CDPD offers data rates up to19.2 kbps.

Central Processing Unit (CPU)

The main processor in a computer.

Certificate

See *Digital Certificate.*

Certification Authority (CA)

A trusted entity that vouches for others by providing certificates.

CF

See *Compact Flash.*

CGA

See *Cellular Geographic Area.*

CGI

See *Common Gateway Interface.*

Channel Switching

Functionality that maintains a session with a user as he or she changes from one terminal to another, or from one network to another.

Character Recognizer

An input mechanism in Pocket PC that interprets individual letters written by hand on the screen.

Chipping Code

In Direct Sequence Spread Spectrum (DSSS) this is the code that determines how data is spread out over the frequency range.

c-HTML

See *Compact HyperText Markup Language.*

Ciphertext

An encrypted message; the opposite of cleartext and plaintext.

Circuit Switched Data (CSD)

A data transmission service that works by sending data over a voice circuit. Because the circuit requires resources to be reserved even when there is no data to send, this is an inefficient way of implementing a data service.

Circuit Switching

A networking technology whereby a dedicated channel is reserved to provide a steady, consistent communication service between two parties. A circuit is established through a connection process, which reserves network resources. The circuit is discontinued through a termination process, which frees the resources. Up until recently, circuit switching has been the ideal technique for providing voice communications, which require a steady flow. The disadvantage is that even when no information is being communicated, network resources cannot generally be used for other purposes. For this reason, packet switching is a better way of communicating data—and it also promises to be a better way of providing phone services. See also *Packet Switching.*

Cleartext

Data in unencrypted form, therefore readable by anybody. Synonym for *plaintext* and antonym of *ciphertext.*

Client

An application, process, or computer that requests services from a network and/or server.

Clustering

Grouping of computers, storage media, and other hardware in a way that permits fail-over (one system taking over the tasks of another in the event of system failure), load balancing, and parallel processing. A cluster appears as a single system to the outside world.

Code Division Multiple Access (CDMA)

(1) A spread spectrum air interface technology. Channels are defined by unique codes that determine how a signal is to be spread out over the available frequency. (2) Networks implementing the IS-95 standard.

Common Gateway Interface (CGI)

A standard way for generating dynamic Web pages by allowing clients to pass information to the Web server, and for the server to use that information to generate a page.

Compact Flash (CF)

A popular, small memory card that uses nonvolatile memory and is therefore able to retain data in the absence of power. These cards are a popular choice for use with personal digital assistants (PDAs).

Compact HyperText Markup Language (c-HTML)

A markup language designed for use with small devices with small screens. C-HTML is used by the popular iMode, which originated in Japan.

Component

In Java, this is a self-contained, reusable software unit. Components can be manipulated using visual application builder tools.

Composite Capabilities/Preferences Profile (CC/PP)

Specification developed by the W3C.

Compression

The process of reducing the number of bits needed to represent a given set of information. This is accomplished by minimizing redundancy.

Confidentiality

The situation in which only the intended participants in a communication are able to understand the communication.

Contact Management

Enterprise application functions that help users manage contacts.

Container

In Java this is an application program or subsystem in which a component is run. For example, a browser is a container that might run a list box, which is implemented as a component.

Content Transformation

The process of extracting data in one form and transforming the way it is formatted to adapt the presentation to features of a specific device. Typically this technique is used to convert HTML web pages into a markup language for a mobile device.

Cookie

A file stored on a computer containing information passed between a Web client and server to relate transactions in a way that mimics a session.

Countermeasure

A feature or function of a security system that works to counter one or more threats.

CPU

See *Central Processing Unit.*

CRM

See *Customer Relationship Management.*

Cross-Selling

Selling products that are related to one or more products already selected by a customer.

Cryptographic Key

A digital code that can be used to encrypt, decrypt, and sign information.

Cryptography

The use of mathematics to provide mechanisms for obscuring data values. Cryptography helps ensure confidentiality, data integrity, and legitimate use.

Cryptosystem

A set of keys and encryption and decryption algorithms used in conjunction to provide cryptographic functions.

CSD

See *Circuit Switched Data.*

CTP

See *Capable-to-Promise.*

Customer Relationship Management (CRM)

A suite of applications that helps enterprises understand customers from multiple perspectives. The intent is to improve customer retention and to increase revenues from existing customers.

Customer-Office Application

Enterprise application that addresses business activities that occur at the customer site, such as quoting prices, upselling, cross-selling, and order taking.

D-AMPS

See *Digital Advanced Mobile Phone System.*

Data Encryption Standard (DES)

A symmetric cryptographic scheme developed by IBM in the 1970s and standardized by NIST.

Data Integrity

The situation in which data is whole and unaltered.

Database

A collection of data structured for quick retrieval by applications.

Data Rate

The amount of data that can be communicated in a given interval. The amount is usually expressed in bits, and the interval in seconds, giving bits per second (bps).

DataTac

Wireless network technology developed by Motorola and IBM to give IBM service employees remote access to mainframes. The ARDIS network, now owned by Motient, is based on DataTac.

DCCH

See *Digital Control Channel.*

Decryption

The process of rendering an encrypted message readable.

Demodulation

The process of detecting changes on a regular signal (carrier) to receive data. Three properties of the carrier that are changed are its amplitude (AM), its frequency (FM), and its phase (PM).

Denial of Service Attack

Any malicious action that reduces system availability or completely shuts down a system. Such action is said to deny service to legitimate users.

DES

See *Data Encryption Standard.*

Detachable

Mode of operation in which the device is not connected to a network, and the user works using data stored on the device. Synonym for *disconnected* and *offline*.

Device

A computer that can be easily carried around.

Device Management

The set of functions for managing devices. This might include functions such as software configuration, application upgrade, device tracking, and data backup.

Diffie-Hellman Key Exchange

A mechanism allowing two parties to establish a shared secret (symmetric key) over an insecure channel.

Digital

Signaling in which data is encoded as discreet values—ones and zeros—onto the carrier.

Digest

See *Message Digest.*

Digital Advanced Mobile Phone System (D-AMPS)

An upgrade to AMPS that divides each analog channel into three time slots, each of which defines a digital channel. This upgrade triples the network capacity.

Digital Certificate

An electronic document, certifying information about an individual or entity. A certificate is digitally signed by a trusted third party. See *Certification Authority.*

Digital Signature

A string of bits appended to a message to prove the message came from a source and to prove the message has not been changed.

Digital Subscriber Line (DSL)

Technology for providing high-bandwidth data communication over ordinary copper telephone lines.

Direct-Sequence Spread Spectrum (DSSS)

A transmission technology where data signals are combined with a higher bit rate sequence (chipping code) that divides the user data according to a spreading ratio. Redundancies in the chipping code allow recovery from transmission errors, caused, for example, by signal interference.

Disconnected

Mode of operation in which the device is not connected to a network, and the user works using data stored on the device. Synonym for *detachable* and *offline.*

Dispatch

The process of assigning an engineer to a job.

DM

See *Document Management.*

Document Management (DM)

System that collects and catalogs documents and makes them retrievable through an intuitive interface. DM systems often also include workflow functionality to route documents to a series of employees, each of whom might modify the documents.

Document Object Model (DOM)

A platform- and language-neutral representation of an XML document and the interface allowing applications to access the document dynamically.

Document Type Definition (DTD)

A specification written in standard generalized markup language (SGML) to define how another document is to be processed and presented.

DOM

See *Document Object Model.*

Downstream

The direction of transmission from the network to a handset.

DSL

See *Digital Subscriber Line.*

DSSS

See *Direct-Sequence Spread Spectrum.*

DTD

See *Document Type Definition.*

Dual-band

A handset that is able to operate in two frequency bands.

Dual-mode

A handset that is able to operate using two different network standards.

E-911

See *Enhanced 911.*

E-Business

Business connected over the Internet, typically involving a browser to provide the user interface.

EAI

See *Enterprise Application Integration.*

EDGE

See *Enhanced Data Rates for Global Evolution.*

EIP

See *Enterprise Information Portal.*

EJB

See *Enterprise Java Beans.*

Electromagnetic Radiation (EMR)

The transmission of energy in waves that have both electric and magnetic fields. Radio frequencies and visible light are forms of electromagnetic radiation.

Elliptic Curve Cryptosystem

A public key cryptosystem that uses relatively small keys, and is therefore appropriate for small devices.

EMR

See *Electromagnetic Radiation.*

Encryption

The process of rendering a message unreadable by unauthorized parties.

Enhanced 911 (E-911)

An FCC mandate requiring wireless network operators to provide location information on callers using wireless handsets. The motivation for this mandate was to allow public safety answering points (PSAPs) to be able to locate a person calling 911 in an emergency.

Enhanced Data Rates for Global Evolution (EDGE)

A fast data service that can be implemented as an upgrade to GSM and TDMA (IS-136) networks. This protocol is built on the GPRS air interface, but improves on GPRS to provide data rates up to 384 kbps.

Enhanced Observed Time Difference (E-OTD)

A method for determining the location of a wireless handset by measuring the amount of time it takes for signals to travel from at least three different base stations to the handset. With this information, and knowledge of the locations of the base stations, software in the handset is able to compute its own location.

Enterprise Application Integration (EAI)

The methods and tools used to integrate enterprise applications.

Enterprise Application

A large business application, or suite of applications, for example, enterprise resource planning (ERP), customer relationship management (CRM), or supply chain management (SCM).

Enterprise Information Portal (EIP)

A Web site that serves as a single gateway to a company's information and knowledge base. Through the portal, users can enter and retrieve information or administer the information store.

Enterprise Java Beans (EJB)

A Java-based model for development of distributed object-oriented business applications by allowing developers to assemble reusable components to create an application.

Enterprise Resource Planning (ERP)

An integrated suite of applications that addresses a variety of business activities, including finance, manufacturing, purchasing, distribution, and human resources.

Entity Bean

Enterprise Java bean that represents persistent resources, such as databases, customers, and prices.

E-OTD

See *Enhanced Observed Time Difference.*

EPOC

One of the three major operating systems used by PDAs. EPOC is licensed by the British company Symbian Ltd.

ERP

See *Enterprise Resource Planning.*

eXtensible Markup Language (XML)

A language for defining other markup languages. XML provides syntax for using tags (words enclosed in "<" and ">") and attributes (name = value). It does not define semantics and it does not define how the data is presented. The semantics and presentation are up to the applications using XML.

FCC

See *Federal Communications Commission.*

FDMA

See *Frequency Division Multiple Access.*

Federal Communications Commission (FCC)

The United States federal agency that regulates interstate and international communications by radio, television, wire, satellite, and cable.

FHSS

See *Frequency Hopping Spread Spectrum.*

Firewall

A hardware or software security system that separates an intranet from the Internet by controlling access.

First Time Fix Rate

A metric for field service engineers that measures the rate at which they are able to fix equipment on the first visit.

Fixed Wireless

Wireless communication between a network and a fixed station. An example of fixed wireless is a broadband wireless link from a phone network to a business.

Fixed-line

Communication over wires or cables. Such communication is said to be *directed;* that is, it travels along a single path. See *Wireless.*

FLEX

A wireless one-way paging technology developed by Motorola and introduced in 1993.

FM

See *Frequency Modulation.*

Forward Channel

The channel used for downstream communication, that is, from the network to the handset.

Forward Caching

Process by which a server makes decisions about which data is most likely to be required by a client. The server sends that data to the client to be cached in advanced.

Frequency

The number of complete cycles per unit of time.

Frequency Division Multiple Access (FDMA)

An air interface technology in which channels are defined by frequency ranges. FDMA is used in AMPS networks.

Frequency Hopping Spread Spectrum (FHSS)

A type of spread-spectrum technology in which the data signal is encoded on a narrowband carrier signal that hops from one frequency to another as a function of time. The transmitter and receiver must be set to the same hopping code, which determines the transmission frequencies.

Frequency Modulation (FM)

Modulation technique in which the frequency of a carrier wave is varied to communicate data values. See also *Amplitude Modulation* and *Phase Modulation*.

Front-Office Application

Enterprise application that addresses business activities involving customers, such as market analysis, sales funnel tracking, and sales forecasting.

Full Duplex

Allowing data transmission in both directions at the same time.

Gateway

Hardware and software for bridging two networks that operate using protocols—or having different performance characteristics.

Gateway GPRS Support Node (GGSN)

An essential component of a GPRS-enabled GSM network. This packet router connects the GSM network to other data networks.

General Packet Radio Service (GPRS)

A packet network overlay for GSM networks. This technology provides relatively high data rates—theoretically as high as 144 kbps, but in practice 28 to 40 kbps. GPRS is considered the 2.5G technology for GSM networks.

GGSN

See *Gateway GPRS Support Node*.

GHz

See *Gigahertz*.

Giga

Prefix taken from the Greek word meaning "giant." This prefix now means billion. It is used, for example, in Gigahertz (GHz).

Gigahertz (GHz)

One billion cycles per second.

Global Positioning System (GPS)

A satellite-based navigation system sponsored by the U.S. Department of Defense. GPS works by measuring the time it takes to communicate with three satellites, and using this information to compute longitude, latitude, and elevation. GPS requires line-of-sight, and therefore does not work in buildings.

Global System for Mobile Communications (GSM)

The wireless network standard adopted in Europe and much of the rest of the world to implement mobile phone networks.

GML

See *Generalized Markup Language.*

GPRS

See *General Packet Radio Service.*

GPS

See *Global Positioning System.*

Graffiti™

The special alphabet used on the PALM OS to allow users to input letters and words by writing on the screen.

GSM

See *Global System for Mobile Communications.*

Handheld Device

A device that is small enough to be held with one hand.

Handoff

The procedure for passing a mobile call from one cell to another as a subscriber moves about.

Handover

Synonym for *handoff.*

Hash

The value returned by a hash function (same as a message digest).

Hash Function

A function that takes a variable length message and generates a smaller data value called a hash. The function is such that if the message changes, the function is likely to generate a different hash value.

Header

The part of a packet that tells the network what to do with the packet. This is analogous to an envelope, which tells the postal service what to do with a letter. Headers usually contain a destination address, a source address, an application identifier, packet sequencing information, quality of service parameters, and error-correction parameters.

Hertz (Hz)

Unit of measurement of frequency named after German physicist Heinrich Hertz. One hertz is equal to one cycle per second.

High Availability (HA)

Describes a system or component that is continuously operational. No system can achieve this 100%, but a widely held standard is 99.999% (5-nines) availability.

High-Speed Circuit-Switched Data (HSCSD)

Wireless data transmission technology that works by combining transmission channels to achieve data rates of up to 58 kbps. A major disadvantage is the reduction in voice capacity, since extra voice channels are taken for data transmission.

HiperLAN2

A wireless LAN technology that provides data rates of 23.5 Mbps and operates in the 5 GHz band.

HLR

See *Home Location Registry.*

Home Location Registry (HLR)

Database in a mobile phone network that stores information about subscribers within the operator's home service area. This information includes details on how to reach the subscriber.

HomeRF

A wireless LAN technology designed for use in homes.

Hot Spot

A business or public meeting place where wireless LAN access is provided to clients or visitors. Examples of Hot Spots are airports, cafes, and shopping centers.

HSCSD

See *High-Speed Circuit-Switched Data.*

HTML

See *HyperText Markup Language*.

HTTP

See *HyperText Transfer Protocol.*

HyperText Markup Language (HTML)

The principal markup language for documents on the World Wide Web.

HyperText Transfer Protocol (HTTP)

The principal protocol providing the functions for document exchange on the World Wide Web.

IEEE

See *Institute of Electrical and Electronics Engineers.*

IEEE 802.11

See *802.11.*

IM

See *Instant Messaging.*

Independent Configuration

A mode of operation defined in 802.11b whereby two stations are directly connected and do not require an access point (AP).

Independent Software Vendor (ISV)

A business that sells software without also being a computer systems or hardware manufacturer.

Industrial, Scientific, and Medical (ISM)

Unlicensed frequency, named for some of its intended beneficiaries.

Information Technology (IT)

Technology dealing with information. Computer and software technology.

Infrared (IR)

A short-range wireless communication protocol allowing two devices to connect and exchange data. Because of the relatively high frequency of infrared, line-of-sight is required, meaning the infrared ports of the two devices have to be pointed at one another.

Infrastructure Configuration

A mode of operation defined in 802.11b whereby a station connects to one or more access points (APs).

Ingress Protection (IP)

An aspect of device ruggedization involving protection against incoming (ingress) particles, such as dust or water drops.

Instant Messaging (IM)

Text-based conferencing between two or more people, all of whom are online.

Institute of Electrical and Electronics Engineers (IEEE)

Organization fostering the development of technology standards, including 802.11. The IEEE publishes a number of technical journals.

Interference

The process by which one or more signals acts on another signal in such a way as to distort or cancel the latter.

Interim Standard 41 (IS-41)

A specification providing guidelines for switches to exchange information about subscribers. This makes roaming possible.

Interim Standard 95 (IS-95)

Wireless network standard defining the networks commonly referred to as CDMA.

Interim Standard 136 (IS-136)

Wireless network standard defining the networks commonly referred to as TDMA.

Internet

The public computer network based on TCP/IP and made up of smaller, interconnected networks.

Internet Protocol (IP)

A fundamental part of the TCP/IP suite of protocols. This protocol includes addressing and other elements that facilitate the routing of a message from one computer to any other computer on the Internet.

Internet Service Provider (ISP)

Company that provides Internet access to individuals or businesses.

Intranet

Enterprise network based on the same technologies as the Internet, but to which access is restricted. Since typically only employees are allowed access, an intranet serves as a means for sharing company-internal documents.

Invoice Generation

Enterprise application functions for generating invoices.

IP

See *Ingress Protection* and *Internet Protocol.*

IR

See *Infrared.*

IS-41

See *Interim Standard 41.*

IS-95

See *Interim Standard 95.*

IS-136

See *Interim Standard 136.*

ISM

See *Industrial, Scientific, and Medical.*

ISP

See *Internet Service Provider.*

ISV

See *Independent Software Vendor.*

IT

See *Information Technology.*

iTAP™

A predictive text entry scheme proprietary to Motorola.

J2EE

See *Java 2 Enterprise Edition.*

J2ME

See *Java 2 Micro Edition.*

J2SE

See *Java 2 Standard Edition.*

Java

An object-oriented programming language developed by Sun with the intent to achieve a platform-independent environment for application development and execution.

Java 2

A version of the Java specifications released in 1998.

Java 2 Enterprise Edition (J2EE)

A Java 2 platform that simplifies application development through the use of standardized, reusable components.

Java 2 Micro Edition (J2ME)

A Java 2 platform designed for use on mobile wireless devices, such as cell phones and personal digital assistants (PDAs).

Java Database Connectivity (JDBC)

A Java application programming interface (API) that provides a consistent approach for applications to access relational databases.

Java Message Service (JMS)

A Java application programming interface (API) that provides a consistent approach to using messaging middleware.

Java Server Page (JSP)

A page addressed by a uniform resource locator (URL) with the suffix ".jsp". JSPs contain a mixture of dynamic scripting content and static content, allowing a dynamically generated page to be created in response to an HTTP request. Similar to active server pages (ASPs) and common gateway interface (CGI) scripts.

Java Virtual Machine (JVM)

A Java interpreter.

JDBC

See *Java Database Connectivity.*

JMS

See *Java Message Service.*

JSP

See *Java Server Page.*

JVM

See *Java Virtual Machine.*

Kbps

See *Kilo-bits per second.*

Key

A value used to encrypt and/or decrypt a message.

Key Pair

A public key and the corresponding private key.

Keyspace

All possible key values for a given cryptosystem.

KHz

See *Kilohertz.*

Kilo

Greek prefix for one thousand. Used, for example, for Kilo-bits per seconds (kbps) or Kilohertz (KHz).

Kilo-bits per second (Kbps)

One thousand bits per second.

Kilohertz (KHz)

One thousand cycles per second.

KM

See *Knowledge Management.*

Knowledge Management (KM)

An umbrella term for applications that capture, catalog, store, protect, and disseminate information.

LAN

See *Local Area Network.*

Latency

The amount of time it takes for data to get from one place to another, usually from a server to a client, or from a client to a server.

Lead Management

A set of functions provided in customer relationship management (CRM) systems to help capture, prioritize, and track sales leads. In some systems, lead management functions help drive leads to closure by providing incentive for salespeople to act promptly. This can be done, for example, by providing more and better leads to those who respond quickly and by reporting response time to management.

Legacy Integration

Integration with existing (legacy) enterprise applications.

Line-of-Sight (LoS)

Situation in which there are no obstacles along a straight line between two points, usually between a transmitter and a receiver.

Lithium Polymer

Light and malleable material used to make batteries.

Lithium-Ion

Light material used to make batteries.

Load Balancing

The process of distributing workload among several computer systems.

Local Area Network (LAN)

A computer network usually owned and operated by a single entity and confined to a relatively small area, such as a business office or college campus. Access to a local area network (LAN) is usually limited either by physical means, or through security measures that mimic physical security.

Location Determination

The process of identifying the coordinates of a mobile terminal, and hence those of the user.

Location-Based Services (LBS)

Services tailored to the user's geographic context; that is, the vicinity and features of the vicinity.

Location Technology

Location determination and location-based services.

LoS

See *Line-of-Sight*.

Major Trading Area (MTA)

One of 51 geographic areas defined by Rand McNally & Company as large trading centers that include one or more big cities. The FCC grants personal communications system (PCS) licenses based on MTAs and Basic Trading Areas (BTAs). See also *Basic Trading Areas*.

Man-in-the-Middle Attack

Attack on a system that involves intercepting a message, altering it in some way, and then passing it on to the recipient in hopes that the recipient cannot tell it has been altered.

Mbps

See *Mega-bits per second*.

Mega

Prefix taken from the Greek word meaning "large" or "great." This prefix now means million. It is used, for example, for Mega-bits per seconds (Mbps) or MegaHertz (MHz).

Mega-bits per second (Mbps)

One million bits per second.

Megahertz (MHz)

One million cycles per second.

Message-Driven Bean

Enterprise Java bean that represents a single message.

Message-Oriented Middleware (MoM)

Software that facilitates the exchange of messages between two applications.

Message Digest (MD)

The value returned by a hash function (same as a hash).

Metropolitan Statistical Area (MSA)

One of 306 geographic areas defined by the FCC in populous parts of the United States for the purposes of allocating cellular licenses. In each MSA, licenses are given to two wireless operators. See also *Rural Service Area.*

MHz

See *Megahertz.*

Mobile Telephone Service (MTS)

Early wireless telephone system, predating commercial use of the cellular model.

Mobile Wireless

Wireless communication allowing the user to move about. An example of mobile wireless is cell phone communication. Mobile wireless can be further broken down according to how fast the user is moving: stationary wireless, pedestrian wireless, and vehicular wireless.

Mobile Technology

Technology to assist people who are on the go. This includes portable computing devices, wireless network technology, and synchronization technology for offline access.

Mobitex

A standard developed by Ericsson and Swedish Telecom Radio in the early 1980s to provide a wireless data service. This standard is implemented by Cingular Interactive (formerly BellSouth Wireless Data). Mobitex offers data rates up to 19.2 kbps.

Modem

Modulator/Demodulator. Device that modulates signals to transmit data over a voice channel. It demodulates signals on the voice channel to receive data.

Modulation

The process of changing a regular signal (carrier) to represent data. Three properties of the carrier that are changed are its amplitude (AM), its frequency (FM), and its phase (PM).

MoM

See *Message-Oriented Middleware.*

MSA

See *Metropolitan Statistical Area.*

MTA

See *Major Trading Area.*

MTS

See *Mobile Telephone Service.*

Multipath

Phenomenon where a signal bounces off obstacles and takes several paths. The result is that the receiver gets several copies of the same signal, some of which may distort or cancel one another.

Multiplexing

Combining several channels for transmission over a single medium.

National Electrical Manufacturers Association (NEMA)

A forum for the standardization of electrical equipment in the United States.

NEMA

See *National Electrical Manufacturers Association.*

NiCad

See *Nickel Cadmium.*

Nickel Cadmium (NiCad)

Material with which batteries are made for portable devices.

Nickel Metal Hydride (NiMH)

Material with which batteries are made for portable devices.

NiMH

See *Nickel Metal Hydride.*

NLP

See *Natural Language Processing.*

Nonrepudiation

The situation where a user cannot deny having performed a certain action.

Notebook Computer

A computer that is about the size of a large notebook. Also called a laptop computer.

Notification

A message pushed to a user to notify him or her of an event, for example, the arrival of an email message, a document update, or a price change. Synonym for *alert*.

Object

Data and a set of operations on that data.

Object Request Broker

A program that mediates the exchange of objects between applications.

OFDM

See *Orthogonal Frequency Division Multiplexing.*

Offline

Mode of operation in which the device is not connected to a network, and the user works using data stored on the device. Synonym for *detachable* and *disconnected*.

Online

Mode of operation in which the devices are connected to a network.

Operating System (OS)

The software that governs a computer and provides a runtime environment for applications.

ORB

See *Object Request Broker.*

Order Status

Enterprise application functions that provide the status of previously placed orders.

Orthogonal Frequency Division Multiplexing (OFDM)

A transmission technology that works by splitting the radio signal into multiple smaller subsignals that are then transmitted simultaneously at different frequencies. 802.11a uses OFDM.

Packet

The smallest routable unit of data. A packet contains a header, which tells the network how to route the packet, and a body, which is the actual data payload.

Packet Switching

The transmission of data in packets without establishing a dedicated connection or circuit. The result is a more efficient use of network resources than when circuit switching is used. See also *Circuit Switching*.

PAN

See *Personal Area Network*.

Parts Ordering

Enterprise application functions allowing an authorized user to order parts.

Passive Scanning

The procedure by which an 802.11b client connects to a network by listening for beacons periodically transmitted by access points (APs).

Password

A secret value used to authenticate a person or entity.

Path Loss

The fading of a signal over distance.

PCS

See *Personal Communications Services*.

PDA

See *Personal Digital Assistant*.

Pedestrian Wireless

Wireless communication with a user moving at pedestrian speed. The speed at which a user is moving makes a difference in achievable data rates. See also *Stationary Wireless* and *Vehicular Wireless*.

Personal Communications Service (PCS)

(1) A set of services provided by digital wireless telephone networks. The FCC allocated the 1850–1990 MHz for operators to implement these services, but now PCS is also offered in cellular bands. (2) Wireless telephony in the 1850–1990 MHz band. See also *Cellular*.

Personalization

Tailoring content to an individual user, based on configuration options selected by the user and/or behavior patters observed during previous sessions.

Personal Area Network (PAN)

Short-range wireless network connecting devices on, or very close to, a person.

Personal Digital Assistant (PDA)

A handheld device providing basic functions, such as personal information management (PIM). Most PDAs have an onscreen alphanumeric keyboard and allow input through a touch screen.

Personal Information Management (PIM)

Collection of software tools to manage personal information, such as contact lists and schedules.

Phase Modulation (PM)

Modulation technique in which the phase (starting point) of a carrier wave is varied to communicate data values. See also *Amplitude Modulation* and *Frequency Modulation*.

Piconet

Bluetooth network consisting of one master device and from one to seven active slave devices.

PIM

See *Personal Information Management*.

Plaintext

Data in unencrypted form, therefore readable by anybody. Synonym for *cleartext* and opposite of *ciphertext*.

PM

See *Phase Modulation*.

Portable Computing Device

A computer that is designed to be carried around. Examples include cell phones, PDAs, smart phones, tablet computers, and notebook computers.

Predictive Text Entry

Software running on a portable computing device that eases data entry by predicting a complete version of what the user wants to enter based on abbreviated entries. This is most useful on small devices with limited keyboards; for example, cell phones. See also *iTAP* and *T9*.

Private Key

The key in an asymmetric key pair that is known to only one party. See *Public Key*.

Proxy

A server that sits between a client and a server and performs tasks on behalf of either the client or the server. The purpose of the proxy is to improve performance by offloading work from the client and/or the server.

PSAP

See *Public Safety Access Point*.

PTP

See *Profitable-to-Promise.*

PTT

Public Telephone and Telegraph company. This was the term for the phone company when phone companies were monopolies.

Public Key

The key in an asymmetric key pair that can be distributed widely. See *Private Key.*

Public Key Infrastructure (PKI)

An infrastructure providing key and certificate management. A fundamental aspect of a PKI is the notion of trusted parties.

Public Safety Answering Point (PSAP)

A facility operated by an emergency assistance provider (for example, a local fire or police department) to which 911 calls are directed.

Push

The act of sending data to a device without a request having come from that device. Push requires an always-on service.

QoS

See *Quality of Service.*

Quality of Service (QoS)

A guaranteed level of network service. This is usually used in reference to a guaranteed throughput level.

QWERTY

The standard keyboard for the English language. The name is derived from the letters Q, W, E, R, T, and Y on the top-left alphabetic row.

Radio Frequency (RF)

Electromagnetic radiation in the range from 100 KHz to 300 GHz. This includes the frequencies used for radio, TV, wireless telephony, and wireless LAN.

ReFLEX

A two-way alphanumeric paging protocol developed by Motorola.

ReFLEX 25

Version of ReFLEX with downstream data rates of 9.6 kpbs and upstream rates of 6.4 kbps.

ReFLEX 50

Version of ReFLEX with downstream data rates of 25.6 kbps and upstream rates of 9.6 kbps.

Replay Attack

An attack where an eavesdropper records identification and authentication information (for example, a password), and plays it back later to gain access to a system.

Reverse Channel

The channel used for upstream communication, that is, from the handset to the network.

RF

See *Radio Frequency*.

Rivest, Shamir, Adleman (RSA)

An asymmetric cryptosystem using an algorithm developed in 1977 by Ron Rivest, Adi Shamir, and Leonard Adleman.

Roaming

(1) In cellular networks, this refers to travel in an area covered by an operator other than your own. (2) In Wi-Fi (802.11), this refers to movement from an area covered by one access point (AP) to an area covered by another.

ROI

See *Return On Investment*.

RSA

See *Rural Statistic Area* and *Rivest, Shamir, Adleman*.

Rural Service Area (RSA)

One of 428 geographic areas defined by the FCC in less populous parts of the United States for the purposes of allocating cellular licenses. In each RSA, licenses are granted to two wireless operators. See also *Metropolitan Statistical Area*.

SAN

See *Storage Area Network*.

SAX

See *Simple API for XML*.

SCM

See *Supply Chain Management*.

Screen Scraping

Copying screen output. This technique was used with mainframe applications. This term now refers to transcoding. See also *Transcoding*.

Secret Key

A symmetric key. Both parties use the same key or keys that are easily derived from one another.

Secure Hash Algorithm 1 (SHA-1)

A one-way hash algorithm designed by NIST.

Secure Sockets Layer (SSL)

A cryptographic protocol designed by Netscape to provide a secure communication channel that can be used by a variety of applications, including Web browsers.

Security Policy

A document describing an organization's approach to security.

Serving GPRS Support Node (SGSN)

An essential component of GPRS-enabled GSM networks. The SGSN tracks the subscriber and provides security.

Session

A series of interactions between two computers. A session must be established through an exchange of parameters and it must be terminated to allow the two sides to free up resources.

Session Bean

In J2EE™ this is an enterprise bean that is created by a client and exists for only one client-server session.

Session Key

A symmetric key established and used for a single session. The session key can either be exchanged over a channel secured by asymmetric cryptography, or it can be derived by either side using Diffie-Hellman key exchange.

SGML

See *Standardized General Markup Language*.

SGSN

See *Serving GPRS Support Node*.

SHA1

See *Secure Hash Algorithm 1*.

Short Messaging Service (SMS)

A protocol allowing users to send short messages to one another. This protocol works by borrowing capacity from the network signaling channels.

SIM

See *Subscriber Identity Module.*

Simple API for XML (SAX)

An application programming interface (API) for parsing XML documents.

Single Point of Failure

A system component that is not duplicated. If such a component fails, service is reduced or brought down entirely.

Sled

A device into which a PDA can be inserted to make additional functions available. For example, sleds might add data communication functions.

Smart Card

A plastic card within an embedded computer chip with storage capacity. Smart cards might hold information to authenticate the user and they might also hold data and small programs.

Smart Phone

A device that functions both as a PDA and a phone.

SMR

See *Specialized Mobile Radio.*

SMS

See *Short Messaging Service.*

Specialized Mobile Radio (SMR)

A dispatch radio and interconnect service operating in 800 MHz and 900 MHz bands. Nextel Communications has developed a nationwide network around SMR licenses.

Spectrum

A range of frequencies.

Spoofing

To fake the identity of an authorized individual or entity in an attempt to gain access to a computer or network resource.

Spread Spectrum

A class of data transmission technologies in which a signal is spread out across a range of frequencies. Because the signal is spread out, it is harder to detect by eavesdroppers, and it is more resistant to interference and jamming. Spread spectrum was first used by the military, where secrecy and resistance to jamming are essential. There are two approaches to spread spectrum: direct sequence spread spectrum (DSSS) and frequency hopping spread spectrum (FHSS).

SSL

See *Secure Sockets Layer.*

Standardized General Markup Language (SGML)

A standard for specifying a markup language. For example, HTML can be defined using SGML.

Stationary Wireless

Wireless communication with a user who is standing still. The speed at which a user is moving makes a difference in achievable data rates. See also *Pedestrian Wireless* and *Vehicular Wireless.*

Storage Area Network (SAN)

Short-range network (usually a wired network) consisting of one or more computers and several storage devices. These networks are used with application servers to provide high-capacity, fault-tolerant data storage.

Storage Density

The amount of storage capacity a battery has per unit of weight.

Streaming

Communications service that provides a steady, continuous stream of data. This is useful for transmission of video and audio.

Stylesheet

A template that specifies how a source document is transformed to another format.

Stylus

A pen-like tool that allows users to write on a device screen.

Subscriber Identity Module (SIM)

A small card that stores subscriber information for use in GSM phones. This card can be removed and placed in another phone to transfer the subscription to the second phone.

Supply Chain Management (SCM)

A suite of applications run by business partners to coordinate and optimize activities along a supply chain.

Symmetric Algorithm

A cryptographic algorithm for which the encryption and decryption processes use either the same key or two different keys, which are easily derived from one another. Such an algorithm assumes the sender and receiver exchange key values in secret. The sender and receiver are said to have a *shared secret*.

Synchronization

The process by which data on two or more computers are brought up to date with one another. This might occur in only one direction. For example, a portable computing device might receive updates from enterprise applications. It might also occur in both directions. The device might also post updates to enterprise applications.

T9™

The predictive text entry scheme devised by Tegic and now used on most cell phones.

Tablet Computer

Portable computing device that is similar to a notebook computer, but has the screen facing outward. In this way the screen is always viewable. These devices can be carried around somewhat like a thick tablet of paper.

Taxonomy

In regard to knowledge management (KM), a subject-specific vocabulary used to catalog information into categories and subcategories.

TCO

See *Total Cost of Ownership*.

TCP/IP

See *Transmission Control Protocol/Internet Protocol*.

TDMA

See *Time Division Multiple Access*.

Thick Client

A device with enough software to run meaningful applications on its own. Thick clients do not require a connection to a server.

Thin Client

A device with just enough software to provide a user interface. Thin clients depend on a connection to a server to run applications.

Threat

The potential to violate a computer or a network. Security systems seek to counter threats.

Time Division Multiple Access (TDMA)

(1) An air interface technology in which channels are defined by time slots. TDMA is used in TDMA (IS-136) and GSM networks. (2) Networks implementing the IS-136 standard.

Total Cost of Ownership (TCO)

Total cost associated with owning a system. This includes initial purchase of system components, training, support, and ongoing usage charges.

Transceiver

A device that acts as both a transmitter and a receiver.

Transcoding

A method of content transformation whereby data is picked out of pre-configured fields from an HTML document and transformed to another format. This is similar to screen scraping. See also *Screen Scraping*.

Transcriber

An input mechanism used by Pocket PC that interprets words written by hand on the screen.

Transmission Control Protocol/Internet Protocol (TCP/IP)

The suite of communications protocols on which the Internet is based. The suite gets its name from the two most prominent protocols, Transmission Control Protocol and Internet Protocol, which provide end-to-end error-free transmission and routable packets, respectfully.

Triple DES

A cryptographic algorithm that improves on the strength of DES.

Tunneling

Technique of encapsulating a packet within another packet. The second packet is used to route the data to another point in the network, where the original packet is extracted and passed to a destination. The result is a virtual network with the source and the destination as points on that virtual network. To provide privacy, and thus a virtual private network

(VPN), the original packet is encapsulated in encrypted form to render it unreadable by all computers not on the VPN.

Two-Way Paging

Paging system that allows messages to be sent in both directions—from the network to a paging device and from the paging device to the network.

UAProf

See *User Agent Profile.*

UM

See *Unified Messaging.*

UMTS

See *Universal Mobile Telecommunications System.*

Unified Messaging (UM)

Technology that consolidates different kinds of mail—voice, fax, and text—so the user can use one interface to access different kinds of messages.

Uniform Resource Locator (URL)

The address of a Web-based resource, such as a document or an image.

Universal Mobile Telecommunications System (UMTS)

A 3G network standard designed to deliver high-speed wireless voice and data services. The terms 3G, UMTS, and IMT-2000 are often used interchangeably.

Upselling

Selling a customer a higher-end product based on some previous selection on the part of the customer.

Upstream

The direction of transmission from a handset to the network.

URL

See *Uniform Resource Locator.*

Vehicular Wireless

Wireless communication with a user moving at car speed. The speed at which a user is moving makes a difference in achievable data rates. See also *Pedestrian Wireless* and *Stationary Wireless.*

Virus

A piece of code that replicates to spread onto other computers. Viruses are designed to cause various degrees of harm, from displaying annoying messages to deleting all data on a computer.

Virtual Private Network (VPN)

A private network overlaid on a public network. Security systems are put into place to ensure confidentiality and legitimate use.

Visiting Location Registry (VLR)

A database that tracks all visiting subscribers; that is, all subscribers roaming into the network to which the VLR belongs. The VLR forwards information back to the HLR of each visiting subscriber to indicate how the subscriber can be reached.

VLR

See *Visiting Location Registry.*

Vulnerability

A weakness in a computer or network system that can be potentially exploited by individuals with malicious intent. Security systems seek to cover vulnerabilities.

VPN

See *Virtual Private Network.*

W3C

See *World Wide Web Consortium.*

WAG

See *Wireless Application Gateway.*

WAP

See *Wireless Application Protocol.*

WAP-Enabled Phone

A cell phone with a WAP browser and wireless data capabilities.

Wavelength

The distance a wave travels to complete a cycle. For RF signals, wavelength is equal to frequency times the speed of light.

Wi-Fi

Short for Wireless Fidelity. Synonym for *802.11b.*

Wireless

Communication using radio frequency (RF) signals. This includes fixed wireless—for example, a broadband wireless link from the phone company to your business—and mobile wireless, for example, cell phone services, wireless LAN, and Bluetooth. Such communication is usually implied to be *undirected* or *omnidirectional;* that is, the signal moves in all directions along the medium. Consequently, the signal is easy to intercept and cryptographic measures must be taken to ensure privacy. See also *Fixed-Line.*

Wireless Application Gateway (WAG)

A term coined by the research advisory firm Gartner to refer to platforms that extract data from enterprise applications and repackage it for use on a portable computing device.

Wireless Application Protocol (WAP)

A set of specifications to standardize the way Internet-like services can be provided on cell phones. These specifications take into account the constraints of the cell phone (small screen and keyboard and limited processing power) and wireless networks (low bandwidth, high latency, and unstable connections).

Wireless Data

Wireless communication of text, images, audio, video, or large files.

Wireless Internet

Internet access over wireless media. Usually this access is constrained by the wireless interface (high latency, low bandwidth, and unstable connections) and the small devices used (small screen and keyboard and limited processing power).

Wireless Local Area Network (WLAN)

A local area network (LAN) using a wireless interface between stations and the network. The three popular WLAN standards are 802.11, HiperLAN2, and HomeRF.

Wireless Markup Language (WML)

A markup language defined as part of WAP for presentation of information on cell phones. WML takes into account the limitations of wireless networks and cell phones.

WLAN

See *Wireless Local Area Network*

WML

See *Wireless Markup Language.*

Workflow

The ordered set of tasks, procedures, and people needed to process information.

World Wide Web (WWW)

A network overlaid on the Internet to facilitate the sharing of documents and provide a relatively intuitive user interface. Two fundamental technologies used for the WWW are HTTP (for transfer of documents) and HTML (for presentation of documents). Also refered to simply as the Web.

World Wide Web Consortium (W3C)

An industry consortium that develops and promotes standards for the World Wide Web (WWW).

WWW

See *World Wide Web.*

XML

See *eXtensible Markup Language.*

XSL

See *eXtensible Markup Language.*

Index